THE VIEW
FROM ALGER'S
WINDOW

THE VIEW
FROM ALGER'S
WINDOW

■❙■

A Son's Memoir

TONY HISS

■❙■

ALFRED A. KNOPF

NEW YORK

1999

THIS IS A BORZOI BOOK
PUBLISHED BY ALFRED A. KNOPF, INC.

Library of Congress Cataloging-in-Publication Data
Hiss, Tony.
The view from Alger's window : a son's memoir / by Tony Hiss. — 1st ed.
p. cm.
ISBN 0-375-40127-X (alk. paper)
1. Hiss, Alger. 2. Hiss, Alger—Trials, litigation, etc.
3. Hiss, Alger—Correspondence. 4. Hiss, Tony. 5. Fathers and
sons—United States—Biography. 6. Trials (Perjury)—New York
(State)—New York. 7. Prisoners—United States—Biography.
8. United States. Dept. of State—Officials and employees—
Biography. 9. Subversive activities—United States—
History—20th century. I. Title.
E743.5.H55H57 1999
364.1'31'092—dc21
[B]   98-50911
CIP

Manufactured in the United States of America
First Edition

To my brother, Tim, and my son, Jacob

THE VIEW
FROM ALGER'S
WINDOW

ON A muted, misty late-November morning in 1997, I made an unremarkable, unmarked right turn off a suburban highway strip in north-central Pennsylvania—and abruptly, a year after his death, began a strange, rewarding period of vividly renewed contact with my father, Alger Hiss. I've seen again the full person he was, his strengths and gaps and the ways he changed, and I've revisited the rich inner world that sustained him and that only a very few people ever got to see. I've been learning how much of him there is in me, particularly in areas I've liked to think were my own invention. He's also been jogging my mind, it seems, posing questions, pointing out possibilities, suggesting strategies and next steps. From out of the any-where, it arrived—this wild rose, this lovely, sweet-smelling, prickly gift—with nothing more complicated than a right turn.

The only explicit piece of fatherly advice I can remember my father giving me was: *Whatever you're going to do, get it up and running before you're seventy, because that's when the machin-ery inside starts to break down.* Now I've collected a second piece of advice for my own son to think about someday (he's still only seven): *You won't—can't—know ahead of time when some not-to-be-ignored idea may overtake you.*

Since once-upon-a-time wishes, like wanting to spend more time with your father, don't expire just because you haven't thought about them for decades—the fairy tales that deal with the subject of wish-granting don't spell out all the rules, such as the fact that deliveries are erratic and unscheduled. So try not to let your calendar get too cluttered.

I don't think there's anything either unique or spooky (or ennobling or neurotic, for that matter) about what's been happening to me. My father himself even had a name for a kind of ongoing closeness between people in which death is sometimes only an irrelevance. He called it "the Great Span," a sort of bucket brigade or relay race across time, a way for adjacent generations to let ideas and goals move intact from one mind to another across a couple of hundred years or more. He thought its purpose was to keep unifying memories alive.

As Alger explained it, it had been his privilege as a young lawyer to hear a series of Great Span stories from Oliver Wendell Holmes, the man he most admired in life—Holmes was then eighty-eight, ramrod straight, with a booming voice and an elegant white handlebar mustache, and still a Supreme Court Justice. Alger was his clerk. Alger could repeat these stories, word for word, for the rest of his life. In the Civil War, the young Lieutenant Holmes, from the 20th Massachusetts Volunteers, was wounded three times, and at Ball's Bluff, when he was twenty, he was shot in the breast and left for dead when the Union forces retreated across the Potomac. His sergeant, who had heard him moaning, "How will I get to the other side?" said, "Well, Holmesy, you don't have to worry about that. You believe in Jesus Christ and all that, so you'll be all right." "I got so damn mad," Holmes said later, "that I decided to live!"

In the Holmes story Alger treasured above all others, the Justice told him that when he had been very young, his grandmother, a woman he revered, had shared her memories of the day at the beginning of the American Revolution when she was five and had stood in her father's front window on Beacon Hill in Boston and watched rank after rank of Redcoats marching through town. Ever after, my father said, the awed, scared experience of a little girl born more than a century and a quarter before him had been a bright presence in his own mind.

The Beacon Hill house later became headquarters for Lord Howe, the British commandant, and Holmes owned an old mirror from that house. Holmes left the mirror to Alger, and it now hangs in my living room. "Sometimes when I look into the glass, I think I can see Lord Howe's bewigged face staring back at me," Holmes told Alger. "Can you see it, sonny? Can you see it?"

Although I've thought of the Great Span as an illuminating idea, blazing a sort of Appalachian Trail across time, I wasn't looking to get caught up in such a journey. My father, who had become physically frail for the first time in his final year, died in November 1996, four days after his ninety-second birthday. Growing up, I would have thought of such an age as not quite old enough for him (I had always assumed that he would try to make it to ninety-three, like Holmes). My Pennsylvania trip, taken a year and five days after Alger's death, had been planned as the end of an ending, a day for making a final, peaceful farewell.

The month after Alger's death there was a long, affectionate memorial service in New York that more than eight hundred people came to—quite a huge crowd, but I would have been surprised only by a smaller turnout; I've never known anyone else with so many and such devoted friends.

Having said that first good-bye in New York, where I'd known Alger for most of my life, and then another one the following summer in Peacham, the tiny town in northern Vermont where we spent summers when I was a small boy, I wanted to go back for the last time ever to Lewisburg, Pennsylvania. To complete my own circle of remembrance from deep inside an enormous, high-walled, red brick building there, the institution in which he'd been confined during what had once upon a time felt like an endless time—the forty-four months between March 1951 and November 1954.

When I made the right turn just north of downtown Lewisburg onto the winding, almost empty country road that leads after a mile to the United States Penitentiary where Alger had once been incarcerated, several things changed—one of them an odd, now ordinary, but still unsettling kind of evaporation. The franchise stores and strip commercial buildings that had felt so inescapable along the highway vanished from sight swiftly and completely; the woods and fields and small, older houses that replaced them seemed so not-near to anything but themselves that it was already hard, only moments later, to hold on to the memory of the highway behind, which had started to break up, like mist in sunlight, and to flatten and fade, like a dream flickering away at daybreak. Dream researchers say that we lose the memory of most dreams not because they're supposed to be forgettable, but because the mind doesn't automatically tag them with a "REMEMBER THIS" label. Maybe we'll find that one of the things wrong with scenes in waking life the eye slides over is that they're built so the mind will slide past them as well.

I slowed down and opened the windows, because every bend in the road seemed to bring with it an intensification and deepening of all the small countryside goings-on around me. There were new streams and hedgerows to see, and hills just beyond; still more late-fall freshness in the air to take deep breaths of; and just enough occasional sounds to punctuate a vast quiet—like the fallen leaves that rustled nearby whenever a breeze pushed them along the road. It was almost like seeing—vastly speeded up, of course—the great, ten thousand-year-old post-glacial process still playing itself out over much of North America, as the land beneath us, once squashed flat under the deep weight of mountains of ice, unfolds, swells, and rights itself, springing back up toward its former height.

It was the kind of thing that delights me. Looking at landscapes, subtle ones and obvious ones, and studying what it is in them that speaks to us—it's part of what I do for a living. Along this unusual road many of the voices of place are almost silent. I had entered, I knew, a rarely encountered and complicated sort of territory, a place gripped by a strong and continuing spell. It is a domain of slowed time and an area where distances are deceptive. It wears a sort of extra-slippery cloak of concealment—long ago deliberately hidden away, but actually not hard to find, it stays invisible primarily because of avoided glances.

The "reservation," as the locals call it, is 950 acres of nationally owned land—one and a half square miles, well cared for for almost seventy years—and almost all of it is beautiful. The "almost-all" is suffused with the kind of unchanging, spirit-restoring serenity that irresistibly pulls people into equally extraordinary national parks. This is rugged, late-settled land for the East Coast, just south of the Appalachian Mountains and close to the bound-to-flood-sooner-or-later West Branch of the Susquehanna River—"the wilds of Pennsylvania," as the area could still be called in the early nineteenth century, long after many settlers were already streaming west far beyond the mountains to make lives out in the more welcoming Mississippi River Valley.

The almost-all, nearly empty before it became federal property in 1930, except for a few farmers, and still farmed and still lightly settled today, has for well over a century been changing only as new crops or new farming methods are brought to it. It has kept an old countryside feeling that pre–World War II farmers would easily recognize. But the slow tick of time that governs the almost-all and the strong taproots of rural continuity burrowing through it—qualities that in any other landscape would bring people from miles around—are really only coincidental occurrences, unintended by-products of the fundamental purpose of these fields and hills.

There is continuity here not to support a great span, but to serve an even greater divide. The fields and hills are an enormous perimeter, an incalculable moat of remoteness between the outside world and the reservation's official assignment, which is to function as a place of confinement for twelve hundred or more federal prisoners. At the center of the reservation is, unmistakably, an exact square of land. Along each edge of this square, east, north, west, and south (where the road comes in), stands an abruptly impassable barrier, a massive concrete wall thirty feet high and more than one thousand feet long. There are red brick watchtowers at the four corners where they meet. The walls enclose factories, ball fields, lawns, and the huge main prison building, also built of brick.

You might call it out of place—but where on earth could it possibly seem *in* place, this beached whale, this skyscraper on its side, almost elegant but dangerously overweight, this ugly structure struggling to look handsome, this scowl trying so hard to smile? It's as long as three football fields, quite vast enough to deserve one of its nicknames—"the Big House." It's also known, but chiefly among guards and Federal Bureau of Prisons officials, as "the Great Experiment" and "the Center-piece of the Federal Bureau of Prisons." From beyond the walls there's a seemingly endless series of red tile roofs, dominated by a square at the very center of the square, a too tall, four-sided brick smokestack oddly elaborated and crenelated at the very top so that it becomes an oversized, unmusical Italian Renaissance bell tower.

For inmates within the United States Penitentiary at Lewisburg, as for all prisoners, time moves in ways that are

United States Penitentiary, Lewisburg, 1930s

almost unimaginable to those whose lives are less confined. *Diary of a Self-Made Convict*, a profound study of American prison life that's also the only book about Lewisburg written by an ex-Lewisburg inmate, tries to describe a prisoner's sense of time. The author, Alfred Hassler, later in life became executive secretary of the Fellowship of Reconciliation, a now venerable pacifist group. In his youth, he was one of about four thousand American conscientious objectors who served federal prison sentences when they refused to be drafted during World War II. During his eight months at Lewisburg, Hassler kept a seventy-thousand-word diary; his book appeared in 1954—the same year Alger was set free. I looked it up and read it; the New York University library, which I can see from my living-room window, has a perfectly preserved copy that appears as though it could have been printed just last week.

"Time in here," Hassler wrote, "drags with an indescribable slowness. I used to get up in the morning with a sense of anticipation for what the new day would bring; here one begins with the knowledge that the overall pattern of the day will be precisely what the overall pattern was yesterday, and the day before, and the day before that. And what it will be tomorrow, of course!" Several months later Hassler wrote that "time in prison simply cannot be measured by the standards used outside. The unvarying routine, the constant tension, the sense of humiliation—all these make every day a week and every week a year."

Another kind of slowness pervades the Lewisburg reservation—the core and the outside landscape. Prison systems seem to change even less rapidly than other large-scale, long-lived institutions. Hospitals and armies are driven by the need to incorporate the latest equipment every year. Colleges embrace new disciplines every decade or so. But Lewisburg, which opened in 1932, and which doesn't need to keep up with events but only to remain endlessly separate from them, could in 1970 be described, without irony, as "new," in the memoir of James V. Bennett, a former director of the Federal Bureau of Prisons. In late 1997 I could be shown the 1932-built cell with its intact 1932-installed furnishings to which my father had been assigned in late 1951.

For something like the last 2,500 years—pegging the date to one of the earliest prisons we know about, the vast underground Mamertine Prison in ancient Rome, a connected group of dungeons excavated below the main sewer of the city and completed in 640 B.C.—we have been efficiently removing prisoners from our midst. Less noticeably, and just as effectively, we have also been disconnecting our own lives from theirs.

Of all the *us* and *them* pairings that pop up whenever we think about other people, there's one that seems to carry over invariably from one society to another, from one era to the next. Prisoners are perhaps the most indelibly *them*-ish people in the world. Their absence from society gives the rest of us some protection—but not all that much, since decades ago it was estimated that at any given moment 75 percent of the people who commit crimes are at large. Nonetheless, the confinement of prisoners is a powerful force in keeping people's fears at bay. Remote from our daily thinking, barely reaching our most abstract sympathies, prisoners for the most part register only as a faint scariness at the far edges of the mind.

It's for this reason that the quick, mile-long journey from the right turn to the Big House invariably brings its own kind of endlessness, since it's a trip between realms that are at least a planet's width apart. This is also why the refreshment and nourishment of the spirit available in such abundance in the reservation's perimeter goes begging. Some inmates get occasional over-the-wall glimpses of the almost-all out there; none of them ever actually gets to move around in it. The general public, for security reasons, is expected to keep its distance, but outsiders shun this great gulf without being told to stay away. There are no gates, guardhouses, or barricades at the entrance to the reservation. The reluctance people bring with them is deterrence enough.

IT'S ONE thing to have put together a general working knowledge of everyday places that vanish from the mind like dreams, or to have contact with sad, odd, and moving places that linger under spells no one yet knows how to lift. I knew—had known for many years—that driving along a pleasant country road is, when that road leads to the Big House, the crossing of a narrow bridge over an invisible chasm, a miniaturized banishment. As I passed through the reservation, however, I seemed to have left dry land behind and was moving far beyond anything I had been expecting to encounter.

I knew some things about the landscape around me, but I hadn't seen it for forty-three years. I've never dreamed about it, and I've spent only minimal amounts of time in it—a sum total of a few dozen, five-minute-long drive-throughs in the early 1950s, either taxi rides from the town of Lewisburg or lifts from family friends driving west from New York. Not one of the bare trees or pine trees or pastures or tidy, white, frame houses looked recognizable, or evoked any images whatsoever, however faded, fragmented, or momentary. I thought I remembered that it was in Lewisburg taxis that I first heard drivers and dispatchers squawking at each other over two-way radios, something New York City cabs didn't have.

So I had the entirely accurate sense of finding again after a long absence a place that had never been more than vaguely familiar. How was it possible that every second I was, without meaning to, swaying very precisely into each twist and turn the road took? I couldn't explain it at first. From at least the middle of my drive through the reservation to the end, I felt as though I were swinging down a path I followed every day, and knew like the palm of my hand, meaning the exact and fully rounded knowledge that seeps into you in the places, usually only a few, that you've known in all weathers and in every season.

I seemed—this was very dreamlike—even to know what was going to happen next, correctly anticipating many of the road's jolts and sways and slowdowns. There was a tension straight across my shoulders and a feeling of urgency; my teeth were clenched and my breathing almost stopped. I would have been willing to bet, in this place I hadn't even come close to for three-quarters of my life, that on a moonless night I could walk this road blindfolded without a single misstep.

Drifting into my head came a name for the larger valley the reservation is only a piece of—Buffalo Valley, a place which bison herds had called home until they were killed off 200 years ago. Had someone once mentioned that name and that fact to my father, and he'd then passed them on to me? And wasn't there a well-known poem somewhere about the Buffalo Valley, and the way it looked from the air? It wasn't until I got home and tried to find the poem in a book of American poetry that I remembered that no one knew it, that it had never appeared in print but only in pencil, as an item included in *The Family Eagle*, pieces of paper that as a boy I laboriously compiled and called a newspaper, writing them out by hand, originally for only my parents to read.

The poem, "Near and Far," was something my father wrote for me in the spring of 1951, shortly after his arrival at Lewisburg, in response to a *Family Eagle* announcement of a poetry contest (limit ten lines). As far as I know, it's the only poem he ever wrote; it describes his view from a third-floor window that faces east, in a cell in the so-called quarantine wing of the prison, where incoming inmates are assigned. I found the piece of paper, now brittle, in a box at the top of the living-room closet:

Near and Far

I see from my window long ridges of dark woods;
But nearer fields roll away over hill after hill,
Now green, now brown. Against the black ridges a little
    train
Drags behind it a thin cloud of soft white;
But nearer a big crow lumbers much faster over the
    fields.
Off to the south the toy steeples are Milton, they say;
But nearer are large red barns and a blue house.

(April 6, 1951)

Driving toward the Big House, words seemed to float like a mist around what I was discovering I already knew about this road and the valley it ran through. An intense awareness had been tucked away inside me—where and how?—and I hadn't felt its presence (or even its absence) throughout my entire adult life. Yet it had assimilated this small roadway so accurately and so indelibly that my trip felt like taking up again—continuing, that is, rather than resuming—a regular and unbroken pattern from the early 1950s.

The full New York–Lewisburg trip is now no more than a three-hour breeze on I-80. Back before the interstates—which somehow sounds like a far earlier period in history than saying "fifty years ago"—Lewisburg seemed almost inaccessible to New Yorkers: It took seven or eight hours by car, and the alternative was several trains or several buses, or some combination of trains, cars, buses, and taxis. For my mother and me, with most of our thoughts reaching out to my father, the drive through the reservation was the sprint at the end of a tough monthly commute that led to a don't-waste-even-a-drop-of-it visit with Alger. In the early 1950s, federal regulations—they're now far more generous—limited visiting time with inmates to a maximum of two hours every month.

My old awareness must have been prepared to re-emerge the moment it was given half a chance. Some years ago, I found myself looking again and again at a magazine photograph of Conversation Hall, a very grand, late-Victorian ceremonial room in Philadelphia City Hall, ornate and glittering, that had just been rededicated after its almost fluke rediscovery. Decades before, to create space, the single immense room had been divided by partitions into two floors of small, drab offices. In the years since, whole generations of city workers had spent their entire working lives without so much as an inkling they were separated from grandeur by no more than a quarter inch of plasterboard. Until, one day, someone with a long enough memory began to yearn for the return of the great hall. Was it even possible? Workmen punched a hole in one of the flimsy cubicle walls, peered behind it with flashlights, and saw something glinting. . . .

How many things in life are we closer to than we think? And how many improbable events have to go right before we can rejoin them? Maybe the Philadelphia room was bound to be stumbled across, sooner or later. It could have been found again practically any day something needed fixing. For me, this road—a hundred miles from Philadelphia, a road most people never use in a lifetime—had to stay very much the same for almost half a century. Then I had to be invited to use it again for five or ten more minutes. But it did stay the same—and I also owe profound thanks to the people who authorized and welcomed my pilgrimage to Lewisburg, people in two institutions I didn't grow up feeling any gratitude toward, the Department of Justice and the Federal Bureau of Prisons.

The dreamlike sense that came to me on the road through the reservation—"Near and Far" is the best way to describe it—persisted for the rest of the day. I had a guide with me, or so it felt, a companion, someone to share notes with. There was a small, bright presence in my mind; was it something like the image my father had carried with him, the continuing contact with the girl who would become Justice Holmes's grandmother? The time I had recaptured, covering a much smaller span, was my own; the child from history I was responding to was myself, a boy, somewhat overweight, dreamy but just as often overly intense, someone who had lived awkwardly and uneasily in the corner of a once-huge event called the "Hiss case," accusations about lying, stealing, and betraying American secrets to communist Russia that led to what fifty years ago was called the "Trial of the Century" and sent Alger Hiss to jail.

If you have some old magazines, or the right selection of History Channel videos, you can occasionally spot this boy—that's right, the one with the crew cut and the silly, too-grown-up porkpie hat—over at the edge of some grainy, jumpy newsreel shots, trotting along several steps behind his father, trying to keep pace with that tall, lean man's long, brisk stride. I hadn't recovered my entire past—only about one-fifteenth of it: the Lewisburg years. Now I was back in touch with some of the thoughts and feelings, things I'd been confused about and things I'd understood, beginning when I was nine and continuing until I was thirteen.

Do people naturally organize their lives into sequences of long moments? If so, maybe we can see only the wakes of these moments as they recede behind us. My wife, who writes novels for teenagers, once told an interviewer that when she was seven she was surprised to wake up one morning and find that her perceptions of the world had changed forever. It happened again on a morning when she was fourteen, which made her expect a further change at twenty-one. But the pattern had completed itself, and she writes books about teenagers because that's what's natural to her; those are the feelings that have stayed fresh in her mind.

Until my return to Lewisburg, I had very few concrete memories of those years to call on. I'd always held on to the fact that it was then I started calling both my parents by their first names—Alger and Prossy (short for Priscilla); "Daddy" and "Mommy" no longer sounded, somehow, like words big enough to cover the kind of super-vigilant-we-must-stay-ready-in-case-there's-more-bad-news-ahead relationship that emerges after three people have been picking their way through an unending situation none of them had any training for. I also knew that Lewisburg had, most unexpectedly, been the place where Alger and I got to be firm friends.

People tell me about becoming grown-up friends with their

November 27, 1954: Alger is released from
prison. Tony is thirteen years old.

parents only after they were already well into their thirties. The Lewisburg visits got Alger and me started much sooner. Even though each visit amounted to one-three-hundredth of any month, for those two hours I finally had my father almost to myself. My world-traveling, dazzling, handsome, hardworking, so-often-away-from-home father, who, when home, had become my so-easily-monopolized-by-others father, had now been fastened to one fixed spot, and for almost the next four years could be seen, if you don't count occasional visits from his lawyers or the director of the Federal Bureau of Prisons, only by his family. But . . . since my friendship with Alger endured for more than half a century after he left Lewisburg, I would confidently have said, up until a year ago, that, having long ago gained the only thing of value from that time—pock-

eting the lone jewel I'd seen lying on a barren, stony plain—
what I particularly didn't need back was all those extra rocks.
This was the one part of my life I was overjoyed to have put
behind me.

My new guide, the boy in the porkpie hat, has been bringing that discarded time back. He himself has taken some getting to know. There were huge gaps in his information base, as
I already suspected—and other gaps, just as large, in memory.
His deepest feelings were at first below the reach of any words
and thoughts I would send down as hooks or bait to lure them
up into the light of day, surfacing only as vague, irrelevant
physical sensations—a tightening in the jaw, an ache along the
spine. It's been a kind of internal alchemy, this recovering of
experiences.

I'VE BEEN helped along by a couple of extraordinary circumstances—things already mine to make use of whenever I chose
to, but whose magic I'd never quite seen or needed before. Yet,
providentially, I'd held on to them tight since receiving them
from my mother a dozen years ago, just as she had never let go
of them for many years, either.

My Greenwich Village apartment in lower Manhattan is the
same old, third-floor, two-bedroom, last-renovated-midway-
through-World-War-I walk-up apartment that my parents
rented when they moved to New York City from Washington,
D.C., in 1947. I was six. "Starter apartment" wasn't a term that
existed a half century ago, but that's what my parents originally
assumed it would be. They settled there because they were too
busy even to look around (a sister-in-law found it for them),
and because apartments were so hard to find in New York in
the late 1940s you'd take just about anything; they stayed on in
the 1950s because they no longer had enough money to think
about moving to a bigger place. It was their home until 1959,

when they separated, about a month after their twenty-ninth wedding anniversary. It continued to be my mother's home for almost another quarter century; she died in 1984, a day after her eighty-first birthday. Now my wife and I share the place with our seven-year-old son, who sleeps in what long ago was my bed and my bedroom.

When I got back from Lewisburg, accompanied by the boy I had been, one of my first discoveries was that, by great good luck, the modest and comfortable apartment he and I had grown up in has during the last fifty years become a kind of time funnel, meaning a place where the "here and now" and the "there and then" can live side by side. The first time funnel I ever heard of was in *Mr. Wicker's Window*, a children's book I read while Alger was in Lewisburg; it revolved around a tumbledown shop that could take you back in time, but only to a single, specific point. In the book, the time funnel was presented as a wholly magical idea, the kind of invention that as a child makes you think: *How unfair that it's not real.* It wasn't until recently that I realized they're so real and so increasingly widespread that they're probably going to emerge as a real estate and planning problem, with conferences being held on how to operate them properly.

Real-world time funnels, some of them publicly owned, some in private hands, are bound to turn up in just about any American city or suburb now that change arrives at two different rates of speed—incrementally in protected historic districts, and overnight in free-for-all redevelopment areas. Look for time funnels wherever slow change and wholesale change bump up against each other. In *Mr. Wicker's Window*, one specially attuned boy looks out the front window of a dusty antique shop in Georgetown, the pre-revolutionary Washington neighborhood I'd been born in, and sees eighteenth-century sailing ships on the Potomac River instead of twentieth-century trucks and buses on an elevated highway that had been rumbling by just moments before he had entered the store. Real-life time funnels, I've now found, follow more of a front-door/back-door pattern.

A particularly dramatic time funnel presented itself to me recently—in the Peter Augustus Jay House in Rye, New York, on a day when a distinguished group of historians and museum curators had gathered to think about how the building, now a museum, might best serve the public. One answer seemed obvious enough—pop as many people as possible through the house's four-hundred-year-long time gateway. The front door of the Peter Augustus Jay House, which is a white nineteenth-century, Greek Revival mansion built by the son of the first Chief Justice of the United States, opens, like many suburban front doors, onto a twentieth-century scene, specifically in this case the noise and traffic on busy, oblivious Route 1, the shore road along the Long Island Sound.

But the Peter Augustus Jay House back door, two rooms and no more than forty feet behind the front door, opens directly onto a breathtakingly unchanged and now carefully guarded landscape that dates to the seventeenth century, and before that to the receding of the glaciers ten thousand years ago. There's a porch, a lawn, the sound of birdsong and of bees (not of cars), a sloping, half-mile-long salt meadow, a clump of woods beyond, and in the far distance a sparkling glimpse of the Sound. When I looked out this back door eight miles north of New York City during a break, a family of deer, entirely relaxed, moved slowly across the lawn, browsing, followed closely by a strutting line of wild turkeys.

My apartment is only a fifty-year-long funnel, but that makes it a good listening post for family matters. I've been using it as a small bathysphere for daily bobbing up and down through the second half of the twentieth century, which although only a thin layer of time is already dense and opaque. The apartment still has a lot of the old furniture my parents brought when they moved north from Washington, but it's the views from the edges of the apartment, not the chairs and tables in the middle of it, that bring me closer to what went before.

When you look out the three front windows of the apartment, there's nothing to see that connects to my boyhood or to Alger's pre-Lewisburg or post-Lewisburg occupancy— nothing Alger would even recognize, except perhaps the shape of the street, and the waving plumes of diesel fumes from the buses, and the fact that there are people walking by at almost every hour of the day and night. Everything else, sights and sounds, is a recent arrival: high-rises, boom boxes, car alarms, an all-night deli, a Starbucks.

But when I look through the back windows in my son's room or the little kitchen, I'm reminded that I'm seeing again almost exactly what I used to see. Sitting at the small kitchen table, with its old, chipped, green enamel top, a spot where my father's values poured into me through the letters he wrote home from Lewisburg, it's not much of a stretch to think that I could actually be looking through Alger's eyes. This is a view he admired when he lived next to it, and he kept it with him and saw it with his mind's eye throughout his time in jail.

There were reports after World War II that some British prisoners of war had stayed fit in Japanese internment camps, even though they never had enough to eat, by imagining preparing and consuming enormous feasts of their favorite foods. Alger frequently nourished himself with remembered landscapes—the interlacing bays and flat peninsulas of the Eastern Shore of Maryland, where he had spent summers as a boy; the gorge of Rock Creek Park, just below Georgetown in Washington; the hill farms and mountain ranges of the northern Vermont countryside around Peacham; and, from New York, our back view and Washington Square, the old Greenwich Village park a block from our house.

A friend of mine, a creative geographer who teaches at Texas A & M University, has written a much-cited study showing that if you're in a hospital recovering from an operation and can see trees out the window instead of a blank brick wall, you actually heal more quickly. No one's yet looked at the healing powers of views or landscapes so intensively loved that they've been entirely committed to memory, like a poem or a Bible verse—but it was interesting to find out, from a letter Prossy wrote Alger in Lewisburg in 1954, that she had been startled to discover, while reading a brand-new book by E. B. White, *The Second Tree from the Corner*, that our view had also left a permanent impression on him. From the book it appeared that White must have lived on our block sometime before we moved here. A number of apartments later in his own life, he found himself, in the mid-1950s, reaching back and savoring this particular and "infinitely refreshing" view, as he called it, when, for a short story, he needed a special image of peacefulness in the heart of the city. For White, in retrospect, even the summer air coming in through the back windows seemed cool and "filtered of all devils."

This old back view of mine, once Alger's and before that E. B. White's, happens, although it's completely urban, to be full, like the back-door view from the Peter Augustus Jay House, of sunshine and singing birds. It even has a surprising amount of quiet and green. The top half of this view is all sky—a great, arching, almost Western-sized sky—and the bottom half is, in the background, the low rooftops of nineteenth-century rowhouses and stables that the early twentieth century tinkered with. These eye-level rooftops have slanting skylights that glisten brightly and echo dully every time rain hits them; and thin, black chimney pots, some with conical hats and some with rounded tops that whirl like a globe whenever a wind comes by. It's a scene that Edward Hopper, who for many years lived a block away, painted and sketched, over and over.

. . .

IT'S THE foreground and bottom half of the view—my favorite part—that anchors it firmly to the past. Within three feet of these windows is what feels like woodland. There's a forest-canopy view of a miniature orchard of ten ornamental Japanese crabapple trees, tightly bunched, surprisingly tall, and, as the years go by, increasingly expansive, sturdy, and lush. Every spring, before leafing out, this tiny grove puts forth exuberant sprays of intensely colored, spicy-sweet, pink-shading-into-purple blossoms that I could actually lean out and pick, if it weren't for the window guards we installed when my son was a baby.

New York City's back-window, time-funnel views—like mine, they often point straight into the cherished, private center of small-scale, older city blocks where time has been allowed to eddy—can put people in touch with a number of friendly forces. You can sense the humming, the momentum of community-building projects started and continued by a chain of people long departed. These views give glimpses of the city's never-quite-obliterated small-town (or smaller-town) "first face," reminding us that New York, the "city of the twentieth century," as it used to be called in the 1940s and 1950s, has strengths that the twentieth century barely contributed to. New York's vitality reaches deep, and many neighborhoods were up and running so long ago that the newcomers who arrived with each passing decade needed only to add a few touches here and there, or correct the false strokes they found, rather than repaint the entire canvas.

Every time I look out my son's window, and every time I sit in my kitchen and have a sandwich or a cup of tea, I'm looking at everything that has been sustaining this block since it stopped being farmland six generations back. There's a brand-new rooftop air-conditioning duct three buildings away and, in the same glance, the place where, one building nearer, a set of old art studios had to be shored up after a fire in the 1960s big enough to light up the sky. But I can also see the point where our family entered the story of this block, and how it has since kept step with us.

Up to now, whenever I've looked out back, it's been my habit to glance first at the treetops, just to make sure that the trees were still in good health. Now I've realized this is also a way of taking my own pulse, by peering into a living mirror. The ten crabapple trees—there were originally twelve—grow in a shared backyard that, although large enough to be surrounded by and available to twelve small buildings, is nearly invisible from the street. When my parents and I moved to the block, this garden had no trees at all, only three small, green, roofless summerhouses E. B. White had once admired. But in March 1951, right at the beginning of the second half of Alger's life, and less than a month before he left for Lewisburg, two of the summerhouses were removed so that—overnight—apple saplings could be planted.

Of course this improvement to the property by the landlord had nothing to do with what was happening to my family. But the timing of it gave us something to measure our lives by from that moment forward. I hadn't remembered this coinciding of dates until I found that my mother had written my father about it in one of her early letters to him in jail.

For the boy who watched these trees when they were very young, each time they came into bud and flowered again marked a full year subtracted from the time that had to be spent waiting for his father's return. Beauty meant more than hope, it meant accomplishment—progress toward an always present goal. "Overshadowing everything else," Alfred Hassler has written about the Lewisburg prisoners' sense of time, "is the distant release date. I have not met a man in here yet who does not know to the day how long he has still to serve!" The same clocks, wound up on the day a sentence begins, tick steadily inside the families of prisoners as well.

For a middle-aged man glancing out the back window, the trees celebrate a different kind of anniversary. One of the titles Alger considered for his second book, *Recollections of a Life*, the reminiscences he published a decade ago, was "Memoirs of a Diverted Life." It was a title I remember admiring as very *Alger-ish*, because it embraced the fact that the second half of his life had started off with a prison term, but continued to unfold for him, unshattered, changed but still full of wonder. When I look out the window, half my view is of that moment of diversion and of what it's grown into. I see a grove of trees that's been constantly gathering strength through forty-nine flowerings; an early friendship with my father that might otherwise never have blossomed; and the recent reunion with the boy who forged that friendship—the whole trajectory of unforeseen and unfinished events flowing through time from that turning point on.

AFTER I got home from Lewisburg, I hauled out the heap of family papers, mostly old letters and photographs, that since my mother's death had been sitting much as she left them— carelessly organized, it had always seemed to me, but at the same time quite carefully put aside in the collection of cartons, file boxes, legal folders, and shopping bags I'd packed away at the top of the front closet. By now they were behind the supplies my family had been accumulating for a dozen years: the star for the top of the Christmas tree; the plastic jack-o'- lantern my son still uses for trick-or-treating; the night-light he no longer needs.

Some of the old letters were easily retrieved—"Near and Far," Alger's poem, close to the front of the first carton I opened, seemed to spring into my hands; and Prossy's letter referring to E. B. White was part of a bundle in the box under that. The aged rubber bands my mother had slapped around dozens of packets of letters now crumbled even before I touched them, like a sand castle when a breeze picks up. I couldn't stop until I'd looked at everything there was to look at, something that took twice as long as it should have, because two of us, a man and a boy, had to finish each page before it could be turned over. He wants to know what's going to happen next; he's reading to catch up on what for him are still current events; he's finding out more about his new friend, Alger.

Arranging the thousand or more photographs Prossy left behind in big albums (and adding some never-sorted pictures of my own) took only a couple of weeks: The snapshots now march in unison with each innovation to hit the market the family could afford, moving from brown-and-white to black-and-white to color, from daguerreotype to Brownie to Polaroid. I can now see lives in great bursts. My brother, Tim Hobson, who was born in 1926 during Prossy's short first marriage (to a man named Thayer Hobson), and who is now a retired surgeon and a grandfather living in San Francisco, enters as a chubby, blond toddler in a little boy's sailor suit in New York, and long after that, having grown into a slim, dark-haired, crew-cut teenager in a real naval uniform, holds me when I was a chubby, blond baby in Washington. Much later, during the Lewisburg years, he's a confident-looking medical student standing on a lawn in Switzerland, hands in his pockets, and at the end of another twenty years, a father of four setting up a practice in Rawlins, Wyoming.

There's also my father's slowly reblossoming smile. He'd grinned delightedly at fourteen, wearing a full Indian war bonnet for a summer camp assembly. But in most pictures of Alger as a young man the smile has disappeared, its place taken by a grave and steadfast look, although occasionally you can catch sight of a wondering, wistful look. Then comes the one por-

Alger at summer camp

Alger's official prison portrait

trait for families sent back from Lewisburg, where Alger's small smile matches the officially sanctioned, awkward, artificial occasion—the prisoners, one at a time, had to put on borrowed clothes, a local photographer's white dress shirt, striped tie, and enormously too large tweed jacket. But Alger used the moment to smuggle something home—the smile in his eyes is unforced, merry, and bright. Now I can match these to a relaxed picture he gave me years ago, which shows him in his early eighties sitting, arms folded, on a lawn chair in a V-neck sweater over a turtleneck and corduroy pants, and his eyes are glowing, and he's laughing.

There were more than 2,500 old letters and postcards. Although the voices they record have stayed as fresh and clear as during those far-off seasons of solitude when, pen in hand, thoughts or feelings or insights or sillinesses just bubbled up and had to be transcribed at once, scribbled out post haste, poured forth on paper before they would forever fade beyond recall—the ink and paper are less resilient. Given this situation, that the containers we hand on are more perishable than their contents, it seemed sensible to be gingerly and photocopy every page.

With tall piles of copied letters covering the twelve-foot-long living-room windowsill in my apartment (and the real letters, carefully repacked, back in the closet), I found I had almost the entire output of a voluminous family correspondence sustained across six different decades. There were letters of Alger's to Prossy from 1924 through 1971; hers to him dating back to the mid-1940s; postwar letters and cards to all of us from my brother; from Alger's brother, Donie; from Prossy's brother, Tommy; from cousins, aunts, devoted friends, lawyers, ministers, and complete strangers. Lewisburg unmistakably formed the heart of the collection: the 445 letters that Alger had mailed home from prison, along with the 919 letters and cards he'd received there from us and from others, which he'd kept in neat stacks in his cell month after month, and, by special arrangement with the warden, had been allowed to send home shortly before his release. These letters were filled with so many concisely rendered details of daily life—all prison letters, in and out, were by regulation confined to two pages— that they added up to what was nearly an hour-by-hour re-creation of an almost four-year span in my family's history.

Except for a handful of letters I scanned a few years ago when writing a quick magazine article about Alger, no one has seen these letters, which Prossy kept after she and Alger separated, since the early 1960s. It was then that Prossy, always a very private person, stopped showing anything from her life to friends or family. During all the time I could have looked at the letters and didn't—for years, of course (such is the nature of New York City apartment life), they had practically hovered over my shoulder every time I sat down to dinner—I had thought of the Lewisburg letters, when I remembered them at all, with exasperation. I felt going through and putting them in order was a chore that eventually I'd have to do, if it was going to be done, simply because my mother had never gotten around to it. I even thought I'd learned something: *Be careful*, I had pointedly (and smugly) said to myself, *of the work you leave behind for others*.

No, not so. The letters have been as valuable as the time funnel I live in. Now I have a reliable chronicle of certain once-upon-a-time events within and beyond a high wall in Pennsylvania; and what amounts to a printout of so many memories that I and the boy in me have been groping to reconstruct. And I'm lastingly back in touch—this feels like real luck; there hadn't seemed any way to conjure this up—with an Alger who didn't or couldn't in most of life's circumstances fully show himself, even to those who meant most to him. I'd only as a small child seen occasional glimpses of him myself. But the Alger of the letters, who came to the front at Lewisburg—and before then and after that was almost always partially hidden—was, as things played out, the man I'd made friends with in the spring of 1951.

I had remembered Alger's letters as supportive, cheerful, chatty, and little more—a distancing memory at several removes from the letters themselves. What I was remembering was a post-Lewisburg teenager's tough-guy assumption about the intended effect the letters were supposed to have. I had not remembered how greatly that teenager, or the man he eventually grew into, had been molded by reading those letters. Whatever the full intentions their author may have had, I could now see the more intricate reality below the memory. The boy who had received those letters had gulped them down whole, rejoiced in them, used their values to fortify his values, memorized everything understandable he could find in them with his soul—and then, being a boy, and not wanting to feel too lonely (since, when you thought about it, there were so many miles and such a high wall standing between the reader and the writer), had instructed his conscious mind to forget the matter entirely, rather than admit that something extraordinary had taken place.

Similarly, I was not prepared to find that Alger's Lewisburg letters, the great majority of which were jointly addressed to Prossy and me (with passages that were specially for me in printed-out words, and the paragraphs for both of us in Alger's flowing script), seemed now on second reading to be jointly addressed to me as I am at present and to the boy who'd just hitched a ride home from Lewisburg. While engaged in this bifocal rereading, I also had to shift in an instant from being the son in an old story to being the father in a new one—the very afternoon, for instance, that I read the letter in which Alger talked about how much fun he'd had, just before I got home from school, waiting for me to ring the lobby doorbell four times (the family ring), so he could charge downstairs and see if he could get to the second floor before I could get up to the second floor, our daily game, the doorbell buzzed four times.

The family ring. My son, Jacob, was home from school. I had to rush out to the hall and get to the second floor before he did. Our daily game. I was sure I had made it up, or Jacob had. I had taught him the family ring—but, even so, I felt I'd been sailing for most of my life, certainly throughout the forty-year interval that elapsed between first reading and second reading, under sealed orders. Also hidden was the fact that the sealing off had been my own idea.

It's not that I've suddenly been granted 20/20 vision into my family's doings. But it seems I've been handed something that may prove equally useful: a kind of '50s/'90s vision of events, in which both decades keep unspooling, side by side, each one showing how to peer more deeply into the other. You know more about the shape and moods of a mountain after you've climbed it from both the north and the south. Both the roundedness and singularities in people get clearer, too—or at least reveal a very different set of lights and shadows—once you've looked up at them from the past and back at them from the present. At any rate, I'm beginning to have a new understanding of what it means to know a subject "backwards and forwards."

Alger's first letters home, in March and April of 1951, were mainly informational—getting acquainted with Lewisburg and spelling out some of its odd, rigid procedures and unchallengeable customs. Here are a few extracts, run together: "This place is quite large. It is set in its own farm of several hundred acres. As one approaches it, it looks like a European castle, with a great wall (thirty feet high) around it with guard towers at the corners that have crenelated tops. The main building, set back from the wall for fifty yards or so, is a large square structure that looks like a college or military school.

"For the next 30 days or so I will be filling out forms, getting typhoid shots + the like, having physical exams and I.Q. tests, and finally being assigned to a job. During that period I may have no visits. After that I am permitted 2 hours of visiting time a month. . . . the visits are in a group of easy chairs—no glass partition or telephones—and 'handshaking, embracing and kissing by immediate members of the family only, will be permitted within the bounds of good taste at greeting and parting.' So, we can certainly have our family hugs, hooray!

"I have listed as my seven permitted correspondents: you two, Moby [my nickname for my brother, Tim; when I was little I couldn't say "my brother," so I said "Mobo," which became "Moby"], Mimmie [Mary Livinia Hiss, my grand-mother], Donie [Alger's younger brother], Anna [his older sister, director of the women's phys ed program at the University of Texas for many decades] and Helen [Helen L. Buttenwieser, one of his lawyers]. But I have just written Mimmie (who sent me two letters to West St. [the Federal Detention Headquarters, New York, in Greenwich Village, originally a garage and now demolished, that he'd been sent to his first week, a place where prisoners and visitors did have to speak to each other on telephones while looking at each other through plate glass]) that she must write only once a week, otherwise she will cut off some of your letters—as I can receive a total of only 7 letters a week from my 7 permitted correspondents. . . . I may write but 3 a week to all my correspondents combined, so all but you two will understand that I will write the others very rarely" (March 28, 1951).

"As you can see, I have now my Wearever [pen] back again [the previous two letters had been written in pencil]. I also have my Westclox pocket Ben, my pipe, my photographs, and

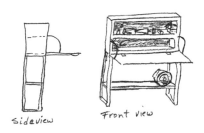

Moby's nail clippers. The writing pad + the three nickels Tony gave me for my birthday are being returned collect from here with my shoes, gloves & nail file. Tony, will you please save the three nickels for me in a little envelope in your cash register. . . . Tony: please don't feel bad that I can't have the three nickels here. The rule is that none of us can have money in our possession. . . . Tony: My room is almost as big as yours. I have my own toilet and wash basin (with hot and cold water), a comfortable iron cot, a broom to sweep it with, a chair and a metal desk, called a locker.

"On the top shelf of the desk I keep my shaving brush,

razor, shaving cream, blades, nail clippers in their box, packs of cigarettes, etc. On the bottom shelf I keep my letters stacked up and will have room for cookies, candy bars, etc. I write on the open desk flap which folds up as the front of the locker when I'm not writing. On the open bottom shelf I keep a bath robe (given to me to use in going to take a shower) rolled and soon will have a white (dress) shirt to add to it.

"The room is heated by a large pipe that runs from floor to ceiling in one corner and it is cooled simply by opening the window" (March 30, 1951).

"Today is a beautiful sunny day and after two gray days I was able to confirm that my window faces due East—toward New York, toward you. The country air is mild & sweet and I keep my window open a good deal" (March 31, 1951).

"Today, Tony started back to school. I get up at quarter of seven, make my bed, get dressed and finish breakfast before eight—just the way Tony does. So we'll all be doing the same things at the same time each school morning" (April 2, 1951).

EARLY ON in life, my mother devised her own strategy for extending the present moment indefinitely. She used her front door to wall off the passage of time. It was her habit—maddening, unsystematic, but in the end more effective than you might think—to hang on tight to almost anything written down or printed that had been handed to her. As a result, I'm now the owner of ration books from World War II; a 1931 postcard telling her a book she had reserved was being held at the Columbia University Library; her 1948 contract as a middle school English teacher at the Dalton Schools; her 1974 appointment to Manhattan's Community Planning Board No. 2—and all the faces and voices that spring forth with such strength from all the photographs and letters.

She lived in the middle of increasing amounts of clutter—in

her final years it threatened to swamp her—but all the time she held fast to an idea about how and when to measure the worth of things: *Don't foreclose your options; don't put too much stock in first impressions; don't give up on anything prematurely; the true value of many a day becomes apparent only long after the sun has set.* Prossy's stubbornness did not always serve her well—long after my father had found happiness with the beautiful Isabel Johnson (who later became his second wife), Prossy clung to a belief that Alger would someday return.

At the same time—what a truly unmixed blessing it has proved to be that both my parents were born early enough in the twentieth century (Prossy in 1903; Alger a year later), and loved literature enough, and were so unswayed by technology, and so seldom had enough money to be extravagant with, that they both spent their lives as letter writers. They mastered, rejoiced at, reveled in an everyday art form that even in their own generation had already begun to disappear. Leisurely, discursive letter writing, undertaken whenever a spare, calm half hour presented itself (and not a telegram, which hides nuances, or a hurried long-distance phone call, which leaves no record at all), was for them unquestionably the most natural, the least distorting, and the only fully rewarding way to stay in touch during any separation. Rewarding because sender and recipient each took equal pleasure from the creating and the savoring of a letter exchanged. More pleasure again from putting just-opened letters aside for future rereading.

What a serious commitment of time this kind of staying in touch entails—it probably took my parents a full half-year of their lives to produce. I hadn't realized just how many separations my parents had to endure during their three decades together, and how lengthy some of them were. But devoted writing during each time apart had become their habit even before they were married—which is why the Lewisburg letters are preceded by a warm-up correspondence of more than 150 letters. In the fall of 1929, for instance, Alger moved to Washington to become Justice Holmes's secretary; but Prossy, who over the summer had become his fiancée, and Tim, her three-year-old son, were living in New York. In June of the following year, Alger went to Massachusetts to the Justice's Cape Ann summer house in Beverly Farms, while Prossy, who'd been his wife since December, stayed in Washington with Tim. A year later, Alger, who'd been practicing law in Boston since his term with Holmes was up, accepted a job in New York—but then, to finish work on an antitrust suit, stayed in Boston for eight months after Prossy and Tim had moved to New York.

Alger went to Washington in the spring of 1933 to join President Roosevelt's New Deal while Prossy and Tim were still in New York; in the summer of 1944 he had to stay in Washington for the Dumbarton Oaks Conference while Prossy was in Peacham (Tim was now on his own); the following spring he was in San Francisco as Secretary-General of the conference setting up the United Nations while she was in Washington; and the next winter she was in Washington when he went to London for the first meeting of the U.N. General Assembly.

Alger and Prossy had actually been exchanging letters for twenty-six years before Lewisburg—they met on an ocean liner bound for England in the summer of 1924. That was one of the first years cheap vacation fares were offered to college students, and Alger wrote Prossy for the first time on the way home—they were on different ships this time, but had made an arrangement to think of each other, and, through some kind of oceanic telepathy, to try to touch each other's thoughts every afternoon at four. (Alger wrote to say that it hadn't worked, but only because he had forgotten that the two ships' clocks were set to different times.)

Many themes that flow through the Lewisburg letters—notes about paintings, about concerts and records, thoughts prompted by books just read and suggestions for books to catch up on, reports on articles in the latest issues of *The New Yorker* and *Punch* and a few other magazines, reminiscences about Justice Holmes, a list of birds seen and heard—make their appearance in this preliminary, prior correspondence. So do a number of shared conventions and special usages: Prossy's nickname for Alger—"Hill"—seems to date back to the beginning of their relationship, but since I never thought to ask them where it came from, it's always going to be one of the things I can only guess at.

A hill of strength? A play on "Hiss"? One of the South Downs they climbed together in the summer of 1924 when they scarcely knew each other, when he was nineteen and she was twenty? I have to keep reminding myself—this is such a big stretch, one I can never quite get used to—how very much younger they were in almost all their letters than I have somehow already become. So were almost all the people they were writing about—my brother, Tim, for instance, the retired surgeon, was twenty-four when Alger entered Lewisburg, and just thinking about taking a crack at some pre-med courses at New York University. Everyone seems to have been moving through life so rapidly, too: When he got to Lewisburg (where, in pickup softball games in the yard, he was part of the "old-timers" team), Alger, at forty-six, had been married for twenty-one years and had a young son and a grown stepson. He'd been Holmes's clerk in Washington and then a lawyer in Boston and in New York.

As a New Dealer, a champion of the reforms Franklin D. Roosevelt brought to Washington to pull the country out of the Great Depression, Alger had lived again in Washington, this time serving as a federal official for fourteen years, working for Congress and for three different agencies in the executive branch—the Agriculture Department, the Justice Department, and the State Department. He'd been a New

York foundation administrator for two years, serving as president of the Carnegie Endowment for International Peace. And, as the defendant in two of the most sensational criminal trials in American history—accused and eventually convicted of a crime that amounted to treason: denying that in the mid-1930s he had passed State Department documents to a man who said he had been a spy for the Soviet Union—Alger had appeared on the front pages of every newspaper in the country for almost three years running.

At forty-six, I'd had one job and had been married for a couple of years; no kids yet. By the time Alger was the age I am now, his pre-Lewisburg existence was a thing of the past, and he had already settled with great contentment into the stable patterns of the second half of his life: He had met my stepmother; he was spending summers in a tiny cottage on Long Island; he was surrounded by a large devoted circle of loving friends; and he was working for a New York printing business, S. Novick and Son, Inc., as a salesman. At the end, he was, I think, equally proud of what he had accomplished in both halves of his life.

Although neither of my parents was ever formally a Quaker, they began using the "little language," as the Quakers call it—meaning *thee*s and *thy*s—in their letters as soon as they got married; they were both attached to Prossy's college roommate and lifelong and generous friend, Roberta Murray, who was also for a while her sister-in-law. Bobby, a "Birthright Friend" from an old New York Quaker family, the Murrays of Murray Hill, had already incorporated Alger and Prossy into the "little language" she used within her own family. The early Alger-to-Prossy letters were also where Alger invented the principal space saver he later returned to in Lewisburg—writing "x" or "x-x" to indicate a shift in thought, and "x-x-x" between paragraphs rather than waste paper by dropping down to the next line.

The many shared references that turn up as catchphrases in Alger's Lewisburg letters are a later acquisition, picked up from many years of the family tradition of reading aloud to each other on holidays: "Dear March, come in, I've so much to tell" (sometimes used at the beginning of letters, it comes from an Emily Dickinson poem); "I'm certain, I think" (used throughout, it comes from the Golux, the lovable magician who kept getting his spells muddled in James Thurber's fable *The Thirteen Clocks*); "No more twist" (found at the end of letters, it's from the English children's book we always read on Christmas Eve—*The Tailor of Gloucester*, by Beatrix Potter, author of the Peter Rabbit stories, an unforgettable fairy tale of redemption and Christmas cheer about how small animals speak in human tongues every Christmas Eve; industrious mice work invisibly behind the walls of Gloucester's old houses to rescue an exhausted old man at his wit's end).

So, for instance, from Alger's letter home of May 9, 1951:

"x-x-x We have been busy in our 'store' [Alger's recently assigned prison job was assisting in the storeroom]—the first 3 days of every 2nd week are devoted to stationery orders from all departments + offices and this week they coincided with numerous receipts of incoming supplies to be unloaded, unpacked & stored on shelves. Tony: Today I ran the freight elevator by myself for the first time + made good level landings—well, almost always. And from my windows in the storeroom I can see a real Diesel switching engine every now + then, shunting freight cars that bring supplies & haul away the things made in the shops here. x-x-x Last night there was a clear clean fingernail moon, in fairly close conjunction to a brilliant planet (Venus?). Did thee see it? The maintenance crew has been putting several round plots of 'geraniums red' into the grounds. On Sunday the altar had two large bowls of the most beautiful blue-violet iris I have ever seen. From my nearby choir-seat I stared at them as I would have at a new Van Gogh. . . . Back to nature—my bird list continues to grow. The chimney swifts arrived over the week-end + last night I'm sure, I think, I saw a night hawk + the night before a short-tailed swallow (bank, cliff, rough-winged?)"

Since Alger spent the second half of his life trying repeatedly—and always unsuccessfully—to get his perjury conviction reversed, and because there are still many people who, when they think of him, see a law case and not a life, a question naturally arises about the contents of the family letters: There is nothing in any of the six decades of letters that in any way either corroborates the accusations of treason and espionage brought against Alger or gives even a suggestion or hint that he was the kind of man willing to betray his country. There are frequent musings about the virtues of a foreign country—but it's usually England (my parents even gave me what they considered a quintessential English name, Anthony), or France, not Russia (even in the 1930s, when it was commonplace to talk about communism). There are recurrent references, especially in the Lewisburg letters, to a nineteenth-century European thinker who changed the world—but the man Alger had come to admire so greatly was Sigmund Freud, not Karl Marx.

What does this prove? To me, nothing at all—and a great deal. It used to be said by some of Alger's enemies that he was "the greatest actor that America has ever produced." If that's what he was, then he would, of course, have been quite capable of writing and leaving in his wife's care 650 letters over the course of forty-seven years (while at the same time sending to my brother dozens of letters which he's carefully preserved, not to mention dozens of cards and letters to me throughout my life) in which he deliberately presents himself as a loyal American devoted to his country's welfare—even if it never occurred to him to retrieve these letters and use them as evidence to support his cover story of having been an upright man all along.

Of course, that kind of argument needs a little elaboration, because if Alger was the greatest actor in America—that is to say until now, since of course records, as sportswriters like to remind us, are made to be broken—my mother must have been the second greatest actor, because she wrote, preserved, and left behind (and refused to make public) 742 letters to her husband which, while seeming to deal with the ups and downs of normal family life and extraordinary family circumstances, by this logic must inevitably have carried the constant and always hidden purpose of bolstering the lies in Alger's letters. Similarly, my uncle Donald, who, like my mother, was accused by Whittaker Chambers of underground communist activities but never formally charged with any crimes (Donie was a successful Washington lawyer for the rest of his days), must have been the third greatest actor, because, although not much of a letter writer, he did go to the trouble of writing Alger a dozen letters at Lewisburg, all of which express only admiration for Alger's steadfastness and continuing efforts to clear his name.

You can't prove a negative, as students of the Hiss case have often pointed out, and under that premise the letters—their existence, their content—probably have minor standing and maybe even add more muddle to the increasingly bitter argument on which the case has always turned: *Did he, or didn't he?* It's now more than fifty years since that controversy first raged and dominated front-page headlines, and yet "the case will not close," according to a recent report by a historian hostile to Alger. Another historian with some sympathies for Alger concurs—for her the case "is not fully resolved and may never be." On the other hand, the Lewisburg letters shine forth with qualities that, while they may or may not have a bearing on the "either-or" question, far transcend it.

They are a window flung wide open onto a life, a bird of the spirit springing into the air, a heart made plain—and I know that because I recognize it. The spirit that was set down on paper three times a week for forty-four months, the one I've been re-encountering, appears exactly as it did when first shown to me, and I slowly got to know it, month after month, for two hours at a stretch in the Lewisburg visitors' room.

It's not that I was completely dazzled, even back then. Not everything I saw was admirable—there were blind spots as big as a barn, and Alger could be maddeningly obstinate and obtuse about people and their actions. The wonder of it came from seeing so clearly straight into the inner substance of another person.

Because these prison letters invite us to hold an entire life by the hand—perhaps that, at some later point, can help us find a path through what in the end will prove not to be such an eternally unresolvable quagmire. A life speaks to us through so many more dimensions than a law case can, so maybe when, having been surrounded for a time by all its flavors and textures, we've at length got the taste of it down in our marrow, we could find we've gained a new capacity to weigh the likelihood of whether that individual life could have included the particular actions of which Alger stood accused.

What is the opposite of a "smoking gun," the conclusive, clinching negative that sews everything up? We haven't come up with the phrase for such a situation; perhaps we haven't run across enough of them to need one. Swords get beaten into plowshares, or so at least the prophet Isaiah, who saw far into the future, predicted, on a day beyond his time (and still awaited by our own). Maybe the phrase "shining plowshare" will do.

"The silver swan, who living had no note"—so began an Elizabethan madrigal that my Quaker Aunt Bobby's family liked to sing—"when death approached unlocked her silent throat. Leaning her breast against the reedy shore, thus sang her first and last, and sang no more." People who liked Alger used to complain that he never told his story properly in either of his two books, one written in his fifties, the other in his eighties. The first book, *In the Court of Public Opinion*, about living through the Hiss case, received savage reviews, particularly from critics who had already taken sides against Alger. Sidney Hook, for instance, reviewing the book for the Sunday *New York Times Book Review*, said both that "Chambers must have been telling the truth," and that Alger's writing was "curiously flat": It "has no warmth or color and contains little of his life, thought, or the drama of his downfall."

Reviews like these, Alger's friends would tell me with sighs, were half right. Alger's writing was so wooden or leaden, so chilly and detached, you would think he had no feelings to express. We hear his denials, they'd say, but why wasn't he as emphatic about the positives—we want to hear about what he did do, what he does believe in. He sounds (some of them would go on to say, lowering their voices), almost inhuman, as if he had something to hide after all. Where was his true voice, the one whose ring they often caught in private conversations?

The half-million words that Alger sent home from prison were the book he never wrote, or, more accurately, the book that in later years he had already written and couldn't afterwards duplicate. The letters were the one outpouring when his words consistently caught fire. Why was this? Now that his journey is complete, I think I know. A fast-flowing stream making its way from the mountains to the sea found the middle of its passage unexpectedly blocked by a temporary dam. For forty-four months, as it was held in one place for the first time, its banks rose to form a pool, and its purest waters welled up from below. At one edge of the new pool, with their current slowed, they lapped quietly against a beach where I was learning to swim.

THE ESSENCE that Alger had kept private for so long that it seemed suspect and deliberately hidden was not a contradiction or negation of his public self—it held the same values, pursued the same goals. But the inmost Alger was so much more effervescent and playful than the outward Alger, and could express itself so much more forcefully and pungently, that the publicly presented Alger—slower, more stilted, careful, cautious, polished, punctilious, and so lawyerly—seems like an incomplete person. Perhaps the contrast is more vivid for me, knowing how much of the other Alger, my friend, was omitted from the Alger the world got to see.

The difference between the two Algers was brought vividly to mind when I needed to check a Holmes reference. I pulled out a copy of the paperback version of the *Holmes-Laski Letters*, a collection of the twenty-year correspondence between two people for whom, living on different continents, letter writing was the only way to establish and sustain a close friendship—Justice Holmes and Harold J. Laski, a dazzlingly brilliant English scholar fifty-two years younger than Holmes. Their many hundreds of letters, carefully preserved by both recipients, became a two-volume book which Alger abridged for paperback in the early 1960s.

I'd been reading two of Alger's letters that dealt with Holmes—the Lewisburg letters, incidentally, are all first drafts, uncorrected except for very occasional interlineations. The first letter, from 1952, was responding to a picture postcard my mother had just sent him. It was an old family tradition to refer to Mr. Justice Holmes simply as "Justice." This dated back to the summer of 1930, when my brother, Tim, then three, was introduced to Felix Frankfurter, at that time the Harvard Law School professor who chose Holmes's new secretaries every year. Tim asked him brightly, "Do you know

Justice?"—meaning, of course, Holmes. Frankfurter, the story went, was momentarily staggered by this infant's profound metaphysical inquiry.

"The Morisot 'Edouard Manet + sa fille,' " Alger wrote home on December 4, 1952, "*is* charming + was unknown to me, too. [It's a picture of the painter sitting primly, one hand in

Shore, passing not far from Chestertown. The winter wheat is green, the "magnolia bushes popping" + the F.S. "as flat and charming as ever". He crossed to Virginia on the wonderful (full of flowers + wisteria) ferry Mommy can tell you about + visited Charleston, S.C., which he thought "perhaps the prettiest city" he's seen, —like Georgetown. In Florida he got sunburned "lobster pink" right away. He saw parrots in the woods + a lazy pelican who doesn't catch his own fish - eats these the fishermen give him - + a red-headed woodpecker has a nest right outside his window. He's been swimming, of course, the lucky duck, + this week they are going to visit the state parks, leaving on Fri. t. be back for his classes on the 14th. There was lots more - all very good + interesting, especially a description of a long discussion about life on the drive down in which our Tim, of course, was on the side that people must grow up + live on the basis of "love-trust-truth" instead of "fear-distrust-lies." But there isn't any more room for the rest of it. x-x-x I'm so glad you heard the peepers. x-x Here's a spring idea. Why don't you ask Mommy to ride up to school in the bus with you one or two mornings a week, so she can see Spring changing the Park week by week? x-x Now I have to save the rest of the twist for tomorrow, though - as with our visits. there's lots more to tell x-x-x Continued Tues. evening at 2:00 p.m. x I have just come back from the library where I was studying Hogben's "Science for the Citizen", trying to understand why the constellations rise, + of course set, earlier each night - so that Sirius the friendly dog star will in a little over 1 more month set before it is dark and therefore not be visible at all during June. I've got it all clear in my head once again - it's really very simple, as you know, merely the result of the earth's swinging completely round the sun once a year. Naturally, the sun's brightness makes it impossible for us to see the stars that are from month to month more or less behind it, as the sun gets between them + the earth. Sirius in June / Earth in Dec. / Sun / Earth in June — The distances in my sketch are not nearly so much in proportion (nor the sizes of Sirius, Earth + Sun) as Peter K:S.'s pasture diagram! x The nearby trees all have fat buds or catkins + the maples look quite pinkish. This morning, before breakfast, a dove sat on the wall + turned about, bobbing + ducking his head like a male pigeon in the park. I've never seen a timid dove do this before - probably because I have never been so close to one that didn't realize people were nearby x Mommy's Mon. afternoon letter came today. She wrote out the chorale that is repeated again + again in the St. Matthew Passion. And she told me that the lettuce is already up in your window box! Also that the first rush-seating Alger Hiss 1913?/ project has started. 8th St. sounds very busy. Trucks, stones, + bushels of love,

his jacket pocket, playing a game with his small daughter on a park bench in springtime.] I notice that Les Editions Nomis [the Parisian postcard printers] include Berthe Morisot's dates, 1841–1895. She (?) was born in the same year as 'Justice' +, as the painting emphasizes, grew to maturity as he did in a world, inner as well as outer, that was fragile + myopic. Those like

B.M. + O.W.H., Jr.'s set (Henry Adams, Henry James as bell-wethers) who could afford to cultivate beauty did so with charm + surface complexity. Blessed few of that generation looked at their world with clarity, profundity + vigor sufficient to see man's potentialities as a distant grandeur dwarfing their miniature minority culture. O.W.H. + Cezanne are among the blessed few in their fields—O.W.H. capable of the grand perspective coupled with hearty relish of all healthy processes of growth; Cezanne with a simplicity of outlook undistorted by the rationalized conventions of a provincial, smug + self-imprisoned society."

On March 3, 1953, Mark DeWolfe Howe, Jr., Harvard Law School professor, former Holmes secretary (the next-to-last one, in 1933–1934), and editor of the unabridged, hardcover *Holmes-Laski Letters*, had just sent Alger a copy of this then brand-new book: "x-x Thy dear letter of Sun. just come. Thee + O.W.H. have the gift of making letters a true extension of your personality. In both cases the letters bring the writer with them. Thee can imagine the pleasure thy letters give when thee comes to read his. Mark has done a superb job of editing—notes which enrich the text by explanation but never burden it, no 'display' learning— + the dust jacket, even, is a delightful part of the book (the lovely photograph, taken in 'our' year [1929–1930] or close thereto, of the Justice seated before a well-remembered section of his shelves).

"Never having been Laskivious, I find L's letters the bread to the sandwich. They are interesting as journalistic + gossipy mental excursions, but Holmes' letters shine on the page with the light of his fullness of life. To be sure H.L. brought out only one side of H's rich nature but all sides were so integrated that the full glow illuminates whatever he gave himself to. And he had an immediate intensity + fullness of focus in all personal relations—no divided or wandering mind for him. That quality, so notable in his talk, informs the letters with his warm +

vital personality—hard of head + sensitive of spirit. And to think that he didn't value Cezanne, whom he calls the 'goddest God,' rightly, of the 'modernist painters.' And that music, too, meant little to him—'I do not believe that music is the highest expression of man' he says in the judicial backhand that means, as with diplomatic usage, what it does not say."

For comparative purposes, here is a brief excerpt (it's dated February 1963) from the Alger of the printed page, the public Alger on whom so many of the world's judgments, the supportive as well as the disparaging, have been based. It's from "The Methodology of the Abridgement," his introduction to the paperback edition of the *Holmes-Laski Letters:*

"It is appropriate to set out the criteria I have tried to follow in deciding upon the extensive excisions made necessary by limitations of space. First, I have sought to present without disfigurement the rich and varied contents of these widely-ranging, highly-civilized letters. Next, I have tried to preserve the tone of responsive dialogue which is the matrix for the self-portraits sketched by the two authors as they revealed to each other, through this prolonged correspondence, their personal tastes and traits."

Further complicating Alger's story, there has been a shadowy "third Alger" floating through the world for the past half century. The 1950 perjury conviction of Alger Hiss derived from allegations by a man who said that he and Alger had been intimate friends in the 1930s. According to Alger's accuser—Whittaker Chambers—"Alger Hiss and his wife I had come to regard as friends as close as a man ever makes in life." This is an extract from *Witness,* Chambers's autobiography, a hugely successful best-seller which came out in 1952, while Alger was in Lewisburg. The same passage continues: "By unnumbered little acts of kindness and affection, by the pleasure, freely expressed, which they took simply in being together with my wife and me, they had given us every reason to believe that their feeling for us was of the same kind as our feeling for them."

Alger, when the charges surfaced in the 1940s, had only a dim recollection of this person, who had been merely a Washington, D.C., acquaintance, who had introduced himself under a different name, and who was now exaggerating and inventing memories from thirteen years before. Alger remembered having tried to be helpful to the man and his family on several occasions; and he also remembered dropping him abruptly, because the loans Alger had extended never got paid back.

However, these weren't the principal contradictions between statements by Whittaker Chambers about Alger Hiss, and statements by Alger about George Crosley, the name Chambers used when the two men met:

Chambers contended that he and Alger, as close friends, had been partners in a criminal communist conspiracy that included Alger regularly bringing home State Department documents and retyping them. When Chambers found out that Alger couldn't type, he said that Prossy, yearning to be a participant, retyped them, and Chambers stopped by the house to collect the copies, which were then taken to Baltimore to be photographed; the photographs were then turned over to a Soviet intelligence agent. Under this amended story, Prossy, who was never charged with any crime, was as guilty as Alger and must have lied under oath when she denied Chambers's accusations.

It was communism, Chambers said, that had forged both the friendship and the criminal partnership. As *Whittaker Chambers*, an admiring new biography, puts it: "What had drawn Chambers to Hiss—and drew him still—was his powerful resolve combined with a tragic view of life. It was the ideal makeup for a Bolshevik. To Chambers, Hiss was the supreme *ernste Mensch* [a "serious man," someone invincibly dedicated, as Chambers used the phrase, to achieving communist goals], possibly surpassing himself. 'No other Communist but Alger Hiss,' " the biographer quoted Chambers directly, " 'understood so quietly, or accepted with so little fuss or question the fact that the revolutionist cannot change the course of history without taking upon himself the crimes of history.' "

Chambers told variations of his two Alger Hiss stories—the first about the personal life of his friend Alger; and the second about their traitorous underground activities together—over and over: in appearances before the House Committee on Un-American Activities; as a witness before the federal grand jury that indicted Alger and at both perjury trials; in his book, *Witness*. Friendship is a great joy, not a crime, and claiming more of a friendship than ever existed is a failing that's so widespread and usually so harmless that it generally comes across as comical and certainly forgivable. In one old Middle Eastern joke, a villager returns home from the capital and announces: "The king spoke to me!" Only one person thinks to ask, "And what did he say?" The answer: "Well, he said, 'Get out of the way!' "

But the intimate knowledge about Alger that Chambers offered seemed to buttress in a quite formidable way his closely entwined contentions about their successful and most creative joint plunge into espionage. The case, after all, although a mountain of circumstantial and other evidence was introduced in court by both sides—including copies of State Department documents and films of other documents that Chambers had famously hidden in a pumpkin—essentially turned on whether to credit the words of one man or the words of another. (Prossy's testimony supported Alger; Mrs. Chambers on the witness stand supported her husband—so the two wives, in effect, cancelled each other out.) For nine years, Chambers's story had been that he and Alger had been communists but not spies. But because Chambers's subsequent story, the one about both of them spying, was in the end taken to be true by the jurors in Alger's second trial (the first trial had ended in a hung jury), many people came to accept as equally trustworthy Chambers's frequently repeated and seemingly precise descriptions of both Alger's home life and his mind and values and beliefs.

Especially so, since the only alternative Alger was the aloof face he presented to the public. As a result, the Chambers-defined Alger—the "third Alger"—has hovered over Hiss case debates ever since, only occasionally challenged as a character portrait, even by many Hiss upholders, who have concentrated their attention on the Chambers accusations about Alger's part in a communist plot. The third Alger is set forth at some length by Chambers in *Witness*; this book uses language that, read today, shows itself as flickering from affection and concern to condescension and derision and then back again. Alger is portrayed as a strange, misshapen, mean-spirited, unlovely person—more a jumble of parts than a man—even in his everyday life and thinking, quite apart from the eagerness he showed for betraying his country. Alger was, Chambers said, simple and gentle and kind, although not really very bright or curious or well read; at the same time he was unpredictably cruel, savage, and brutal.

Chambers got enough details right, or half right, to sound informed. As Chambers accurately reported, Alger had beautiful manners and loved birds (although he also claimed that the Hisses "gave up bird walking in 1934"). Prossy called Alger "Hill" and "Hilly." Then again, he never once, as Chambers claimed, called her "Dill" or "Dilly," nor was Alger deaf in one ear. And so what? Misremembering a few facts needn't cloud or compromise an otherwise comprehensive depiction of a person. But manners, birds, and Hill are about the only points of overlap I can find between Chambers's Alger and my Alger.

I can see this Alger, who is for me the first Alger, standing behind the stiff and stilted mask of the second, or public, Alger. Those two figures make sense, as aspects of the same person. They are continuous, or at least flow into each other. But Chambers's portrait, even if it has one of Alger's ears or perhaps both of his eyebrows, is unrecognizable. How can I put this? It would sadden me to learn that Alger was once a spy, and had committed the crimes he was tried for—although I have never, in fact, doubted his innocence. Betrayal of a trust is an idea I find repugnant—was, in fact, brought up by my parents to abhor—but it is at least abstractly conceivable that the man who opened himself up to me could have been someone who had stolen government papers in his safekeeping.

But in any real world there is no way to squeeze together inside one person the translucent father I got to know and the monstrous Alger that Chambers talked and wrote about, the Alger who had taken on the life of a dangerous criminal because his core personality—smoldering, corrupt, disaffected with life—had collapsed into a dangerously unstable form, like some kind of malignant, ashen dwarf star. Chambers himself, close to the end of *Witness* (an eight-hundred-page book), presented very much this same thought in what he called the "jagged fissure" of the Hiss case—though, characteristically, he put it back to front: "It was the enlightened and the powerful, the clamorous proponents of the open mind and the common man, who snapped their minds shut in a pro-Hiss psychosis, of a kind which, in an individual patient, means the simple failure of the ability to distinguish between reality and unreality, and, in a nation, is a warning of the end."

EVER SINCE Alger went to jail, some well-meaning friends have assumed that deep down, if nowhere else, I must have had my doubts about Alger's innocence. After all, how could I know for sure, since the case was about events that had either happened or not happened before I was born? Wasn't it likely that I had been blindly clinging to a belief in him because it would have been too painful to face the truth? Kindly therapists, both those I was referred to during Alger's time in Lewisburg and those I later sought out as an adult, all assured me that it was normal and healthy to question my father's (and my mother's and my uncle's) version of what had taken place, and I would feel stronger and more grounded as soon as I moved beyond denial.

But that was one of the few problems I *wasn't* wrestling with—Tim had filled me in early on. My brother, who is the final living eyewitness in the Hiss case (as well as the only one who didn't testify at the trials), had been seven—my son's age now—when, according to Chambers, he and Alger first met; and Tim had been twelve when, again according to Chambers, he had paid his last call on the Hisses, a meeting, Chambers said, that ended with Alger in tears. Tim, who lived with Alger and Prossy for ten years—in Washington, Cambridge, New York, and Washington again—from the time of their marriage, when he was three, until he went off to high school at George School, a Quaker boarding school outside Philadelphia, had been ten and eleven during the time when, according to Chambers again, Alger had brought home State Department papers; Prossy had stayed up late to retype them; Chambers had arrived to collect them.

Tim assured me that maybe about 1 percent of this was either real or based on something real: In 1935, when he was eight, he said, Chambers, his wife, and their baby daughter did spend a few days with the Hisses in Georgetown. Alger had given them a sublease on an apartment the Hisses had moved out of, and the Chamberses' furniture hadn't arrived yet. They needed a place to stay, and made use of the empty top floor. Chambers's wife had painted Tim's picture; he wasn't sure if he'd ever actually met Chambers or not. Nobody in the family

Tim in the late 1930s

knew them well or had any other connection with them, and none of the Chamberses ever came back, not to that house, on P Street, nor to either of the two Georgetown houses the Hisses lived in later in the 1930s, one on 30th Street, the other on Volta Place. Tim spent months at home in the 30th Street house around the time of his tenth birthday, after breaking his leg badly in a bicycle accident; and even after he was back in school, he was home every night doing homework. No visits then at all, he said. No typing and no documents, either.

Any typing would have resounded through the small 30th Street house—it was flimsily built, with insubstantial walls. Prossy was a poor typist; typing was always a chore for her, not a pleasure. Even when she took some courses at George Washington University, and had to write some papers, she always wrote them out by hand.

As *Witness* tells the story: "At the P Street house I first met Timothy Hobson, Priscilla Hiss's son by a former marriage. Timmie was then about eight or nine years old, a high-strung, rather pathetic little boy, who was strikingly like his mother in features and nervous temperament. Alger was extremely kind and considerate in his treatment of Timmie. No one could have been more so. But my wife and I sometimes commented on the lack of warmth in their relationship.

"Timmie knew me only as Carl. The fact that his eyes were always observing us together, and he was a quiet, watchful little boy, disturbed me. I was afraid that, if there should be any threat to the apparatus, Timmie would be a dangerous witness. I discussed it with Alger. He felt that Timmie was too young to constitute any danger. There was really nothing I could do about it, but Timmie always made me uneasy."

Tim told me: Nothing like this happened. There was only the one short visit by the Chambers family. During it, he and Chambers had scarcely glanced at each other. This seems obvious, since Chambers had described him as puny, whereas Tim had been—in his own words—"a fat, little, bubbly prickly pear" who interjected himself into every conversation and who couldn't stand by observing for even a minute.

One of the most dramatic and vividly rendered passages in *Witness* concerns Chambers's final meeting with the Hisses, the one when "tears came into Alger Hiss's eyes—the only time I ever saw him so moved." Chambers came to Alger's house on Volta Place, he said, after himself breaking with the communist underground, to try to "pry him loose from the party"; his memories of the encounter were so intense it was "the only one of the visits that I can date with certainty. It took place shortly before Christmas, 1938." The Hisses were not at home when he arrived, unannounced, so he turned to leave, but at that moment Prossy drove up. "I decided at once that Alger Hiss had been warned of my break. We went into the house together. Yet there was nothing in Priscilla's manner, as we sat chatting in the living room, that enabled me to tell what Alger really did know. Then Timmie joined us. Timmie is Timothy Hobson, Priscilla Hiss's son by her first marriage. Timmie was delighted to see me."

Chambers had to go to the bathroom. "I closed the bathroom door and thought: 'This situation is tight.'" Prossy was next door, making a phone call "in a very low voice." "At that nerve-tingling moment, Alger Hiss came home." They went in to supper. "The light supper, which had been intended for three, and was stretched for four, was quickly over. With Timmie present and the maid serving, we again made the kind of random talk that Priscilla and I had had before Alger arrived. Again, I do not remember just what we talked about, but I seem to recall that Timmie, who had never taken much interest in athletics, was trying out for the wrestling team at his school, and wanted for Christmas, or had just bought, some wrestling shoes.

"Timmie left the table while we had our coffee and I said good night to him—in effect, good-bye, for I have never seen him since." Chambers then pleaded with Alger: "I begged him to break with the Communist Party." But Alger's response was an "angry flare-up: 'What you have been saying is just mental masturbation.'

"I was shocked by the rawness of the anger revealed and deeply hurt. We drifted from the dining room into the living room, most unhappy people." At the front door, Alger turned away and came back with "a small cylindrical package, three or four inches long, wrapped in Christmas paper. 'For Puggie,' he said. Puggie is my daughter's nickname. That Alger should have thought of the child after the conversation we had just had touched me in a way that I can only describe by saying: I felt hushed." Then the tears came into Alger's eyes. Later Chambers was horrified when the gift turned out to be only "a little wooden rolling pin such as could be bought at the dime store for a nickel."

Tim told me: No 1938 encounter ever took place. It was fabricated without even a seed of truth. People were in and out of Alger and Prossy's houses all the time—some of them memorable figures, like John Lossing Buck, the ex–Mr. Pearl Buck, who had taught English in China and looked distinguished enough to be in a whiskey ad. But not Chambers; he had made only the one visit, and never came back, not for a chat, not for a party, not for dinner. So Chambers and Tim had already said good-bye forever, more than three years previously.

Now when Tim talks to me, on the phone or by e-mail, San Francisco to New York, grown-up to grown-up, he provides more specifics: The maid went home before dinner; Prossy did the cooking; there were no Carls among the many people Alger and Prossy knew. But I'd already taken in the gist of it as a boy. I knew Tim was blunt and to-the-point and no sugar-coater (clearly *not* the fourth greatest actor in America), and, while loving Alger and Prossy, saw their flaws. Of course, as the older child, Tim had had far longer to think about such things than I had. So I'd always thought of Tim as a disinterested witness. I didn't know until I was all grown up that he had been given sodium amytal—a variant of sodium pentothal, "truth serum"—by one of Alger's lawyers in 1953; nothing in his interview contradicted or added to his conscious memories.

PSYCHOLOGICALLY — AND paradoxically—it might have been easier to grow up thinking of Alger as guilty. At least there would have been a more familiar kind of pain to make sense of. His would have been an oft-told tale—the tragedy of a man of great promise who turns away from high purposes has been one of the towering themes of Western literature for the last twenty-five centuries: Sophocles has helped us understand such a man's inevitable humbling; Shakespeare has showed us that after this downfall all can be made right again. Such a story, for all its sadness, has a fitness to it, a rightness. If Chambers's charges had been true, he, too, would be an easily recognizable figure—a scoundrel redeemed, cleansed by his repentance, a prodigal son returned home.

Had Chambers's charges been true, had the third Alger been the real Alger, then Alger's story would today carry an abiding balm and comfort—the knowledge that it now had ended, for better or for worse, and could be laid to rest with his ashes. Because punishment is an atonement, a restitution, a public apology. Punishment balances crime; it fills in holes; it makes a vent for unbearable tensions, heals deep wounds, and lets us get on with life.

Then again—there is also punishment you don't deserve, innocence that can't make itself heard; these remain deeply disturbing, year after year. Their weight doesn't diminish; the hurts keep bleeding. They call out, but they have not been soothed or cheered, remedied or attended to—they are babies in Dumpsters and on doorsteps, refugees inching toward us on endless lines. Such situations leave their mark. Even when we hold back, hesitating to act, they pierce us straight to the heart.

On the third hand . . . It got even more confusing—at least being a Hiss did, back in the early 1950s—when great numbers of people were insisting that anything Alger said to establish his innocence was all part of his cover-up as a Russian spy. Chambers, on the other hand, seemed to become more believable every time he changed his story. In effect, Alger said, "He is a liar," and Chambers said, "I am a liar." And hearing this, a jury said to Alger, "Therefore, *you* are the liar." So by this logic Prossy, too, was a liar—so why wasn't I visiting her once a month in a women's prison?

Those are the kinds of questions that I wrestled with as a nine- and ten-year-old, not whether or not my father was guilty. Where could I turn for guidance? How did I even define to myself what was happening? How often is anyone faced with an "on the third hand" kind of situation, anyway?

Maybe in a fairy tale, because such stories could get very complicated, with things happening either suddenly or for long periods not at all; people were whisked away from places in an instant, transformed into unrecognizable shapes and placed under spells that could last for a century. What about in real life? Plenty of people told me this was one of those when-bad-things-happen-to-good-people occasions (of course, we didn't have that particular phrase around at the time). At least an equal number, it seemed, were prepared, given a chance, to say this was instead a when-bad-things-happen-to-bad-people sort of affair. It was strange—having done nothing, being the exact same person I'd been a moment before, and part of the exact same family it had always been, I was now looked at with sympathy by some people and with hostility by others.

Actually, I already had some experience in this murky area; a few years earlier, up in Peacham, of all places, I had tried—sobbingly, unsuccessfully—to stop an enraged group of farmers from killing a five-foot snake with rakes and shovels. They thought it was venomous, and somehow I had enough information to know (correctly) that it was only a milk snake, shy, harmless, even a friend to farmers, because milk snakes eat rodents. There were times when an idea was stronger than the truth.

A more compelling question than Alger's guilt was: Given what had just happened to Alger, what was likely to happen next?

As a teenager, I was drawn to a curious scene tucked away in a work of modern literature—*The Maltese Falcon*, Dashiell Hammett's famous detective book. The action stops dead in its tracks for several pages so the author can, irrelevantly it seems, tell a completely different story:

A man who had suddenly disappeared for no reason (he'd led a blameless life, was happily married and a successful businessman) was discovered years later in a nearby town leading an almost identical and equally contented life. Sam Spade pieced together the following story: The man had been heading for lunch one day in the first town when a steel beam from a construction site fell ten stories, and he narrowly missed being crushed. He was unnerved; and suddenly his life seemed hollow, a sham; and he vanished: " 'He went like that,' Spade said, 'like a fist when you open your hand.' " The man had never before realized that the nature of the world we live in was such that everything could change in an instant. He waited for more changes to come, but life resumed a placid course. As time went by, he found a job, fell in love, got married again.

As Spade said: "He adjusted himself to beams falling, and then no more of them fell, and he adjusted himself to them not falling." This story without a moral, which I remember even more clearly than the rest of the book, helped me immensely, confirming a notion I'd been reaching out for—that one thing that's maybe not so unusual in life is being asked to grapple with the unusual.

Then, when I was almost thirty, I ran across an eleven-hundred-year-old Egyptian story, anthologized in the late Idries Shah's *Tales of the Dervishes*, that seemed to finally capture some of the isolation that Alger in particular had had to live through. It wasn't so much that he had been publicly attacked—that was duck soup for a New Dealer who had relished his all-out battles with the diehards who had lined up against President Roosevelt's efforts to reinvigorate the American economy.

It was even a family tradition of sorts. Donald Hiss, Holmes's secretary in 1932–1933 (Alger and Donie were the only pair of brothers to both clerk for Holmes), had, after all, been in the room (standing quietly in one corner), when F.D.R., only a few days after his inauguration, came to

Holmes's library at 1720 I Street (Eye Street, as the Washing-tonians call it) to pay a call on "the greatest living American" and seek his counsel. It was the depths of the Depression; two days earlier the President had closed the banks. On the follow-ing day, he would announce his program for dealing with the national emergency to a joint session of Congress. "You have lived through half our country's history; you have seen its great men. This is a dark hour," President Roosevelt said. "Justice Holmes, what is your advice to me?"

"You are in a war, Mr. President," Donie heard the old man reply (Donie, who treasured Holmes's stories as Alger did, later passed this one on to Catherine Drinker Bowen, Holmes's biographer, and it appears in her 1944 book, *Yankee from Olympus*). "I was in a war, too," Holmes went on. "And in a war there is only one rule: *Form your battalions and fight.*"

What Alger hadn't expected was that so soon after banding together in the 1930s to fight the Depression, and such a very short time after battling side by side against Hitler in the 1940s and triumphing over his totalitarianism, so many Americans would seem to have forgotten the common purposes, the deep fellow feeling, the national sense of neighborliness and con-cern, of rolling up sleeves and getting the job done, the golden thread of shared humanity that had seemed, for a time, to forge a permanent sense of community and mutual respect among Americans from all backgrounds. A "we the people" spirit that in the closing days of World War II had even seemed to be enveloping the globe, as the nations of the world gathered in San Francisco to found the United Nations and proclaim their determination, as the preamble to the United Nations Charter declares, "to practice tolerance and live together in peace with one another as good neighbors."

These words hang on the wall of my apartment—because Alger, who had been Secretary-General of the San Francisco conference, and thus, in effect, the first Secretary-General of

The United Nations organizing conference, San Francisco, 1945. Alger is standing, far right. Seated, second and third from left, are Secretary of State Edward R. Stettinius, Jr., and future Secretary of State John Foster Dulles.

The House That Hiss Built

A disparaging postcard printed by the John Birch Society

the U.N., came home with an elegant presentation copy of the preamble, decorated with gold ink. I found it in a closet and had it framed, something Alger had never bothered to do. Alger was always casual about holding on to mementoes, and generous about parting with possessions of all kinds. When I was a boy he gave me the varnished hardwood gavel that Secretary of State Edward R. Stettinius, Jr., had awarded him for his work at the San Francisco conference—in case I ever needed to preside over a middle school assembly.

I'm still finding Alger's effects. When I looked up Catherine Drinker Bowen's story about F.D.R.'s meeting with Holmes, I found a typed letter from her to Alger I'd never known about; it's dated May 23, 1944, a reply to his thank-you note for sending him a copy of *Yankee from Olympus*. He had tucked her letter into the front endpapers of the book, and it stayed there for over fifty years. "It means much to me to have you approve the book," Mrs. Bowen wrote to Alger, "and especially to have you say you found no false note. After all, I never knew him, never saw him." To thank Alger, too, for his help with putting it together:

"I remember every word of our talk; it was one of the most valuable I had about the Justice. Your own enthusiasm about him, your reluctance to leave, because you were in a sense leaving him when you stopped talking about him, revealed to me almost as much as your actual conversation. Irving Olds had the same attitude." Irving S. Olds—Holmes's secretary in 1910–1911—later became chairman of the board of United States Steel. "He sat there behind the big desk in the U.S. Steel offices, and talked for an hour and a half, and then he said not to go, because it meant so much to him to talk about 'the old man.' " There's something touching about being only the second reader of a letter—an attentiveness, a quieting down inside. It happens whether the reading comes the day a letter arrives or half a century later.

And, no, I haven't found any secret documents used as bookmarks by the third Alger, or the third Prossy, or the third Donie—or the third Tim, for that matter. Just the discoveries you make when a father is casual about papers, a mother hangs on to every scrap, and life takes the kind of sudden turn that indefinitely postpones even the normal, cursory, spring cleaning, do-we-have-anything-for-Goodwill sorting through of belongings.

There are actually three inserts in the family copy of *Yankee from Olympus:* Mrs. Bowen's letter; a never-removed "With the Compliments of The Author" card; and Mrs. Bowen's name and address, in pencil and in Alger's handwriting, on a page from a "DEPARTMENT OF STATE/ADVISER ON POLITICAL RELATIONS" memo pad (a government document of sorts, I suppose). Alger must have been thrilled to get the letter, which is why he kept it. But he thought it would be "poomp-poomp-ish," as he liked to say (meaning the sound you make when you blow your own trumpet), to unfold the letter and place it in a desk drawer or file. So he stuck it inside the front of the book.

Mrs. Bowen's letter is also a case of two time funnels, mine and hers, meeting in the middle: She tells Alger that every one of the Holmes secretaries she interviewed "thought of him as 'the old man,' and at the period when I talked with all of you (twelve of you) it was always confusing to have to translate myself from the [Civil War Lieutenant] Holmes of 1861, about whom I was then writing, to this 'old man' I did not yet know."

"When the Waters Were Changed," the dervish teaching story that sounded so much like Alger's story, is a sort of psychological version of the biblical story of Noah and the flood. Humanity is forewarned by a prophet of an impending calamity and told to take precautions. At a certain moment, all the water in the world, except for any supply that has been specially set aside, will disappear for a short time. When it flows again, it will look the same, but it will have been changed, and all who drink it will go mad.

Only one man pays any attention to this warning, and when the waters do run dry, he retreats to a secret place and drinks the water he has been storing. When he sees that the waters have returned, "this man descended among the other sons of men. He found that they were thinking and talking in an entirely different way from before; yet they had no memory of what had happened, nor of having been warned. When he tried to talk to them, he realized that they thought that he was mad, and they showed hostility or compassion, not understanding."

The end of the story diverges markedly from Alger's experience—because after a time the man drinking the stored water can no longer tolerate the pain of living and thinking differently from everyone else. He drinks the new water, whereupon his old friends hail him as "a madman who had been miraculously restored to sanity." While Alger, on his release from Lewisburg, seemed strengthened in his original outlook—that the great, uplifting force in any society, big or small, is neighborliness.

It kept people sane and able to grow and learn, both in jail and in the world. It transcended politics; it carried humanity forward. Individual fulfillment was achieved only by looking beyond individual needs. Holmes, a lifelong Republican, left almost his entire fortune to the United States Government, returning to his fellow citizens what they had been generous enough to offer him. F.D.R.'s Democrats had rescued the country by making the idea of the helping hand national policy—when people around you have fallen, it's everybody's business to find some way to get them back on their feet.

For the rest of his life, Alger liked to call himself an "unre-constructed New Dealer," someone who confidently looked forward to a day when people would be drawn to public life by a new politics of pulling together. At the same time, I think he brought back from Lewisburg a deeper understanding of how to reach out to people—an understanding summed up in a remark he made to me years later, that "three years at Lewis-burg is a good corrective to three years at Harvard." One of the characteristics of the ruthless Alger, the *ernste Mensch* conjured up by Whittaker Chambers, was an ability to sacrifice both country and family without qualms to advance the cause of Marxism-Leninism. The real Alger, in his pre-Lewisburg years, did have trouble seeing that by instantly and vehemently fighting Chambers's false charges of communism, he might also be endangering his own safety as well as the welfare of his family.

Probably the toughest night I've had in recent years hit me when, just before my son Jacob's seventh birthday, I woke up at four in the morning, sweating and with a blinding headache—something that never happens—and overwhelmed by the sudden, dreadful, wrenching thought that I might be so sick I'd be unable to go to Jake's birthday party. I was fine within an hour or so, and lighted the candles on his cake that afternoon; all that had happened was that one of my oldest fears had momentarily resurfaced after fifty years. My seventh birthday party in Peacham, on August 5, 1948, wasn't the first of my birthdays Alger missed—the 1944 Dumbarton Oaks talks that led to the founding of the United Nations had kept him in Washington when I turned three—but it was the first one that hurt so much, and even more in retrospect than at the time.

In early August 1948, instead of coming back to Peacham from New York, which I'd hoped he'd do, and instead of staying in New York to work at his Carnegie Endowment office, as he'd planned to do, Alger decided it was essential to go to Washington and appear before the House Committee on Un-American Activities to deny Chambers's then just-made-public charges of communist activity. Some of Alger's friends applauded his courage in standing up to Chambers and the Un-American Activities Committee; other friends, more politically astute, among them the president of the Carnegie Corporation, Charles Dollard, had counseled him to ignore the charges, reminding him that the House Committee, as its own chairman later admitted, was just trying to generate headlines to make it easier for Dewey to defeat Truman for President in November.

Later that year Alger ignored more good advice—from his brother, Donie, who, along with his partners at Covington & Burling, then and for many years the dominant law firm in Washington, told him not to sue Chambers for libel (it cost more than it was worth; there was no percentage in it because you always wound up looking like the heavy, even if you happened to be right and happened to win). Alger ignored advice from John W. Davis, vice chairman of the Carnegie Endowment's board of trustees and the 1924 Democratic nominee for President against Calvin Coolidge, who told him not to testify before a grand jury looking into Chambers's charges. (If Alger had declined to testify, which was within his rights, he could never have been indicted.)

I didn't know about Chambers's accusations for a couple of weeks after my birthday, and I don't remember the moment my mother gave me the news—but it's in letters she wrote to Alger that summer, telling him how proud she was of him:

"Thee must just think of us as here and happy and sure of ourselves and sure of thee" (August 20, 1948). And: "Remember, darling, thee is not a victim but a champion for all the good folk of this earth." And: "I thought today that I should tell Tony something to reassure him in case some child said

Prossy sent this picture of herself, Tony, and cat Putter to Alger with her letter of August 25, 1948.

anything that might surprise him + Dardar [Doris Soule, a close friend and one of the "summer folk" who, like Alger and Prossy, had been coming to Peacham for years] agreed with me. He listened calmly + serenely when I told him that some evil people were being mean to Daddy + he was working to see that they stopped it. Then he said in his beautiful voice, 'Then why doesn't he do the same right back to them. They are wrong and he is wonderful' " (August 20, 1948).

I remember the love and the pride and the fierce loyalty and the longing—it was already deeply ingrained in me: Two and a half years earlier, on January 12, 1946, when Alger was in London for more than a month attending the first session of the United Nations General Assembly, Prossy had written him that "Tony [I was four] . . . is now living a protest against thy absence," and that "He talks about thee all the time. He said spontaneously: We ought to get another Daddy while Alger's away because I miss him *so* much." But I had not stored away the fact that August 20, 1948, was the day I found out that my own life had just been diverted onto a different course. What I do remember is that as the years passed I always associated this particular missed birthday with the beginning of trouble.

Because the Hiss case never quite went away, and because I had long since seen its resemblance to a fairy tale, I also internalized—and deeply buried, and never repudiated—the notion that if I ever had a son of my own, his seventh birthday would be supremely important; that, whatever else, I would have to be there for it; and, conversely, that despite my best efforts, this might be the day a curse overtook him. Of course, I should have known, having read it so many times—for over a decade I methodically reread every Dashiell Hammett book at least once a year—this was not a steel beam that was going to drop twice. Fortunately, I had also learned a more useful lesson— that sons flourish if you're there for them whenever they need you, not just on their seventh birthdays.

IN THE second half of his life, Alger became exceptionally good at talking with and listening to much younger people. For thirty years and more I've been hearing stories, first from people a little older than me, then from those my age, and finally from an even larger number ten and twenty years younger, about how they will never forget that when they were teenagers, or in college, or working at their first job, how a chance meeting with Alger taught them to see themselves with new purpose.

I've usually had a warm feeling of recognition when hearing these stories—unless it was on a day when Alger had, I was convinced, completely missed the point of something extraordinary I'd just said to him. In that case the feelings would be much hotter, and I'd think, well, you've seen his home runs but not his strikeouts. Followed by a more complicated thought: If you're going to love him, and not just be dazzled by him, you have to stick around and see his full range of behavior, and all the things he understands and doesn't understand about people.

The stories didn't stop with Alger's death. At his memorial service, Leon Botstein, the president of Bard College and a longtime friend of Alger's, spoke about how, when he had just graduated from college and couldn't decide on a career, he spent three days talking only to Alger and then knew what to do with his life. This past summer, John Stonehill, another old friend of Alger's, a New York architect who's the nephew of Alger's friend A. J. Liebling (the great *New Yorker* writer who wrote about war and food and about how the press often made a complete hash out of stories), walked me home from dinner at a Village restaurant so he could tell me how, when he'd been an awkward teenager, Alger, who had never met him before, spent a full hour with him at one of Joe Liebling's famous, crowded, celebrity-filled New Year's Eve parties.

Then, the following New Year's Eve, after not having seen John for a full year, Alger beckoned to him from across the packed room and said, "John, I've been thinking about what you were saying in our last conversation." "That was the first time an adult took me seriously," Stonehill said. "And it happened twice, so that meant the first time couldn't have been a mistake. Later our own children would say to me, 'Why can't all your friends be like Alger?' "

By the way, there's only one reference to the Chambers family in any of Prossy's August 1948 letters to Alger, and it's the very first mention in all of their correspondence. It comes five days after Prossy told me about the coming firestorm—which she and Alger were still confidently and mistakenly treating as a brushfire. From the tone of the letter, it was written at a time Alger was trying to pull together records, memories, any information lodged anywhere within the household, to refute the stories emerging from Chambers: "I'm so sorry I am a complete blank on the leases, dates. What a fool I am. All I remember is that it was summer or at least outdoor weather when those creatures were put up at P St." (August 25, 1948).

It may help first-time readers of all the books by and about Alger Hiss and Whittaker Chambers to realize, in advance, that what you make of them may depend on what waters you've been drinking. Of course, you weren't born into this affair, as I was, so you haven't had to look at it over and over even when you don't want to. But perhaps it will help if you carry along with you—in one pocket, maybe, for future reference—the picture of what this subject looks like if, for one reason or another, you've never drunk from the Chambers cup. Having never had to myself, thanks to my brother's forewarning, I've always seen the Chambers side of the story not even as "a side of a story," but as the strangest kind of dance: There are people out there—it seems almost rude to say this, since so many are sober-minded and decent—who think they are standing on solid ground, when in fact they've been displaced from bedrock and are walking around twelve feet in the air. Up there it looks to them as though they're following a straight path, whereas from down below it's clear they have to keep sidestepping, again and again, so they can hold their original position.

This means finding new ways to tell some of the big American postwar stories. For instance, two of Alger's principal attackers—Richard M. Nixon and J. Edgar Hoover—were national heroes for many Americans for many years. Recently, as their reputations have sagged, it's been necessary to say things like, "Well, they may have been wrong about many things, and perhaps they were not admirable or even honest men after all, men who may well have shown in their public lives a pattern of attacking people for baseless motives. *But of course they were right about Alger Hiss.*"

That's the sound of footsteps overhead, and I've found that you live your life underneath them and get so you don't notice them too often. On the other hand, a few casual remarks have for some reason lodged themselves in my head over the years and still won't go away. At a Dalton School pre-election assembly in the fall of 1954, shortly before Alger came home from Lewisburg, W. Averell Harriman, the grandfather of one of my classmates, Bobby Fisk, and the Democratic candidate for governor of New York, was invited to speak. The school was intensely excited to hear him. One of the other speakers, Manhattan's Republican Congressman, Frederic R. Coudert, Jr., was hissed—literally—when he offhandedly referred to Alger as a traitor. His semi-apology was offered afterwards, when he found out I'd been in the audience: "Tell him that if I'd known he was here, I wouldn't have said it."

What did he mean by that? At first I thought he was saying that Alger's guilt was so poisonous I needed to be shielded from hearing about it, or, on second thought, maybe Alger was less guilty when I was in the room. And why didn't he come speak to me personally? Years later I decided that what hurt was that both Alger and I had had so little to do with either the attack or the retraction. The Congressman was embarrassed at looking like a bully in front of kids, and shocked that he'd been disliked for denouncing Alger Hiss. It was just one of those things you said and in 1954 could expect to get applauded for.

"If Hiss would only admit he was guilty, I'd feel so much better." This was said at a cocktail party in the 1970s by a magazine editor. Another unforgettable line, because it seemed to mean, at its deepest level, that if Alger confessed she could finally have some real confidence in what so far she only hoped she believed.

Other people, who may have drunk only a few drops of the Chambers waters, have produced much queerer comments. This few-drops condition is perhaps even more threatening to people's general health than gulping down Chambers whole, since it seems to lead not just to skewed logic but to reasoning that sounds flash-frozen. The most frequently heard remark— uttered by many good and well-meaning people—is "We'll never know the truth." This seems to mean, when you work it through, that "We're trying to live without drinking water of any kind ever again."

Someone once wrote about Alger, "Guilty or innocent, he's paid the price." My first reaction to that: What price is owed if you're innocent? After much thought over the years, I think I've translated this remark. It means, "At any moment, all you have to do is say 'THE END' and any story will instantly be over." It also contains this notion: "When you really think about it, nobody ever really needs to think about anything."

Some people have speculated that maybe Alger was innocent but Prossy was guilty—which would indicate some kind of collusion or joint cover-up on the part of Chambers and Alger, and elevate Prossy to the status of greatest actor. Or maybe that Prossy and Alger were both innocent, but Chambers had somehow conspired with Tim. Once even I got roped into the act—a few years back, at a public hearing in a small town in upstate New York on then Governor Mario Cuomo's plan to start a Greenway, a kind of regionally cooperative effort, to protect the Hudson River Valley (I'd been hired to put a state commission's ideas into words; the Greenway, now up and running, is considered a success). A man stood up and said, "You let that communist write your report!" Meaning, I guess, that I'm part of a family business or dynasty, or there's a hereditary defect at work.

Every week he was in Lewisburg, Alger got at least four pieces of mail from Prossy. Many of her letters included, at the top of the first page or the bottom of the second, her own pen-and-ink drawings of the place she was writing from. At home in Greenwich Village, she recorded various corners of the apartment—the mantelpiece; the dining-room table. In Peacham, in summer, she looked out the window and drew hollyhocks in bloom; or the nearby lines of blue-green Vermont hills and, above and far beyond them, the high, snow-capped peaks of the Presidentials, meaning the White Mountains way over in New Hampshire, which shimmered into view on only the very clearest days.

Wherever you were—it didn't have to be just in Peacham—days when the sky stayed entirely blue, not a single cloud from sunup to sundown, were known in the family as "Peacham specials." They were like a perfect game in baseball, because they were so rare and because you couldn't know for sure that they were real until they were over. But you kept an eye out for them, because they were so beautiful they seemed to glow from within, and because they somehow confirmed that nothing could really go wrong forever.

Late in life, I discovered after her death, Prossy had started a children's book about things you can always count on: Cows lie down in a field with their backs to the wind. Robins fly north every spring. Lighthouses send messages across dark waters. Prossy was probably more badly injured by the Hiss case than anyone else in the family—the power of the ugliness inside people scared and dismayed her to such an extent that she kept the world at arm's length for the rest of her life.

Here is one of her sketches, showing the mirror Justice Holmes gave Alger:

If the mail Alger got at Lewisburg had a special highlight, it had to have been Prossy's "double-duty postcards," as I think of them; Alger called them "the gallery," and displayed them proudly on top of his locker. They were also an end-run around the prison authorities—Prossy had discovered that a picture postcard didn't count against the rigid seven-letter-a-week quota of what Alger could receive. She bought more than 250 cards by painters Alger loved best—22 Van Goghs, 12 Monets, 9 Cézannes, 8 Vermeers, and more than 50 other great masters. She crammed the backs, message and address space, with almost as many words as a regulation two-page letter (her handwriting got more and more mouselike as it reached the bottom), and mailed them in envelopes. No inmate could get any mail until it had been read by the prison censors, and officially stamped, in purple or black ink, by one of their big, blotchy rubber stamps. But the censors were kind: delicately and helpfully, they stamped the message side of each card, sparing the art.

So my mother became a successful smuggler in contraband—close contacts with home and a distillation of six centuries of beauty. Along with the well-remembered Vermont and Maryland landscapes Alger was holding in his mind, the "gallery" and the letters were daily sources of nourishment within Lewisburg's tall walls. The internal clock that recorded his inner life never lost a beat at Lewisburg.

In Alger's letters home you can hear that clock's steady ticking. Many of the themes he keeps returning to center around how you can best use your time to build a life. He asks himself hard questions: How do people release themselves from self-imprisonment? How does beauty add meaning to life? How do you live so that whatever your setting you see God's world around you every day, and not a world of fear and failings?

Alger paid close attention to the long conversations he had in the yard with the men he met; to the two organized prison activities he signed up for—choir practice and Bible study; to a new group activity he helped set up—weekly classical music concerts on the auditorium's sometimes screechy, sometimes whispering record player (these concerts were sparsely attended); to the early morning and nighttime views from his cell window; and to his reading—books and magazines (primarily *The New Yorker* and a high-minded, Labour Party-supporting British weekly, *The New Statesman & Nation*), and, in addition, a daily scouring of the *New York Times* so thorough that he often sent home tips about upcoming events (planetarium shows, art openings) we might otherwise have missed.

Even with the high purposes Alger set for himself, there were hours and days when, like anyone else, he had to just set his teeth and wait for the moments in front of him to pass. I caught an echo of this ache when reading what Alfred Hassler's Lewisburg book said about the role the *Times* had assumed in his life there: "I read the *New York Times* word by word and page by page, and I still have eons of time to fill. I bet I'm the only reader the *Times* has who reads all the classified ads every day!"

Probably not the only one. Alger also read, again and again, the letters he was getting from home, and I can see now, having done the math, how small a part I played in the business of keeping these lifelines open. There were news and thoughts and pictures from Prossy almost daily, but he was lucky if he got something from me even once a month. Of course, I was only a kid, and I didn't quite know how to say—or whether I was even supposed to be saying—the one thing I really wanted to say, which was "COME HOME NOW." In the more than two and a half years between my seventh birthday, the day Alger went to Washington to repudiate Chambers, and March 22, 1951, the day he entered prison, I'd spent a lot of time practicing reticence, which, although not much spoken about (reticence again!), seemed to be the preferred family approach to adversity.

By the time Alger arrived in Lewisburg, there had already been a half-dozen occasions for closed mouths—beginning

*A newspaper photo of Alger and Prossy
during the trials*

with Alger's perjury indictment, followed by his two trials, his conviction, the denial of his appeal, and the Supreme Court's refusal to take up his case. (Two of the justices, who might have voted to give him a hearing, couldn't take part in this decision because they had appeared as character witnesses for Alger in his trials. One of them was Justice Felix Frankfurter, who had, some twenty years earlier, selected Alger and then Donie as secretaries to Justice Holmes.) My parents, as I gathered from what they were saying and from what they weren't, had met each of these increasingly somber occasions stoically.

Particularly, of course, in public—that was where the second Alger always came into play. They had a sense, probably already hopelessly old-fashioned even back in the late 1940s and early 1950s, that their feelings were nobody's business but their own. They also believed that when you were right about something, it was the rightness itself that mattered and what you wanted people eventually to see. So if you remained modest and dignified, you wouldn't be distracting people while they searched for the truth of what you were saying. My parents also felt uncomfortable with, and even a little ashamed of, their own anger. Alger would take walks around the block rather than express it. On top of that, they had a sense that you didn't comfort your opponents by letting them see you were hurting.

Of course, they were hurting: Prossy's fears of being swamped by what the world had in store for her had come to the forefront the night she'd heard, in early December 1948, that Alger was likely to be indicted, and they never receded. As Alger once said to me about the panic that overwhelmed her (this was in the mid-1970s), "Every day seemed a new wound to her." A pattern emerged: Alger remained, for the most part, composed. Prossy's anxiety escalated. And each deeply resented the other's behavior.

It wasn't that Prossy rejected the idea, expressed most beautifully by Shakespeare, that calamity confers advantages on the willing soul: "Sweet are the uses of adversity," says the exiled duke about his newfound forest life in *As You Like It* (a favorite play of hers). "Which like the toad, ugly and venomous, / bears yet a precious jewel in his head. / And this our life, exempt from public haunt, / finds tongues in trees, books in the running brooks, / sermons in stones, and good in every thing." But the calculating, artificial, deliberately contrived nature of her own affliction and its relentlessness were so encompassing that I think she shrank from embracing some of the opportunities that un-looked-for change had spread before her.

ODDLY, SOME of this became clear from my own scouring of newspapers. There's a famous—well, it was once famous—

*Alger, Prossy, Dardar, and Aunt Bobby leaving court
after Alger's sentencing, January 25, 1950*

United Press photograph that appeared on front pages around
the country on January 26, 1950. It shows what Alger and
Prossy looked like just after noon on the previous day, the day
of Alger's sentencing. In the photo they've just left the federal
courthouse in downtown Manhattan (a friend of Alger's had
posted bail), and they're walking quietly and quickly through—
and away from—a mostly silent group of five hundred reporters, photographers, onlookers, and a few supporters.

They've linked arms with each other and with two close
friends who years before had become more like family. It's a
moment when bravery needs company; and the two loving
friends, as I now realize, are being every bit as courageous as

Alger and Prossy, choosing to stand by, and even stand next to, a man who has just been publicly branded a traitor. Alger's on the left; Prossy's next to him. Then comes Dardar Soule, their Peacham friend since the 1930s and my friend as soon as I joined the family; and next to her is my Aunt Bobby—by the time of this picture she was Bobby Alford, in the middle of a very happy second marriage.

The three women have on sensible shoes; Alger's black shoes are brightly polished, and his gray tweed overcoat is neatly buttoned. Prossy is wearing a jaunty, pert, silly black hat with two long pheasant feathers that point straight up into the air—the family flag flying high; a semaphore signaling to the world that all is still well. They might be sightseeing or Christmas shopping, unless you know them well enough to read the expressions that seem to be giving nothing away.

It's a truly terrible picture of Prossy, taken during the middle of a blink, but that makes it easier to concentrate on the body language of her "bonny" look, as she liked to think of it: crisp, polite, a slight, fixed smile, and all sails set (jaw firm, chin up, shoulders back, heart racing)—a "thee is a son-of-a-bitch look," as Tim once characterized it, although Prossy would have been horrified that it came across that way. Alger appears exhausted, unflappable, unfailingly polite, his mind abstracted and already concentrating on the appeal that will need to be filed.

Dardar, a Quaker like Bobby, is biting back comments, and Bobby has on "the face," as my cousins, her children and grandchildren, still remember calling it, the instantly recognizable and terrifyingly impenetrable mask her usually animated features always assumed whenever any of us had done something that was, at least for the time being, totally unforgivable. I came up with my own rule of thumb for such pictures: The greater the seeming stillness, the more it ached.

I pored over newspaper photographs because for much of

this time I had, for my own good it was thought, been taken out of the picture. It was decided that my life should continue as if nothing had changed, or at least continue as normally as possible; Prossy and Alger didn't see why my life should be disrupted just because they were in trouble. That would be a sign the other side was winning. Also, Alger and Prossy could concentrate more fully on answering the criminal charges against Alger if someone else could look after me for a while. And Alger (this was never said, of course) would have more time to try to calm Prossy down.

It was explained to me that this would be more fun—and in some ways it was. The first trial, which everyone assumed would be the only trial, started, conveniently, just as second grade was ending. So I was sent up to Peacham for the next six weeks, which is where I loved to be and would have expected to be anyway; my mother later remembered that on the way to the train station, I proudly told the cabdriver, "I am going to the place I dream about in the winter." In Peacham, I was under the care of Rena Hunter—"Aunt Rena" to me—the elderly Peacham woman I loved more dearly than anyone in the village, because her bony hugs were the most sheltering thing in the world. She'd lived with us the past several summers first as a housekeeper, then as a friend, and finally as a member of the family; she was in fact old enough to have been one of Alger's or Prossy's aunts.

So nothing had changed, or almost nothing. It was just like being home during a long trip of Alger's, except this time both my parents were away. Of course, that didn't quite make sense: They weren't away, they were home; I was away. Or, no, they weren't home exactly, they were in court; that's what the newspapers kept saying. And I was in a house that became home once one of them got there, too. So where was home in the meantime? In court?

It was then I began to think that maybe I could help most by staying quiet and not getting in the way. Another good reason for silence was that I was already confused about what it was I was keeping all bottled up. The mechanics of everything the family was going through had been explained to me, because the family believed in openness. But at the same time some of the feelings welling up in the family had been left out of the explanations, because how could my parents be open about feelings they hadn't been able to acknowledge within themselves?

The Hiss case wasn't the kind of thing you got angry about—I'd been told that in so many lack of words. This left my parents in a terrible fix of their own, not so much because getting angry would have made them better fighters, but because when you can't listen to feelings inside you, there are so many things you can't sense in the world around you, including your own peril. Only one member of the family seemed to understand this right away—Tom Fansler, Prossy's youngest and best-loved brother (and Bobby Murray's first husband). In August 1948, two weeks after Chambers's first charges had made headlines, Uncle Tommy, who was working in Chicago as head of the Midwest office of the National Safety Council, wrote Alger in New York to expect the worst: "Be prepared for underhanded, sly, dirty, slugging, foul kinds of tactics. Don't rely wholly on the armor of righteousness. You may, and my guess is probably will, be attacked through your personal and domestic relations, Pros, Timmy, Anna, Donnie, etc etc."

And: "I do not think it is personal, but I do think that 'they' will be ruthless and vindictive—and artful." And: "Suppose Chambers comes into the Committee [on Un-American Activities] room and says 'Hello, Alger. Heard from Mimi lately—that's his mother (aside).' Can you imagine the effect that would have on the minds of the committee? Regardless of whether it got into the record, it implants a seed of doubt concerning your denial. Suppose he is permitted to say—for the record—'I remember particularly the night at your house because you and Pross were disturbed by a letter from your sister, Anna.' Regardless of your denial, another seed of doubt. Etc, etc. etc." And: "While you don't have to play dirty in order to beat a dirty team, you have to be on guard against dirty play." And: "Well, anyhow, you get the picture. Your side is our side and the other side are bastards."

Of course, Alger didn't see it that way. Prossy's fears, when they arose, weren't heard as an alarm bell warning of enormous and imminent danger, but were treated instead as an impediment to logical and ordered thinking, to mobilizing an intellect that was trying to function brilliantly in the absence of elementary emotional input. (Here was, it seems to me, the core of Alger's problem—he was not a person who had been blighted by the kind of mental dissociation that would lead him to act dishonorably, and then hide his actions, but he was a person who suffered from an unwariness and a detachment that would cripple his attempts to defend himself effectively against invented charges of this nature.)

Alger's response to his troubles is epitomized in another August 1948 letter—a lovely message to Prossy in Peacham from Melvin J. Fox, a bright young economist who'd recently gone to work for the Carnegie Endowment for International Peace (he later spent twenty-six years at the Ford Foundation): "There is some measure of comfort to be gained during this period from the kind of loyalty and devotion which Alger has developed here at the office. There isn't a person here who would not do everything and anything possible to be of help to him. I personally am more grateful than I can say that I happen to be in this particular spot at this time and to have the opportunity, thereby, of being of whatever small assistance I can. As I told Alger, I would quit my job in a minute if I could work for him more effectively in some other way, and I will do so if the opportunity ever should arise.

"In some ways it is probably just as well, as Alger suggested to me, that it is he and not someone else. Aside from his long experience with legal methods and his understanding of the fundamentals of this case (i.e. it is not so much a personal matter as it is an attack upon the broad issues of the 'New Deal' and the United Nations), he has the confidence which comes out of deep principles, fortitude which comes from utter humility and the strength which comes from faith. I have no question at all as to the eventual outcome of this really terrible business."

But I was in a fix of my own. At seven, up in Peacham during the first trial, I was wrestling with the idea that if I thought I was feeling angry, I wasn't really feeling angry, because, as had been explained, nothing was happening that we needed to feel angry about. So that meant maybe I wasn't feeling anything at all. Which was another reason to keep quiet.

Thanks to Aunt Rena and several of her Peacham near contemporaries, including Elsie Choate, owner of the Choate Inn (where Prossy and Alger stayed during the 1930s), and Ernest Brown, sexton of the Congregational Church, I felt welcomed inside a sturdy, ongoing, northern Vermont form of the Great Span. (My friends, it turned out, were either seven like me or in their seventies and eighties.)

It was Mr. Brown, ancient, gnarled, and incredibly strong, who once a week renewed the town's sense of its heritage, because when he rang the bell for Sunday morning services, the silvery clang that echoed down from the top of the steeple to resound through every ounce of air in the village poured forth from a bell that had, it was always said, been cast in

In Peacham

eighteenth-century Boston by Paul Revere himself, and perhaps during the years when Vermont, before it became the fourteenth state, had proclaimed itself an independent republic. Mr. Brown showed me how eighteenth-century technology called for as much deftness as any—the bell rope down in the church vestry had such a kick to it that unless you planted your feet firmly on each downward pull, the upstroke could pull you clean off your feet.

There were memories almost everywhere you looked in the village, and the most recent, only just older than I was, was the one you couldn't see—above the stubby top of the community center, formerly the Methodist Church, was where the town's second steeple had stood for one hundred years before being blown off during the famous hurricane of 1938. A tradition of learning as the sure foundation for Yankee self-reliance also stretched back to the town's earliest days: The Peacham Academy, a hybrid high school—part private, part public—had been established in 1795, and by Aunt Rena's generation Academy graduates were expected to have a thorough grounding in botany and Greek, among other subjects.

Certainly the letters Aunt Rena and Elsie Choate wrote

Prossy were the equals of any she received. In the early fall of ·
1948, as Alger's problems were mounting, Henry Fansler, one
of Prossy's four brothers, died. Aunt Rena wrote her: "How I
feel for you in the sudden loss of your dear brother. How often
one's troubles and griefs do follow one another and things seem
hard to bear. Yet we go on bravely as it's meant that we should
and another little step is climbed." In early 1949, after Alger's
indictment, Elsie wrote to Alger and Prossy: "Keep up brave
hearts, for there never were kinder, more sincere & earnest &
honorable young people than yourselves—and I know it!"

"We devour the papers daily," Aunt Rena wrote Prossy during the first trial, in one of her regular bulletins to New York
about my health and doings (I was all right, but had started
sleeping downstairs next to her room, instead of upstairs by
myself). "Chambers is certainly showing his colors in a fine
manner, he's simply a liar from the word go—Nuf said, keep up
your courage." Without the words for something like the
Great Span or its disrupter, changed waters, I already sensed
that the old Vermonters who befriended me were no longer
walking in step with many postwar Americans who, although
my elders, were the Peacham people's juniors.

I wasn't sure how long even Peacham could hold on to its
ability to read people aright. I savored the fact that, during
the 1952 Republican National Convention, when everyone
crowded around the village storekeeper, who was the fount of
information because he had a radio, to ask him who General
Eisenhower's running mate would be, he said, "Oh, it looks
like some feller from California, named Nixer or something."
But I also started having a recurring dream, one that took place
in the cellar of the Peacham house we no longer had—we'd
been just about to buy it, for next to nothing, when Alger
needed every penny for legal bills. Not having that house and
not having my father turned out to be the only outward
changes that the Hiss case brought to my childhood—because,

once the family could no longer afford it, Dalton put me on a scholarship.

But losing the house, right in the middle of the village, and very grand by my standards, with its old black horsehair sofas, slippery if you rubbed them one way, and scratchy if you rubbed them the other way, was a wrench. In my dreams we again lived in the house, which felt like a restoration—that blissfully reassuring, wish-fulfilling sense you get in a dream that the waking life that surrounded you just before you fell asleep was the dream, and now everything's been put back to rights, just as you always knew it would be. Except that that was only the beginning of these frequent and always identical nightmares. When I went down the cellar steps to get wood for the stoves, the cellar wasn't there any longer. Instead I was standing on the shore of a vast underground sea. Something huge and ancient, a monster from its depths, was rushing across the water toward me.

However often I dreamed about this—and for a while that was at least once a week—there was nothing I could do to make it better. I couldn't move or speak or warn anyone upstairs. I had the sense that even if I tried, they wouldn't understand. I knew, even in the dream, exactly where that sense came from: There was a harrowing Peacham story, a true story. The younger son of one of the dairy farmers near town had a speech impediment that his family found comical and that got worse when he got excited. One night, while the family was eating supper, the barn caught fire, the worst thing that can happen on a dairy farm. The boy, the only one who had seen the fire, burst into the kitchen, terrified, to tell his family. Who laughed at him.

I was now enmeshed in more confusion—finding that the mere act of living through something as intense as the Hiss case stretches you out of shape in ways that no one has ever told you even exist. Maybe somebody could have said that difficulties that arise out of nowhere test you, let you see what you're made of. Or that in unforeseen situations your strengths will be strengthened and your weaknesses may undermine you. After the fact, it's obvious enough. Look at my mother. Her anxieties nearly crushed her. While my brother—to my parents' intense pride; he himself still sees the timing as coincidental—put himself through pre-med classes at N.Y.U. by working nights as an orderly at Bellevue, and then went on to medical school in Switzerland, where the lectures were in French, a language that had given him fits back in high school.

While my father, throughout the case, got ever more stubborn, rejecting almost all advice that could help him, if it was presented as "something you must do to protect yourself," because that sounded ignoble, unworthy, beneath what he expected of himself. So, after the first trial, the one that ended in a hung jury, he fired his lawyer, Lloyd Paul Stryker, widely considered the ablest criminal lawyer in the country—and warmly recommended by Felix Frankfurter—because Stryker told him, "Alger, I can keep getting you hung juries till doomsday." That wasn't good enough. Alger wanted vindication. The problem, too, was that Alger found Stryker "rather florid," as he put it in *Recollections*. He hired a corporation lawyer from Boston who had never tried a criminal case in his life—a kindly, honest, decent man, who lost the second trial. From *Recollections*: "It looks as if I paid a high price for indulging my taste in courtroom styles." On the other hand, Alger's inner sweetness deepened and intensified, so that when the fires actually surrounded him, he was not consumed or even badly scorched. He emerged intact.

In my case, from my seventh birthday until Alger left for

Lewisburg when I was nine and a half, I was growing up so fast intellectually that I was already evaluating concepts about intergenerational knowledge and national mood swings I couldn't even organize clearly as thoughts, let alone put into words. I mastered legal terms, like "rebuttal witnesses" and "circumstantial evidence." I had learned to read between the lines of newspapers; I could see from the way they constructed the reports they themselves considered objective that most of the local papers, including the *New York Times*, were convinced that the government had a strong case, while the reporter the *New York Herald-Tribune* sent to the trials played it fair.

I could see that my father was almost the mirror image of the man he was accused of being—that far from being someone who secretly believed that the federal government was a capitalist monster that must be thrown down by any means, fair or foul, he was someone who, at his very core, idealized the government as just and courageous and the instrument of his exoneration, who needed to keep on seeing it as something far wiser and more benevolent than it actually is. I had already accepted the fact that many of our assumptions about the underlying integrity or kindliness or insight of official institutions are at bottom only hopes, or perhaps it's more accurate to say promises we are still trying to live up to—when we remember we've made them.

As for my emotional state during this time—what's the opposite of precocious? *Post*-cocious? I was lost, totally out of my depth, struck dumb, frozen solid, a real boy transformed into a block of wood, uncomprehending, and caught in the grip of feelings I had been assured didn't exist. Or, rather, existed only in other people, or if in me only in other situations. Alger's second trial began shortly before Thanksgiving in 1949, and didn't end until the third week of January in 1950. At that point I was already in the middle of third grade at Dalton, so I couldn't very well be sent off to Aunt Rena's little house in East Peacham. Instead, and even more bewilderingly, I continued to live in Manhattan, but in a palace.

That wasn't the right name for it, since the immensely hospitable and extremely well-to-do family who owned it took great pains to present themselves as—and indeed were—altogether unpretentious and unostentatious. But what else could you call it, especially if you were eight and had never seen anything like it? I was living with the Buttenwiesers—Helen (one of my father's lawyers), her husband, Ben (who was out of the country a good deal, serving as Deputy High Commissioner of postwar, American-occupied Germany), and their daughter and three sons—in their Upper East Side town house half a block from Central Park. I immediately associated it not with money, which I knew nothing about, but with happiness and energy. It was a place, I thought, where as soon as you entered it voices sounded stronger and more confident, laughs rang louder and more jovially, and even the light spilling from the table lamps and floor lamps and the cunning little reading lamps, tucked away inside the head of the bed, seemed polished and sparkling and flowing into glowing pools that filled the rooms like warm honey.

Our family, which now had no money at all and was living on loans and donations from uncles and friends (Alger had resigned from the Carnegie Endowment the month he was indicted), had just, inexplicably as far I could see, been borne aloft by the wings of angels. Several sets of angels, at that, in a tightly clustered band. Because practically around the corner from Helen and all the Buttenwiesers, whose living room had twin Steinway grand pianos and still seemed empty, which was the way you might expect a heavenly space to behave, lived another new friend, Dr. Viola W. Bernard, whose Fifth Avenue apartment had a wraparound terrace that seemed to float at

Tony with Prossy and Vi, early 1960s

low-dipping cloud height, or perhaps it was actually angel height, over Central Park.

Looking through my newfound '50s/'90s glasses, I would still rank both Helen and Vi among the most formidable people I will ever meet. They had similar backgrounds but knew each other only slightly (Vi being better friends with one of Helen's sisters). Their families belonged to what was later called, at least by outsiders, "our crowd"—meaning the small group of New York German-Jewish families who were then as well known for their accomplishments and good works as they were for their great fortunes. The "W." in Vi's name meant she was a Wertheim, which was United Cigar Company and banking money; the same "W." appears in the name of her niece, the historian Barbara W. Tuchman. Helen was a Lewisohn (copper and mining products), but the "L." in Helen L. Buttenwieser said specifically that she was a Lehman as well, which spoke both of banking money (Lehman Brothers) and of the fact that one of her uncles, Herbert H. Lehman, was a United States Senator (and former Governor of New York), while the other, Irving Lehman, served as Chief Judge of the New York State Court of Appeals.

But what must be said about Helen and Vi was that at a young age they had each decided the real purpose of having a W. or an L. in your background was that it would let you plunge into and do exceptionally well at careers that were still considered almost exclusively reserved for men (law in Helen's case, psychiatry in Vi's); and that *then*, having been accepted by their fellow practitioners as equals, they could use their chosen professions as vehicles for changing the world. Viola W. Bernard and Helen L. Buttenwieser, as was pointed out at Vi's memorial service in New York (she was ninety-one when she died in 1998; Helen had been eighty-four at her death in 1989), are now recognized as having belonged to a small and shining circle of twentieth-century East Coast women—it also includes Eleanor Roosevelt—who fought on behalf of children, women, and the disenfranchised in America for more than six decades.

Late in life, Helen was the first woman to be chairman of the Legal Aid Society in New York, which represents people who can't afford to hire lawyers, and Vi, in the mid-1950s, helped found the new field of community psychiatry, which works with people by treating whole neighborhoods and changing the environmental conditions that surround impoverished families. The last of Vi's more than a hundred research papers in psychiatry was awaiting publication at the time of her death. Back in the late 1940s, when I met them, Helen and Vi were still—as I now think of them—remarkably young (Helen was forty-four and Vi forty-two) and had only just found the full, furious, flat-out pace they would never again relinquish.

That pace, it seemed, was something of an artful illusion—not that I thought they were really moving and thinking more slowly than that. On the contrary, I was convinced they had to move past other people in a blur because that was the only way to stay visible at all; their true velocities were even more accelerated. It could be an uncomfortable experience having a conversation with them; angels are not big on small talk. You often saw exasperation in their eyes—which I now think they meant as encouragement, as a sincere and urgent invitation to get a wiggle on, to be up and doing, to make something of yourself, to push forward, to join them up at the speeds they found so natural. That was the only way you could ever hope to feel good about yourself or to generate the kind of surplus energy that would let you be useful to someone else.

I found that just being around them added up to yet another powerful argument for holding my silence. Of course, since I was silent, I never knew if other people felt this way, too. Not until Vi's memorial service, where one of the mourners, a woman about my age, confided that whenever her mother was summoned to a small dinner or a large party at Vi's—which could be either at the Fifth Avenue apartment or at what I thought of as her huge country house in Nyack, New York (which was actually only the carriage house down the hill from a truly gigantic estate her father had built)—her mother's hands shook so much she could hardly pick up a fork.

I was sure that Helen, during the time I lived in her house, and Vi, whenever I was asked for a weekend at Sky Island Lodge—that was the name of her Nyack house—could see right through me and read my thoughts. I often hoped that one of them might comment on the things I wasn't talking about. Things that were so confusing in themselves and that were now, more confusingly still, tumbling together inside my head. Things like anger, and fear, and not wanting to damage the family or hurt my father's chances—distracting his attention by asking him what was happening, or telling him I loved him, or yelling at him, or begging him to come get me. But they never raised the subject. This might have convinced me that even angels have limitations, but instead I took it to mean that they had heard what I wasn't saying and concurred with it. Through their own silence, they were expressly confirming the fact that I had thought things through properly, and that what I was feeling was my proper contribution to the family welfare.

The angels, as I could see clearly enough, were required to follow certain rules. Their powers could be exerted only on individuals; sweeping events like the Hiss case were beyond their jurisdiction. So I would sit at the Buttenwiesers' breakfast table and, spooning raspberry jam from a silver pot and spreading it on a piece of toast that had had all four crusts cut off, I would study the newspapers carefully. I found that as for the confusion, although I couldn't make it go away in the present, I could quite easily make it go away in the past—by forgetting much or even all of what had happened the day before, or during the past month or year, for that matter.

The one thing that was hard to forget was dreams, particularly when they came back over and over. By now I was getting another recurring dream. I was in a very blue, very cold swimming pool, down at the shallow end. Which wasn't all that shallow, because I could only keep my head above water by standing on tiptoe. For some reason the pool had a strong undertow, the way an ocean does. This one was almost impossible to swim against, and slowly, despite all efforts to keep myself afloat, I was being drawn under and pulled ever closer to the deep end. I could see the legs of lifeguards standing on the side of the pool. I tried to call out to them but they were too busy talking to one another.

There was a potential ally in the house—Paul Buttenwieser, Helen's youngest son, who was three years older than I was, and whose hand-me-down striped ties and white shirts and blue serge suits I wore for years. They came from DePinna, a long-gone Fifth Avenue store that in those days was a kind of

Brooks Brothers for boys, selling miniature versions of the clothes bankers and lawyers wore. Paul and I were both over-weight, so his clothes fit like a charm (eventually my mother would give them away to some other chubby kid; DePinna suits never wore out). I realized, when I put on a blue suit and a white shirt and a tie with narrow blue and red stripes for Vi's memorial service, that I still, at age fifty-seven, model my ideas of what you ought to wear for formal occasions on Helen's taste in clothes.

For boys, at that. Just as archeologists can generally tell the date of a pot or an arrowhead by measuring how far down into the earth they had to dig for it, I can see now that several of my opinions about places and thoughts about people, which I'd always considered lightly held and subject to change, got fixed into place during 1949 and haven't moved around much since. Reading family letters now, for instance, I am fascinated, and slightly shocked, to find that Prossy had once spent a perfectly miserable summer in our beloved Peacham—in 1944, when I was just turning three and Alger had stayed in Washington for the Dumbarton Oaks talks.

It was the last full year of the war—many of her letters were scribbled on old "V Mail" ("V" for victory) forms—and I had an incurable cold, no available baby-sitters, and there was almost no fresh meat for sale in the village, because of the war. Moreover, Peacham was in the middle of a drought and a heat wave. You could buy vegetables from neighbors' gardens, but they sold only turnips and kept the squash and lima beans for themselves. Prossy wrote that she could quite happily never see the place again, except perhaps for "a short visit"; that even Dardar had been getting increasingly hard to take; that "the weather is not to be counted on + not what we fondly imagined it." No Peacham! No Dardar! No Peacham specials! I noticed that, because of my 1949 attitudes, I was feeling insulted *now* by remarks Prossy had tossed off in a bad moment in 1944.

It was also in 1949 that I acquired fixed opinions about Paul Buttenwieser—they were wrongheaded and remained uncorrected. All the "Buttens," as my parents called them, seemed dazzling in their abilities and polish and ease with people, but Paul, probably because he was closest to me in age, was the one I invariably ended the day comparing myself unfavorably with. He wrote moving and sensitive letters to people that they treasured forever (and I had nothing to say), and he played the piano exquisitely and with unshakable self-assurance (and I could barely pick out a tune).

I wasn't at all surprised when Helen told me briskly that Paul was most likely headed for a brilliant concert career. In my mind, Paul cast a long shadow that was swallowing me up, and I wanted to think that many of my doubts and obscurities would disappear if only I could stand clear of the dark shade he had imposed. It was all projection, of course, this unprovoked jealousy. No comparisons were being made; there was no rivalry; everyone wished me well. The generosity and warmth of the Buttenwiesers was all-encompassing. It was agony, nevertheless. I was holding on for dear life to the idea that I had to stay out of the way, for the good of the family. Which meant— it was one of those overly complicated thoughts you come up with to comfort yourself, especially when the intellect has outstripped the heart—that if I could work hard and get really good at not asking for attention, then my parents would be so grateful, their attention would return to me.

In that state, it was easier to get angry at the serene and much appreciated Paul than at my parents. My most tormented, despairing moment—the lifeguards will never notice me now!—came on the morning Alger was supposed to report to jail, when at the Buttens' there was loud admiration (they always expressed their high regard in full voice) for a quiet, touching, tender going-away letter that Paul had written Alger to tell him how proud everyone was of the way he had carried himself during his ordeal. I spent the next three days, even though I had nothing to put into words, writing and rewriting, again and again, a letter I could send to the prison that would not be calling attention to itself, of course, but that Alger would have to like as much as—oh, is there any way that it could be more than—Paul's.

The echoes of that moment, the overtones, the undertow, the crosscurrents, and the misunderstandings within misunderstandings, all surge back when I read that letter now, but curl into foam at my feet and have no more passion or force. It was a short letter, written on Buttenwieser stationery, and I'd never felt so restless in my life as after mailing it: "Dear Daddy, I have not much to say, but what I have to say is that I think nothing could possibly go wrong at home, and also at the prison, if the walls are painted black in your cell you will turn them white forever. Yours, Tony."

IF I had only known "Carl Gutheim" in those days, rather than the Paul Buttenwieser I was sure I knew all about. What a revelation it was to read the careful descriptions Paul had written in a novel about the fictional "Carl Gutheim"; and what a belated, complicated business I had made of it—through the convoluted double delay of reading about Paul in a book rather than talking to him directly, compounded by putting off reading even the book because I was still afraid, after all the years gone by, that the better it was, the darker the shadow would become.

Their Pride and Joy, Paul's novel, is a powerful, illuminating book. The character of Carl is a stand-in for the young Paul, in a book about a family very much like the Buttenwiesers (the grown-up Paul has become a psychoanalyst and a writer of note, not a concert pianist). Much of the book is about Carl's sister, who dies of anorexia in her early twenties (as Paul's sister also did). That's a story that didn't overlap with mine—Paul's sister, Carol, when I knew her, was simply someone who though already grown up was invariably kind to me; the book also does not mention the Hisses. For me, nevertheless, reading it was like being offered an angel's eye view of the days I had spent at the Buttens'.

Because Paul, from the inside, had written lovingly and honestly about what it was like to be part of a family for whom treating outsiders like angels came more easily than keeping each other clearly in focus. Children who had been knocked loose from their moorings by world events, as he says in *Their Pride and Joy*, were especially welcome in the households of the Buttenwiesers and their relatives, and my arrival had, for instance, been preceded by that of two French refugee children who had been given rooms for the duration of World War II, and, near the end of the war, by German-Jewish twins who had somehow been smuggled out of Nazi-occupied Europe. Being an angel doesn't mean being perfect, since no one is, and instead has a lot more to do with making sure that when pain arrives at the heart of a family, as it always does in time, you don't stop reaching out to other families who've been slowed down by the pain that's come their way.

Being an angel can prove dangerous to your reputation, too. I recently heard, for instance, that long after I left Dalton, the Buttenwiesers were bounced as school trustees by a headmaster who bragged that he had "cleaned out the communists."

Helen remained Alger's friend for life, but Ben after a time stopped inviting Alger to the family's famous Sunday brunches, which were attended by glittering, witty guests and where you were offered almost anything you could possibly think of to eat ("This is Liberty Hall!"). Vi stayed equally close to Prossy for the rest of Prossy's days—after my parents separated, Helen and Vi in their practical way had decided that the easiest thing all around was for each to take over half a friendship. At Vi's memorial service, I learned that most of her close friends never knew she'd even met the Hisses.

"When Carl," Paul writes in his novel, "was discovered, at the age of four, picking out a melody at the keyboard, it was instantly decided that he was gifted. In the family, one didn't have mere aptitude. You were outstanding, or you were nothing. Just how outstanding he was, and how far he would go, remained a plaguing question for him throughout his childhood, but no one else shared his doubts." Eventually Carl avoids playing a much-dreaded recital at Juilliard only by breaking his wrist (accidentally on purpose, as the expression goes). So it turns out that during my time in the cheerful, bustling Buttenwieser house, two kinds of isolation over-lapped, or at least ate breakfast at the same table, side by side. But my attention was glued tight to the morning newspapers. So I never took things to what might have been the next step of real friendship with Paul.

Instead this was when I became a journalist, at least in my own mind. I invented, wrote, illustrated, and edited *The Family Eagle*, my personal newspaper, and found not only that sending occasional issues off to Lewisburg was something that Paul had not thought of doing, but that all the immense amount of work and time involved was hugely less difficult than writing Alger another letter. It was also when I began to admire reporters as the only people who had been bright enough to find an escape hatch, a hiding place, a free pass, a cloak of invulnerability that gave them immunity from the troubles of the world. Immunity and impunity. They could come and go as they pleased, if they had notebooks in their hand, and they could say what they liked, provided they said it in print. They were truly safe, as I saw it— this was the most important thing—because by writing about other people attacking one another, nobody could attack them.

Sometimes, after I was back home from the Buttens', I would look longingly out the front window of our apartment if there were a couple of reporters camped out across the street in front of Riker's, the all-night coffee shop. Prossy avoided even glancing at them, but to me, watching them hunched and stamping their feet and rubbing their hands together to stay warm on a cold night, they were swaggering, heroic figures who had mastered the one secret worth knowing. They could for life always touch bottom in any swimming pool! For some reason, maybe because I never actually saw one, I was not impressed by or scared of F.B.I. men; their presence in or around the house was limited to the annoying series of clicks that for years interrupted our phone calls, signaling that someone was listening in. "Hi, George and everyone from the F.B.I.," I'd say when my best friend from school, George Engel, called up after finishing his homework. Maybe I thought that G-men were vulnerable to things going wrong, like the rest of us. I longed to be a reporter.

The answer to my letter to Alger, the one I'd agonized over, came indirectly. He never referred to it in the letters that began arriving home almost immediately; it seemed to pass directly from my unconscious into his. But almost from the first, and consistently from then on, Alger's letters spoke to all the things I wasn't saying in the newspapers I constructed for him. Whether he was spinning a yarn, or describing someone he'd met, or remembering something he'd read in the *New York Times*, or sketching something he'd seen or remembered, or just commenting on the views he'd glimpsed, he—or something in him—knew exactly how to bypass my defenses. The message was always the same: Aloneness is an illusion. Each moment of joy is a reminder of this truth. Every place and every person are aspects of one another. The real purpose of many otherwise inexplicable events is to reshape us—by drawing us closer while extending the range of our understanding.

Sometimes Alger's didacticism was obvious enough even for me to spot, as in this paragraph from a letter dated September 15, 1951: "Football (touch football) has already started here, although there will be one more week of baseball, and basketball will begin soon. Does basketball start right away at Dalton as soon as school opens? One of the young fellows here isn't much good at sports"—I myself was rotten at sports—"but he plays them all and everybody respects him for trying. I guess he didn't have much chance to play games when he was a small boy. The interesting thing is how quickly he is improving. Probably it's because he doesn't mind it when he's clumsy; he just has fun playing and keeps right on trying and getting better and better."

I found I could also connect to unpremeditated passages that Alger set down exactly as they occurred to him: "x-x We have had an unbroken series of moonlit nights + today, though there were numerous picturesque clouds, the visibility was greater than at any time since a clairvoyant day in April when from the east-facing windows of the quarantine dorm I could see 20–25 miles of wavelet hills marching toward thee + N.Y." (October 18, 1951).

And: "x The day was gloriously bright + the sunset again very exciting. By standing on my bed I can see the rolling fields to the south + the lane of young sycamores that leads to the entrance (all yellow, they are now) + with a sunset glow the view is fair indeed. [The sycamores, dear Alger, have forty-seven years later become quite gigantic and stately! Here's another grove that has grown tall in your absence. But then in your day Lewisburg itself was youthful, and less than a third of its present age.] Skies + the fields + hills are of special importance here because the utilitarian architecture is without any semblance of beauty. The far vistas serve as galleries, gardens,

Cloisters, concerts, home music + the small household bits of beauty" (October 20, 1951).

Earlier, in September 1951, he had written about another sunset, a "particularly beautiful" one, remarking, casually, as an aside, that "sunsets are among the prettiest things we have here so I am on the lookout for them. It's harder for you to see them in the city but whenever you see a very nice one you can be pretty sure I'm looking at it, too." Reading this passage again, I got a jolt. I'd totally forgotten these words, but ever since reading them for the first time, at the age of ten, looking up and catching sight of a sunset has been—well, of course we all respond eagerly to the sudden flood of beauty a sunset spills across the sky. That's built into our minds and souls; it comes with the territory.

But for me every sunset has been—I don't know—something I need to interrupt whatever I'm doing to look at and drink down and store up for later, like rain after a drought. A sunset has been a Peacham special's purity gathered into the essence of a single moment. It's become the instant when everything pauses, and sadness and joy seem evenly balanced and to have found some peace with each other. I stand stock-still, but my mind seems ready to sail off with the sun to some place, to any place just beyond and below the horizon. When it fades, I come back to the next moment renewed and strengthened. Sunset-watching has been—although I hadn't concentrated on it before, I had just *done* it, sort of assuming it must have been self-invented—a key small, personal ritual that I've never let go of.

Alger's spontaneous, offhand gift of sunset watching made me think yet again about gratitude. Once, after I was grown up, or at least physically grown, I tried to thank Helen Buttenwieser for giving me a home during the second trial. She told me there was only one way she'd ever heard of, which was to try to help someone else, somewhere down the line, when the chance came. Helping me out had been one way she'd been able to thank the people who'd helped her out. This was how, she said, the thanks for any act always got pushed ahead, sometimes into the next generation, and always took new forms.

Alger's letters home, this book he never wrote, brought me back to life, and I can't thank him by going back to write the letters I never wrote then (and haven't written anyone else since—Alger and Prossy did not raise a letter writer). But now that it's time for Alger to be resting peacefully, perhaps I could let him get on with his death by showing people for whom he long ago had become a headline and not a person, or who are too young ever to have heard much about him, or even to have heard of him, the man I've had the chance to get back in touch with. I could pass along some of the things that Alger could share with me and his closest friends but held back from public view.

It's strange that one reason I could meet up with Alger again is already evaporating and won't be available to my son's generation. It really didn't last very long, the idea of putting every thought down on paper, of creating a meticulous record of millions of lives that could last longer than the memories transmitted through the Great Span. The early Victorians, when they introduced the penny post in 1839 (buy a one-penny stamp and send a letter anywhere throughout the British Isles), made letters indispensable for a while by transforming them into what computer-speak would call the BFC way of keeping in touch—meaning "Better-Faster-Cheaper."

Holmes, born in 1841, wrote letters daily; my brother, Tim, born in 1926, has the knack, although Alger and Prossy used to complain about his spelling; I came along just too late—a pre–baby boomer, but a post–letter writer. Telephones went on sale in 1876, but 1946, when I was five, was the tipping point, the first year that half the households in the country had a phone. So I grew up disdaining older, slower letters and loving phones—the pre–World War I, wooden Peacham party-line wall phones you rang by turning a crank, and our big, black New York mid-1940s dial phone that weighed as much as a frying pan and that the F.B.I. had bugged. Which turned out to be one of the anomalies of living through a BFC transition period. Because later on the F.B.I., assuming its agents had filed their notes, would be the only attic or basement that might contain a record of exactly what my classmates and I had said to each other about the upcoming Fifth Grade Greek Festival, or about our hopes and fears.

MANY OF Alger's early letters drew us closer just by being so down-to-earth and matter-of-fact. On May 24, 1951, he wrote, "I'm going to *try* to draw a picture of the storeroom where I work. It has a front counter, just like a regular store and rows of high shelves at each side of a long aisle. At the end of the aisle are 5 or 6 windows that look out on the big

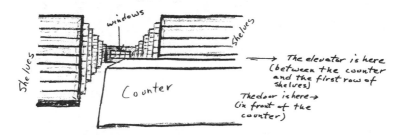

yard where the baseball diamond and the track are. I haven't tried to draw any of the items we stock so the shelves look bare in the sketch. Imagine to the left: paper (in packages), scotch tape, rubber bands, date stamps, bottles of different colored inks, paper clips, etc. and in the rest of the shelves to the left glasses, clothes, soap, etc. while all kinds of hardware, wire, balls of string, plumbing pipes, nails, bolts, etc. are to the right. So when you see Ned Somers in June [Ned kept the general store in Peacham] you can remember that except for food, he and I will be handling the same things. Oh yes, we keep the paints and drums of oil down in the cellar and we have hand trucks   and a table on wheels   (to collect stationery items)

and a little four wheel dolly   (to push heavy packages)."

A month and a half later, on July 7, when I was off at summer camp in Vermont for the first time in my life, Alger wrote: "x-x-x One of our stunts here is to have cocoa + cookie parties in the dorm at night. We make cocoa from chocolate bars and very hot water (like Mr. Gudert's). [Fred Gudert was our superintendent in Greenwich Village, and our building was well known for having the hottest hot water in the neighborhood. Sometimes when you turned on the faucet steam came out.] We can buy chocolate, Graham crackers + other cookies at our store, as well as   ,   ,   ,   ,   ,   ,   ,   ,   , etc."

Alger's drawings could be deliberately silly, such as the "Dearest   +   " at the beginning of his letter on September 15, 1951; he knew I adored rebuses. Other drawings evoked images that had by then entered my mind's eye. Later in the same letter, for instance, he sketched both the Peacham church steeple and the Washington Square arch in Greenwich Village, a block from our apartment, to represent the family's return from Vermont to the city. (The Paul Revere bell, by the way, hangs behind the two arches in the steeple, above the clock.)

Back in July he had sent along a picture of another New York landmark, the Little Red Lighthouse under the George Washington Bridge. In *The Little Red Lighthouse and the Great Gray Bridge*, the already famous children's book that I loved so much Alger had had to read it to me again and again at bedtime, the lighthouse is overawed by the size and strength of the Great Gray Bridge that rises above it, and pines away until it realizes that its own small light is still the only beacon that boats out on the Hudson River on treacherously foggy nights can see and rely on. Most of the kids I knew happily read this book for its intended message, that children are as valuable as

adults. I did, too, when I read it to myself. When Alger read it to me, though, I took it to be a message that the Hisses still had a place in the world, and work to do, and would pull through.

Of course, it wasn't the fact that the lighthouse was *red* that was of importance—the only political group I'd ever heard my parents talk about fondly was the Democrats, who had no colors except red, white, and blue—I just knew this was a structure that could shine from within. Alger's letter had alarming news about the lighthouse (taken from the *New York Times*, no doubt): "The Coast Guard wants to sell the Little Red Lighthouse that lives under George Washington Bridge.

Lots of people, especially children who have read the book, don't want it to be sold and to be moved away. Maybe it won't. One little 4 year old said: 'I wouldn't like that at all. I like that little lighthouse very, very much.' "

But the picture next to these words somehow made it clear that the lighthouse was in no real danger. I didn't at the time know the word "immutable." But I did know that if something is threatened, and then the drawing you make of it is still crisp and sure and tender, it shows that people's affections can be stronger than those forces that might tear the world to pieces. (I was right, too, at least about this small building. So many children wrote letters of protest to the city, the lighthouse was saved and became part of a city park. This successful New York children's crusade preceded the national historic preservation movement by more than a dozen years.)

Every time a letter came from Alger, there was one thing I particularly hoped I would find, and always put in a last-minute, extra special wish for even while tearing open the envelope—a new story in the long-running saga of the Sugar Lump Boy. The Sugar Lump Boy, usually abbreviated to S.L.B. in the letters, to save space—where did he come from? Since sugar lumps were a household rarity by the time I was a small child (granulated having already become the BFC alternative), I've always assumed Alger himself must have heard Sugar Lump Boy stories as a boy growing up in Baltimore and, more likely still, during long summer nights on the Eastern Shore of Maryland, where many early American customs, including the old Southern and Uncle Remus oral traditions of tall tale telling and yarn spinning, survived intact at least until the middle of the twentieth century.

All I know is that, as far back as I can remember, after I climbed into bed, and provided that Alger was actually home that night, when he tucked me in and settled down for a story, the best stories he told were the ones he made up on the spot about the Sugar Lump Boy and his friends, the "little men" (who were the real toys I played with). It was probably my first sustained contact with the playfulness and sweetness and glee-fulness—and the inventiveness and complete lack of self-consciousness—that were the underlying wellsprings of Alger's character. How did he do it? I marveled and delighted at each unexpected twist and turn of a tale. Now that I'm a dad myself, although still a halting, embarrassed, and self-censoring story-teller, I know what Alger was up to and why his stories were so beguiling.

The Sugar Lump Boy—sweet, simple, mischievous, and comically vainglorious—was lovable because, no matter how bad things got for me, he was in worse shape and needed my help right away. Badly. There's a name for this technique, as I found out when it was my turn to read child guidance books—"the child as mentor," Dr. Stanley Turecki, a child psychiatrist and best-selling author of *The Difficult Child* and *Normal Children Have Problems, Too,* calls it in one of his books: "By putting her in the position of a teacher . . . you create in the child an awareness that she's in control, a sense of mastery."

What I got from the S.L.B. stories was that Alger was home, showing me how to do something, or encouraging me to try again when I was feeling defeated. I had only two hours a month with Alger in the visiting room at Lewisburg, but by reading and then rereading every letter several times, and sometimes reading them out loud to Prossy as well, I managed to squeeze in at least another forty minutes with Alger every week, more than doubling the official rations. It was a feast in the midst of a great famine, and there was the added joy of thinking that Lewisburg authorities never noticed that letters annihilate separation twice—I had been with Alger in his mind when he wrote the letters, and then he was present with me as soon as I found them in the mailbox:

"The Sugar Lump Boy Learns to Swim

"One day the S.L.B. said to Tony: 'I want to pass my swimming test.'

"This was quite a stumper—because the S.L.B. *couldn't even swim*. So Tony said: 'Don't you think you'd better learn to swim first?'

" 'Oh,' said the S.L.B., 'do you have to go to school and read books before you can swim? I thought you just got in the water and splashed and said "gurgle, gurgle." '

"Then Tony explained about learning to swim and put about four inches of water in the tub and taught the S.L.B. to put his face down in the water and to dog-paddle with his hands. At first the S.L.B. did *NOT* like it at all. He choked and he spluttered and he said his eyes stung. 'I've got soap in my eyes,' he yelled. But after a while he got so he could put his face under water without minding it.

"Next Tony taught him to float on his face. And how surprised the S.L.B. was when he first floated. Then Tony told him to do the dog-paddle while floating. The S.L.B. was DELIGHTED to find he moved a whole inch and a half. Later Tony taught him to kick his feet. And then Tony said: 'Now you can swim. All you need is practice and learning to lift your face up so you breathe while you're swimming.'

"The S.L.B. could hardly believe it; he was so pleased. He practiced + practiced and after a week or so he learned the crawl and how to float on his back. Then Tony took him to school and swam beside him while the S.L.B. swam across the

WIDTH of the pool. He was very proud: "I swam across the Big Lake." *THE END*

"Much, much, much love, Daddy" (September 15, 1951).

"The Sugar Lump Boy Learns Basketball

"One Saturday morning the S.L.B. said to Tony: 'Please teach me to play basketball. I already know a lot from watching you throw baskets on the back of the front door + bouncing the ball up + down on the floor—dripping you call it, don't you?' x-x-x 'No,' said Tony, smiling, 'dribbling.' x-x-x 'That's what I said, drimpling.' x-x-x 'Well, never mind that,' said Tony, 'but how can you learn without a ball + without any baskets.' x-x-x 'Oh,' said the S.L.B., 'I've thought of that. In fact, I've thought of EVERYTHING. If you'll just borrow a ping pong ball from the Buttens + put some brown crayon on it + some lines like stitches that will take care of the ball—ping pong balls dripple fine; I've tried them. And for baskets—we can make them with paper clips, straightened out + then bent in circles. Your Mommy can sew some cloth on them + then we can tack them up on posts.'

"Tony laughed + told the S.L.B. his ideas were very good but that he could borrow the baskets + a ball from Vi's mechanical basketball game, so they wouldn't have to go to the trouble of making them.

"And he did. x-x-x Then when Tony brought the baskets + the ball home there was great excitement. Now everybody wanted to learn. 'Me first,' cried the S.L.B., 'It's my idea.' x-x-x 'Let's everybody line up + take turns shooting baskets,' said

Tony. x-x-x And *they* did. x-x-x After a little while the S.L.B. said, 'I've changed my mind. I *hate* basketball.' x-x-x Tony had been watching + he had noticed that just before this the S.L.B. had missed 6 shots in a row, because he had got so tired running + shouting + shooting. So, very calmly, he asked the S.L.B. to come + sit by him + watch the others for a while. After the S.L.B. was rested Tony said, 'Please, Sugar Lump Boy, try just once more. But don't worry if you miss. I used to miss a lot when I started, too.' x-x-x Fortunately the S.L.B. didn't miss that time. Of course, he often missed later. But he kept getting better + better + never again got quite *so* discouraged. THE END. All my love, Alger-Daddy" (December 15, 1951).

CLEARLY ALGER, who was a gifted natural athlete, wanted to keep me from dreading the sports I was so disgusted with myself for being bad at. The idea—that it could actually be okay to not be very good at something—didn't click in until many years later. As a boy I preferred my running-away-by-standing-still (or journalism) strategy: If kids were choosing up sides for a softball game, I'd be the umpire. But Alger also knew how to leaven the loaf; sometimes he incorporated pieces of the Eastern Shore tales he'd loved best as a boy, stories about Epaminandus, a wise fool and mirror of humanity who in his eagerness always got everything wrong. (In a January 1954 Alger retelling, the S.L.B. comes home from the grocery store with fresh baked bread that he's squashed so it can fit inside his toy cart. When Tony explains that it would have been easier to ask the grocer to cut the bread in half, the S.L.B. reappears "with half a grapefruit, cut-side down, in the rather dirty wagon. Looking very proud he said, 'I wasn't going to make the same mistake twice!' ")

There were also plenty of Sugar Lump Boy stories that played to my strengths:

"The S.L.B., Piglet & A Rebus

"One Sat. morning Tony heard the S.L.B. say to Piglet: 'What kind of a bus is a rebus? Is it No. 2 or No. 4?' Then he heard Piglet say: 'It's not a rebus, it's a rebush. It grows berries or maybe nuts—AND it has ENORMOUS thorns, I *think*.' x-x 'No,' said the S.L.B., 'you're wrong, Piglet. I've heard Tony say "reBUS" quite plainly, not "reBUSH." But what puzzles me is that when he talks about a rebus he's always reading a letter or writing one. I've never heard him say just before he went out: "Now I'm going to take the rebus to school" or when he comes in: "I've just had a long ride on a rebus with the nicest driver." ' x-x Then the sensible Snow Man said: 'Why don't you ask Tony, instead of arguing?' x-x So they did, each one saying: 'I'm right, Tony?' x-x 'No,' said Tony, smiling, 'you're both wrong. A rebus is picture writing.' x-x 'How perfectly silly,' the S.L.B. answered, 'How can a picture write? It's not alive.' x-x 'I mean writing with pictures instead of words,'

Tony replied, 'Like this: $A +$ $+A+$ $=$ Adorable.' x-x

'Well,' said Piglet quietly, 'it *would* be easier if it *were* a bush. That looks like Ablockapig to me, whatever a Ablockapig is.' x-x Tony laughed + said, 'I'll do another illustration. Look: $+$ $=$ basketball.' " [Alger used a red pencil here to add color to the handle of the basket; the basketball was blue, green, and red.] "x-x 'That's better,' said the S.L.B., 'why

didn't you use colors before? Let me try one: $+$ $=$

fight.' x-x Tony laughed + laughed + explained that colors had nothing to do with it + that the pictures had to take the place of spelling the word. 'Oh, I see that,' said Piglet. 'How about this: $+$ $=$ Ice cream.' x-x Tony praised Piglet for catching on so quickly + asked the S.L.B. to try again + this is the result: $+$ $=$ Peacham." [More red pencil shadings from Alger on the peach and the ham.] " 'Very good,' said Tony, 'and that brings our rebus lesson to THE END' " (February 19, 1952).

READING ALGER'S letters with '50s/'90s hindsight and foresight, I was struck (as I never used to be) by some things that are *not* in them. Perhaps that's because I was also listening to Alfred Hassler, a conscientious objector meditating on the proposition that modern society, when it sets out to reform prisons, is a stone trying to lift itself—since, for Hassler, "the fundamental evils of the prison system are the fundamental evils of the culture of which it is a part." "The criminal," Hassler wrote in his *Diary*, in a passage that's still provocative, "is our own reflection, staring out at us from the mirror of our own desires and ambitions," and "not so much a deviate from the norm"—and the values it honors, such as "aggressiveness, competitiveness, and skepticism"—"as he is its mildly distorted reflection."

"What is lacking," Hassler said, both in our culture and in our prisons, "is love. Not the *eros* type of love, but *agape*—the love that expresses itself in reverence for the personality even of the most depraved, that reacts to evil and cruelty with understanding and sympathy and sorrow, and that forgives *because* it understands and sympathizes and sorrows." Forgiving without forgetting—that would be the goal. But, for now, prisons are instead ruled by anger that has been fused with fear until they have become a single compulsive, corrosively distorting force: an organized "cycle of humiliation-resentment" that consumes both jailers and the jailed. The *Diary*'s foreword, contributed by an eminent American criminologist, Harry Elmer Barnes, explains that the custodial staff, haunted by an "almost morbid fear of convict escapes . . . is always superior to the treatment staff" hired to help prisoners make sense of their future lives. This sets up "a state of perpetual tension and boredom which at all times puts the institutions on the verge of revolt. Latent rebellion is always present, even in a place like Lewisburg."

Hassler's many *Diary* observations were written from this radical pacifist and explicitly Christian sensibility (reading the Sermon on the Mount one night—"You must always treat others as you would like them to treat you, for this sums up the law and the prophets"—it was clear to him that "its implications are so enormous" that if people were ever to "apply it to prisons," then "they would have to be emptied and torn down"). "Unhappiness saturates the place," says Hassler, "and saturates it for twenty-four hours a day, seven days a week." Other entries:

"There *are* only two general subjects of conversation in here: release and sex. It would take a stronger character than I to banish either one from one's thoughts!"

"On the surface, life here appears to run almost placidly, but one needs to go only a very little beneath the surface to find the whirlpools and eddies of anger and frustration. The muttering of discontent and rebellion goes on constantly; the *sotto voce* sneer whenever we pass an official or a guard, the glare carefully calculated to express contempt without arousing overt retaliation, the tempers that rise so swiftly to the breaking point. . . . Arguments obviously provide the needed release for this prison-built tension, but the onlookers keep a wary eye on them while they are in progress. Knifings are not uncommon in here."

"Men do suffer in here, dreadfully. . . . It is impossible to be in prison and escape this. I hear men pace their cells for hour after hour, hear them muttering unhappily to themselves, hear them, sometimes, sobbing quietly or cursing with a deep and bitter loneliness."

"Prison involves a whole sequence of petty humiliations: uniformity in clothing and cells, censorship of mail and reading matter of all kinds, locks and keys and passes and the whole impedimenta of inferiority. The irritation is constant and cumulative."

"During the day, the men maintain the cloak of bravado in which they wrap their self-respect; at night, alone in the darkness, their grief and fright sometimes become too much for them to bear."

"At first one is struck by the magnitude of the tragedy being enacted in here. All one's impulse is to combat and alleviate in some way. It seems intolerable merely to sit and witness such things. . . . But [by] what practical step? . . . The alternatives increasingly become hysteria or callousness. The latter is what develops, of course: to a large extent he [the prisoner] forces himself to ignore the tragedy, adopts the protective shell of the other prisoners, gradually becomes coarsened in speech and sensibilities, and perhaps suffers a major disillusionment in the power of his own beliefs."

Several months after Hassler arrived at Lewisburg, there was an attempted prison break. Three men briefly held the chief medical officer and his secretary at knife point (using a scalpel and the separated blades from a pair of scissors). No one escaped, but fellow inmates warned Hassler that they would all face "much rougher" treatment during the months ahead: "Guards would tighten up, infractions of minor rules would be punished severely, the little existing fraternization between hacks and inmates would disappear." Three men *did* break out of Lewisburg during Alger's second year there, taking advantage of a dense early-morning fog to slip a pipe ladder they'd made over the wall. They were at large for eleven days, and the story of their escape—especially the harrowing day when they held a local family hostage—was national news, and gave rise to a best-selling book, a successful Broadway play, and a hit

1955 Hollywood movie (*The Desperate Hours,* starring Humphrey Bogart and Fredric March).

It's understandable that no part of this event or its aftermath makes an appearance in Alger's letters; prison regulations explicitly prohibited mentioning either fellow inmates or guards by name in outgoing mail, and any comments about lapses in prison security, even if not specifically banned, would certainly have angered the authorities. There was self-censorship at work in Alger's letters, too. Sex and violence—or what Hassler called "the impedimenta of inferiority"—were, temperamentally, not subjects that Alger would ever choose for letters home; in addition, once Alger had found himself stuck trying to raise a son at long distance and sustain a marriage through a correspondence course, one of the clear purposes of the letters had to be giving the morale at home three booster shots a week.

While Prossy at the same time was trying to lift *his* spirits with her four or five letters a week (plus the double-duty "gallery" postcards she spent her lunch hours finding); both my parents, I think, could allow themselves to feel better far more easily when they thought they had just been helping the other one, rather than letting themselves be helped. It was a complicated form of energy exchange (they were right for each other—"equally incompatible," Tim has said), but it worked well enough for quite a long time because they were also, for more than thirty years, best friends; they were bookish, as the rest of their families weren't; and they relied devotedly on each other's strengths—Alger's elegant reasoning, Prossy's resonating feelings.

It was interesting to find out slowly, over a period of years, that Alger had been subjected to some petty humiliations inside—inmates in the laundry, for instance, with the connivance of some guards, routinely gave him pants with one leg cut higher than the other, and refused to issue him the new pair of shoes everyone else got every six months. Alger also resented what he saw as the Cold War politics that had consigned him to Lewisburg rather than the lower security federal correctional facility in Danbury, Connecticut, less than two hours from New York by train (federal prisoners, generally speaking, are sent to the penitentiary closest to home).

Back home in New York, Alger revealed that he had himself occasionally thumbed his nose at the guards, sometimes not shaving, for example, as a subtle and almost undetectable form of disrespect, and once in a while smuggling a steak from the storeroom under his shirt for a late-night feast with a few friends. It was sobering and far more scary to hear that he had once been in real danger—when a guard, who several months later committed suicide, tried to talk two young inmates into killing Alger, telling them, "The Rosenbergs are dead, why should this man Alger Hiss be alive?" (Several of Alger's friends talked them out of it.) It was almost immediately plain, once Alger came home, that he agreed completely and without reservation with Hassler's fundamental conclusion about Lewisburg—"Prisons are no good."

This was a view Alger never modified: Years later, shortly after Watergate had forced Richard Nixon to resign the presidency, he told Donie (the story appears in *Alger Hiss: The True Story*, John Chabot Smith's 1976 book about the Hiss case) not to feel good about the possibility that both Nixon and his former Vice President, Spiro T. Agnew, might spend time in jail: " 'Never! Don't ever send anybody to jail, it's a terrible place!'

" 'Not even Agnew and Nixon?' Donald asked.

" 'No!' said Alger. 'Jail doesn't do anybody any good.' "

But even though Alger came to share Hassler's perceptions about the unredeeming nature of prisons, what's impossible to find in his letters are any signs, or even the faint traces that the strictest sort of self-censorship can never hide, that Alger at

Lewisburg found himself burdened by the feelings Hassler had thought of as the inevitable accompaniments of such a discovery—either the "hysteria" of true despair or a "callousness" deliberately adopted in the face of despair, to mask it and hold it at bay.

Alger made friends easily at Lewisburg; in some cases these friendships lasted the rest of his days. "Hiss," said one such friend in an interview he gave in 1964 to Dr. Meyer A. Zeligs for his Hiss case book, *Friendship and Fratricide*, "always had something good to say about everybody. He could always see the good things in everybody and that's why a lot of fellows like myself accepted Hiss."

This man was an Italian-American New Yorker who had spent his adult life in organized crime. In Hassler's day, half the population at Lewisburg were young soldiers, half of whom came, as Hassler said, "from the hills"—meaning the Appalachian hills and hollows in Kentucky and Tennessee. By Alger's time, about a third of the prisoners were soldiers, another third were young Southerners, and most of the rest were "racket guys" or "regular guys," as they called themselves. Alger admired the way these racketeers did time—they were the least damaged psychologically (jail was an occupational hazard; their families were being well looked after; they had careers to come home to). "A man of 'heart,' " they said, endured troubles "stoically," as Alger more than thirty years later vividly remembered when he wrote *Recollections of a Life:* "Constant complaining—'crying'—was scorned."

It was an attitude, curiously, that brought Alger (and the racket guys) closer in spirit to James V. Bennett—then the director of the United States Bureau of Prisons and a firm believer in the value of imprisonment—than to the insights of Alfred Hassler. Bennett was a favorite of Franklin Delano Roosevelt, who had made him the Bureau's second director in

1937. He helped invent what in the 1930s and 1940s was called the "New Penology"—the prison reform movement that built Lewisburg, championed rehabilitation, changed prison menus to make the food edible, established a thirteen-thousand-volume library at Lewisburg, vastly expanded recreation programs, and doubled visiting hours (Hassler could see his wife for only one hour a month)—and when he retired in 1964, after twenty-seven years as director (under four presidents), Bennett wrote a memoir of his own, *I Chose Prison*.

I Chose Prison is another autobiography I have relied on to help me see further into an enormous prison system I knew only from one of its visiting rooms. Bennett was ten years older than Alger; his father had been an Episcopal clergyman. The son still found it natural to use biblical language to describe the qualities that could carry someone through the ordeal of incarceration: "Whatsoever is brought upon thee, take cheerfully, and be not cast down when thou art changed to a low estate, for gold is tried in fire and acceptable men in the furnace of adversity."

In his book Bennett pointedly contrasted, almost in the cadences of a short sermon or homily, the very different prison experiences of two "VIPs" that he had had in his charge and had carefully watched from Washington—Alger and Congressman J. Parnell Thomas, who had been sent to Danbury briefly in 1949 "for padding his congressional payroll and taking kickbacks from his staff. The powerful chairman of the Un-American Activities Committee was a difficult prisoner, belligerent and stubborn, and he seethed with resentment when he was told he would get no special privileges. Thomas was disliked by his fellow prisoners and this contributed to a persecution complex." "Thomas's problem," Bennett concluded, "was that he had few of the inner resources upon which men are able to fall back in adversity."

On the other hand, Bennett wrote, "Hiss, prisoner No.

19137, was assigned to Lewisburg and as well as any man I had known he accepted his lowly lot. He was assigned to one of the storerooms as a clerk, was active in the choir and Bible discussion groups, and he spent most of his spare time reading and studying in the prison library" (a point Alger would have disputed—his friendships left him little time for reading, and the only way he could break away from a conversation was by saying he had to write home, an act considered almost sacred by the inmates he knew). "His fellow prisoners," Bennett recorded, in his scrupulous way, "unquestionably liked him."

I thought it was honorable of Bennett to have said this— since it echoed an avowedly sympathetic profile about Alger by Brock Brower that had once appeared in *Esquire:* "When he went out of the [Lewisburg] gates on November 27, 1954 . . . there were rousing cheers from the bleak prison windows. Hiss's success in prison derived from human qualities that it would be hard to fake. Possibly for some days, or some weeks, but not for almost four years."

What I wasn't prepared for, and was shocked by, were the paragraphs that followed—it was necessary to read them several times before they sank in fully.

I was finding out, first, that Bennett had not been, as Alger had assumed (and I had therefore followed him in assuming), a faceless bureaucrat who bent with every change in the wind, a man who had penalized Alger in order to curry favor with his adversaries. On the contrary—Bennett saw himself as someone who in defense of the New Penology had at great peril been swimming upstream against the changed and now icy waters so that he could protect Alger. Such a thought had never occurred to either Alger or me—that the federal government, in the person of James V. Bennett, had at one point soberly concluded that Alger might be in physical danger, not in Lewisburg, but *outside* it:

"Although the reports that reached me from Lewisburg

about Hiss were good, the correspondence from the public was vitriolic. The consensus of my mail was that Hiss had been saved from treason charges only by the statute of limitations, and ought to be treated severely in prison.

"The Hiss issue reached its height when, as a model prisoner, he was granted time off his sentence for good behavior. This reduced his time to be served in prison to three years, eight months. There was a public uproar of which I was the principal victim. Speaking into the wind, I explained that time off for good behavior was one of the crucial elements of prison reform and that all men must be given an incentive for rehabilitation. As far as I was concerned, Hiss was just another prisoner.

"When Hiss was due for release in 1954, the letters took on a violent tone, and I could not disregard the possibility that someone might try to kill him as he left Lewisburg. So we closed off the prison and the grounds, stationed armed guards around the entrance gate, and worked out a combined security plan with the Pennsylvania state police. Fortunately, Hiss was set free uneventfully and, after making a brief statement and posing for press photographs, he drove off with his wife and his attorneys."

The well-remembered morning of November 27, 1954, the day of Alger's release from Lewisburg, took on new meaning. Now, when I thought of the waves and cheers from the windows inside the prison walls, and how excited I'd been about seeing a helicopter hovering overhead (helicopters were a great rarity in those days), I had to add on the idea that the helicopter was very likely carrying sharpshooters on the lookout for possible murderers. One of the standing family jokes from that day was about how, as Prossy and I rode sedately, as required, up to the prison in the back seat of Chester Lane's red convertible—Chester, Alger's flamboyant appeals lawyer, had decided that driving a red car would be his public Bronx cheer to the charges of communism against Alger—my excitable mother kept pounding the back of the front seat and shouting, "Keep calm, Chester! Keep calm!"

But her panic during those years, the fears that seemed so unreasonable because they were so urgent that they made her ungainly, and pushed her awkwardly and too quickly through even the happiest of days—in the climate of those times, I now realize, being fearful was not necessarily a misreading of events, and not always irrational.

Five pages of Bennett's book tell the story, also previously unknown to me, of how, during the years of Alger's troubles, the anti-communist suspicions that "spread through Washington like a plague" had almost cost him his own job: "One nerve-wracking episode began for me, as it must have for many public servants, when a disgruntled ex-employee publicly charged me with softness on Communism and offered no evidence to support the preposterous accusation. He was a prison warden whom I had let go for nonperformance of duties. I was hailed before Senator Pat McCarren's Senate subcommittee on appropriations without any notice of the subject of the inquiry. I was not allowed to bring any of my associates, even though it was presumably an open session.

"To my astonishment, Senator Homer Ferguson of Michigan began pugnaciously to read off questions from sheets of typescript that had been supplied to him, as I learned later, from the ex-warden. He was accusatory and gruff in his cross-examination for reasons I could not understand, but because he was a United States senator with a voice in our funding I struggled to hold my temper lest our employees and the innocent inmates of our prisons would suffer. Ferguson's general point of attack was that I had made it easy for prisoners in Danbury to maintain Communist connections and that my whole bureau was soft on Communism."

These particular charges went nowhere: A Republican senator who admired Bennett passionately defended him on the Senate floor, and "I was told," he later wrote, "that Ferguson was merely attempting to make a political case against the Truman administration and its attorneys general." Later when, just before President Eisenhower took office, "FBI agents appeared at our reformatory at Petersburg, Virginia, without prior reference to me, . . . I concluded that the FBI had now been brought into the 'softness on Communism' campaign and I was sure the matter was now serious." Bennett ultimately survived the "Petersburg probe" as well—about the worst thing twenty FBI special agents turned up during their "hostile and unwarranted investigation" was "the disappearance of several hams." He considered his reappointment by the Eisenhower administration "a vindication of my integrity as a public servant."

Bennett never forgot what he had seen "McCarthyism," as he called it, do to the administration of justice—one federal law enforcement agency had without compunction sought to undermine the integrity of another: "The warden felt sure his phone was tapped," Bennett wrote, "but he talked on and on to me, hoping, as he wrote me privately, that the FBI would get an earful.

"The prisoners were aware of all this and some were delighted to see their guards under fire. Others resented the intrusion. The situation grew so delicate that the warden feared a riot or disturbance of some other kind."

In Washington itself, he noted, as scrupulously as ever, "the steadfastness of our friendships and our mutual loyalties were put to the test as rarely before."

IN HIS first months at Lewisburg, Alger was offered several pieces of advice by friends and strangers about how to approach prison life: "This afternoon," he wrote home on April 10, 1951, "I received a fine letter from Prof. Robert S. Lynd of Columbia [the censors had passed it on as a "special" letter from an unauthorized correspondent]. 'A great many of us decent Americans are enduring this night march with you. We have taken strength from the fact that you have stood-to as you have in this shattering experience. Don't become bitter. We need those back among us who have looked harshness in the face + and can *still* affirm man. . . . But you are not alone.' Pros, dear, thee has had to answer so many letters for me, including those received at home! Please thank Mr. L. for his message and assure him that the walls of my cell are not black—as a matter of fact I don't believe I've yet told you that they are green—nor is the taste of my confinement bitter."

In the fall, there was a letter from the Rev. Ruth M. Horsman, Peacham's new Congregational minister. (Letters from members of the clergy were exempt from the usual restrictions. Ms. Horsman was the village's first woman minister; she was also young and pretty. Initially aghast at the concept, Peachamites became warmly admiring after meeting her.) Most of her letter was about settling in and adjusting to an early winter (the parsonage had no furnace), and about goings-on in the community. The last sentence said: "I think often of the tremendous opportunity for good which is yours under present conditions" (November 6, 1951).

At Christmastime Alger received a "Keep your chin up" note—passed through by the associate warden as a "special" holiday letter—from Professor George Boas, a world-famous philosopher who had taught him at Johns Hopkins almost thirty years before: "Dear Hiss, It will probably surprise you to get a letter from me, but I didn't want the Christmas season to pass by without your receiving a word from an old teacher and friend. It would be grotesque to wish a merry Christmas, but at any rate I can wish you a peaceful one. And I do with all sincerity. I don't want to be preachy, but I still think Socrates hit the nail on the head in his comments on doing and suffering injustice."

Socrates was unjustly condemned to death during the unraveling of the Periclean age of Athens after its defeat by Sparta—"sacrificed," as the second edition of *The Columbia Encyclopedia* says, "to the bigotry and chagrin of the fallen city." (I've had to reacquaint myself with Socrates—Professor Boas, with a scholar's pride, assumed that what he and Alger had studied together in the mid-1920s would of course still be fresh in Alger's mind.) Socrates refused to escape execution because he believed in the rule of law, even when the law was wrong. "But you're innocent," his wife protested. "Would you rather I was guilty?" Socrates asked her.

Uncle Tommy's thoughts were more detailed and specific, and provoked a circuitous Chicago-to-Lewisburg-to-New-York-to-Chicago dialogue. Tom Fansler had early on been added to Alger's official list of correspondents, and wrote him faithfully, month after month—"We think of you every day and speak of you with pride in our hearts and a firm faith"— without once receiving a direct answer. Or at least not until September 1954, when Alger's letter-writing quota was doubled, a privilege extended to prisoners going home soon. Until then, Alger dedicated his letters entirely to Prossy and me, creating the intensely focused beam of energy that swept over us three times a week, like ships at sea taking their bearings from a slowly revolving lighthouse; the only exceptions to this rule were the occasional letters to Tim and birthday letters he mailed to Mimi and Donie. If he needed to send Tom or anyone else a message, he tucked it into one of his letters to us.

Uncle Tommy's suggestions for Alger derived from his own experiences seven years earlier during World War II. In August 1951, he wrote: "One thing I found very helpful when I was in the Naval Hospital at Key West was to treat each day as a separate unit—so many hours of this, a brief walk in the garden and it was lunch time. A couple of hours for letters and some time for helping the nurses and it was evening. Each day just a unit in itself, with no particular past or future."

Alger (on August 22, 1951) replied through Prossy and me: " '. . . no particular past or future.' That is almost exactly the attitude of the more mature + integrated men here—time is something to get through with in as much of a benumbed daze or attention distracting way as possible. The greatest mutual compliment is for the members of a group to say after a bull-session 'That hour (or 2 hours) went fast.' . . . As for me, I of course have my share of boredom—but most of that comes from other men trying to kill time by aimless + rather pathetic chatter, not unique to prisons. But basically I find the concept of consciously killing time (a very literally true phrase, here) as repugnant + alien as ever. It strikes me as being partial suicide here as elsewhere. This is—and I fear must needs be for all too many persons of goodwill before the hysteria (which even the President now does not hesitate to call by name) runs its course—a part of my life as any other experience. . . . As at any other time I shall endeavor to husband as much 'time' as possible for the available activities which mean most to me—here: writing to thee, reading, exercise, purposeful relationships, 'sweet singing in the choir,' . . . etc."

Uncle Tommy—unconvinced and still concerned—returned to this theme just after Thanksgiving: "We thought of you many times on Thanksgiving Day and wondered what kind of day you were having. That particular festival you could probably take in your stride, but the month of December will prove more difficult. While I was in the hospital at Key West I found that concentrating on the immediate minute task in front of me was a salvation. . . . The same way on board ship in oiling and polishing up the working parts of a gun and the gun carriage. I remember taking the hinges and hasp off the ready-ammunition boxes and grinding and polishing the bearings so that they would open almost at a finger-touch. One of the bosun's mates kicked like a steer when he was transferred to another gun crew. He said he knew that anything around one of Fansler's guns would *work*. . . . Well, all that was probably a waste of whatever creative or intellectual talents I may have but at any rate the days went by surprisingly fast."

Alger (on December 4, 1951) replied, again through Prossy and me: "Thee must tell him that while I 'want out' without the minutest reservation, I find that here as elsewhere there is large opportunity for learning + growing. He was *sick* at Key West +, as thee so well learned this fall, a serious illness can indeed be a suspension of living or at least a major contraction of vital functions. I am experiencing prison life with full health + vigor, physically + mentally."

Alger had found out how to stay in touch with the newness that each sunrise brought, and this daily renewal and refreshment freed him from the constant weight of the sameness that prisons imposed on time, making each day seem to be nothing more than a replica of the one before. What Alger had managed to do, it seems to me now, and if I can put this the right way, was to begin living in God's world rather than in the more customary one. Now, I'm not trying to put a halo behind his head, because I don't think of Alger as a perfected person, then or ever. Also, he was doing something that all of us do at least sometimes, and that for many people is the most ordinary thing they can think of, and that doesn't have to be called "God's world" to make use of it.

What's different about the two worlds? They look exactly alike; but in God's world every person and thing and place and moment is both itself and a kind of precursor, someone or something that may have a message you've never heard before. "Learning + growing," Alger's phrase, takes place when you can open yourself up so fully to the familiar that it seems ready to shine with a light you've never seen before:

"Austin McCormick was, for me, also wrong in his dictum that small matters assume large proportions in jail." Before Alger went to prison, Vi had arranged for him to meet McCormick, an assistant director of the Federal Bureau of Prisons in early New Deal days and later the New York City Corrections Commissioner under Mayor La Guardia, so Alger would know what to expect; Alger said he felt like a nineteenth-century traveler seeking advice from a famous explorer before setting off for an unknown land. McCormick had already figured out that Alger would wind up in Lewisburg and not Danbury, which had a reputation as a country club; that he would be assigned to the storeroom, rather than to the prison's education department—because, as McCormick said, even if Alger Hiss taught only mathematics, rumors would insist that he was teaching communist mathematics. McCormick also predicted that Alger would find the racket guys more congenial than most of the other prisoners, and ended with what he said was "the best advice I can give you": "You'll be the new boy in school, and you'll have a lot to learn. The others will all be experienced upperclassmen. Listen and learn."

McCormick's "other errors," Alger wrote, "I have mentioned earlier: the isolation of quarantine was in no sense demoralizing; I am not over-slept; I haven't enough time for reading—not nearly as much as when busiest outside; etc. But all these mis-forecasts (Bill Soule [Dardar's son] would say mis-firecasts) are in the realm of the subjective; on all objective matters he was crisply accurate. The large matters remain those of the human spirit, here as elsewhere. And man's potentialities + accomplishments shine on occasion even more brightly here than in hum-drum ordinary life" (August 10, 1951).

"The most admirable psychological trait displayed here seems to me to be moral courage. It is relatively infrequent (but more frequent than among the large numbers of ordinary people I have known equally well) + most varied. Its manifestations depend upon the nature of the individual's inner resources—codes, religious patterns, pride, family relations are the usual ingredients. The weaker and/or emptier men react to the boredom, frustration + loneliness by talking continuously of their cases (like not-so-ancient mariners or have-I-told-you-of-my-operationers). This reaction is not surprising: like the summer-hotel-veranda paraders or rockers, they are merely verbalizing what is their most significant psychic experience in an otherwise emotionally barren life. x In general, there is a significant paucity of consideration for others deriving from a real inability to project or generalize their own experiences. (But I'm not sure that the average is really lower than outside—it's perhaps just that the lack is more noticeable when a large number of men are arbitrarily forced to be constantly together.) And side by side with this self-imprisonment there are moving instances of sharing the pitifully limited material objects of jail life—cigarettes, candy, cookies, oranges—and instances of helpfulness in terms of information to newcomers, assisting others in hard tasks + the like. x-x And genuine consideration for others is appreciated in almost 100% fashion; while sharing + help is reciprocated with earnest diligence" (August 16, 1951).

"x-x-x Our yard group frequently includes the grizzled but startlingly blue-eyed Sicilian of whom I have told thee. . . . The Sicilian still observes on July 31 the anniversary of the death in 1905 of a beloved patrician priest (a 'baron') of his native village, which he left as a youth not many years later. . . . I believe I am the only one here who has been told the story of the 'baron' (+ the children who adored him) and who has been shown a treasured tinted photograph of him. There is always so much to be learned everywhere + so many unheralded teachers" (August 19, 1951).

"I think never have I been such a confidant—letters, family photos, reminiscences, future plans, personal problems. (All unasked + unencouraged, of course.) Inmate + officer; loneliness is, I realize, not a prison flower but it certainly flourishes in gaol" (August 28, 1951).

"x-x-x Our bible-forum meetings (before choir practice on Friday nights) have brought strongly back to my mind one of O.W.H.'s aperçus. He used to say that the conventional concept is that it is always easy to know right from wrong but that it is hard to do right. He said that, on the contrary, his chief difficulty was in determining what was right. Once determined, a detailed course of conduct was relatively easy. The conventional concept has full sway among those here who are religiously inclined: 'right' is clear but 'temptation,' 'sin,' 'weakness' are powerful deterrents from following what is right. It seems to me so *clear*, as I follow the often rambling discussion, that in fact no clear choice of values has been made by the individual who holds the concept—even, that his major value choice (unacknowledged to himself) is that the so-called 'temptation' is 'right' for him + that the competing value is artificially imposed from without, not really a part of him. The judge's aperçu now seems meaningful + penetrating; at the time I could not grasp it fully in the light of my own psychic experience. . . . A clear sense of regret + shame for an act which injures another is, to my way of thinking, normal + healthy. But if such acts continue + with them follows a constant train of guilt feeling, it is obvious that the value system of the individual concerned is out of kilter + needs scientific remedying, not that such falls from 'grace' are a normal series of phenomena for 'sinful man' " (August 30, 1951).

THESE PASSAGES mark a kind of tree ring of growth for Alger, a turning point at the start of the second half of his life that set a course for the life he led after Lewisburg. He was now a traveler in a faraway land; he was schooling himself to become a phenomenal listener; he had given himself over to "unheralded teachers"; and in every encounter he looked for whatever might emerge that lay beyond his previous experience. The summer of 1951 was, I think, the moment when listening and responding to other people became what Alger did best ("I've never in my life met anyone with such good manners," a well-traveled English journalist remarked to me in the 1970s). It was when he stopped defining himself as an "experienced upperclassman," preferring, more Socratically, to think of himself for the rest of his days as a "new boy in school." (When Socrates was thirty, the Delphic Oracle told the world he was the wisest of men; Socrates said that what this meant was that nobody knew anything, but he had the advantage because he knew that he didn't know anything.)

This was also when Alger began to put less faith in government as a force for moving humanity forward and more trust in private acts of friendship and in the study of the human heart. In his State Department years, there was a joke that "the writ of the New Deal runs everywhere—except through the Department of State!" Meaning that although F.D.R.'s reforms had been accepted by almost everyone else in government, the two hundred or so conservatively minded career foreign service officers who administered the department liked to think they belonged to a club that outranked any mere president. Nevertheless, it had been hard for Alger, for whom government was a benevolent word, to accept, even after seeing it during his two trials, that prosecutors from the Justice Department, where he had himself served, would ever try to finesse a point and hoodwink a jury.

Tim, who sat in court for some days during Alger's second trial, remembers watching Alger at lunch with his lawyers after Thomas F. Murphy, the chief federal prosecutor, used some legal maneuver that had infuriated the defense. At lunch Alger's lawyers were still fuming and sputtering and calling for Murphy's disbarment. While Alger, the only one sitting there quietly, shook his head and said, "You know, when I was in the Justice Department, we just wouldn't have touched a case like this!" I think the first real shock of prison for Alger had been finding himself in the hands of a federal agency whose fundamental mission wasn't simply to help people. Overnight he had gone from being a "do-gooder" to being a "done-unto-er."

Over the years many people, trying sympathetically to get to the heart of Alger, have said to me that, given the radical climate of the 1930s, it would have been "perfectly natural" for him to have at least flirted with communism. In the depths of the Depression so many highly intelligent Americans felt the pull of desperate, revolutionary measures that you might wonder why it was that Alger didn't. I can see perhaps a couple of reasons.

For at least some people attracted to communist ideas in the 1930s, even a few New Dealers, part of the pull had to do with the excitement of finding, and being accepted by, a small, semi-secret elite of remarkable people. But in the words of an old Central Asian proverb, you can't fill anything unless it happens to be empty. Alger had already been enrolled, by Felix Frankfurter, the gatekeeper, into two elite groups in quick succession. For the rest of his days Alger was intensely proud of both associations, and when he talked about them you always heard that special, unmistakable, lit-up-from-within voice that comes to people when they're discussing the peak experiences of their lives.

Justice Holmes had just thirty secretaries during his tenure on the Supreme Court, and Alger was one of them. This club was known only to its own members, and to Holmes and Frankfurter. Just three and a half years after that, Alger was selected to join the "Happy Hot Dogs," a very public group that in retrospect seems almost as exclusive as the Holmesians, the 350-odd men and women "with their hair ablaze," as it was said, whom Frankfurter recruited—by telegram, in Alger's case ("ON BASIS NATIONAL EMERGENCY," said the wire)—to staff the New Deal's newly invented relief agencies during the famous, whirlwind "First Hundred Days" of the first Roosevelt administration.

Holmes's secretaries flourished after leaving the old man— Irving Olds, the man Catherine Drinker Bowen interviewed, was perhaps as chairman of U.S. Steel the most prominent; but another man became Attorney General, a third a Congress-man, and one of Alger's Lewisburg letters mentions with delight that Chappie Rose (H. Chapman Rose) had just been named Under Secretary of the Treasury by President Eisen-hower.

Many secretaries formed close friendships with one another—Robert M. Benjamin, for instance, who clerked for the Justice in 1922–1923, was one of Alger's appeals lawyers almost on a pro bono basis, and saw him in Lewisburg a num-ber of times (legal counsel were the only authorized nonfamily visitors). Intellectually, all the secretaries agreed, their year with the old man—who never had children of his own, and called each of them "lad," "sonny," "young feller," and "idiot boy"—had marked them indelibly. They had been initiated into the Great Span; "We all imbibed that tremendous sense of the continuity of history, that we were all part of one woven strip," Congressman Laurence Curtis said years later. "I don't think any of the anniversaries of the great Civil War battles went by without his remembering them."

As they heard the stories of Ball's Bluff and Antietam and Chancellorsville, the secretaries also picked up, as Professor Paul Freund of Harvard Law School once expressed it to me, the unexpected understanding of human nature that Captain

Oliver Wendell Holmes and Alger, Beverly Farms,
Massachusetts, June 1930

Holmes (a rank he achieved in 1862), by birth a proper Bostonian, had acquired under fire—that doubters could be as brave as believers; that poor men without advantages were often better leaders than Harvard graduates. In addition, although Holmes never spoke about such matters directly, the secretaries felt, Alger and Donie both told me, that they had now personally, Harvard graduates though they were, been entrusted with a mission—whatever it was they set their hands to, they would carry history forward honorably, keeping faith with the American purposes that had been forged during this country's original Great Span, and staying true to the Union that Holmes had fought to preserve.

Alger's and Donie's secretaryships had yet another meaning. "A year of radiance," Alger called his days with Holmes a quarter of a century after they began, in a 1954 letter home from Lewisburg, and the same image rose in his mind thirty years after that, in *Recollections:*

"No other honor or piece of good fortune has been such a

source of delight for me as was that enchanted year I spent with Holmes beginning in October 1929. And no other relationship has had a deeper or more lasting influence." And "No young lawyer who spent a year with this model of the upright man could fail to wish to emulate him in conduct and character. Certainly Holmes was the most profound influence in my life." As Alger remembered it in his book, he barely noticed the great stock market crash on October 24, except to note that there was "an air of agitation" when he went to the theater that night, "because I was completely preoccupied with a wholly different world."

Charles Alger Hiss, Alger's and Donie's father, my grandfather, committed suicide when they were both very small children—Alger not yet two and a half and Donie barely three months. The fact of their father's suicide was withheld from the two boys for years, an almost invariable practice at the beginning of the twentieth century, so I think the truly grievous, lasting psychic wound that touched their growing up was the aching void of fatherlessness, rather than an emptiness made even more inexplicable by the violence and irrationality of self-destruction.

In Alger's case, being a "suicide survivor," as they are called today, may have shaped his character profoundly. Several years ago I met someone—a young computer genius—whose concern for the people around him irresistibly reminded me of Alger. I was allowed to know him for only a short time, because he died suddenly during the next summer, but for a year I got to watch his passionate, lovable thoughtfulness for people he'd known all his life and for people he'd just met—offering rides, lending books, telling jokes, organizing trips, baking bread to comfort someone who'd suffered a loss, steering people through the intricacies of computers, and refusing almost peremptorily to let you decline his help ("I'm going to pretend I didn't hear that!").

He took on too much; he probably undermined his own health; and after his death his wife told me she thought he'd been tremendously transformed by having grown up as a suicide survivor (his mother killed herself when he was thirteen). After that, his wife said—which made me think even harder about Alger—it was as if he couldn't bear for anyone he came across to feel, even for a moment, any of the pain and abandonment he'd grown up with. Books on suicide have little to say about this as part of the aftermath of a suicide, although a recent essay by Dr. Norman L. Farberow, director of the Los Angeles Suicide Prevention Center's Survivors After Suicide program, published in a book called *Suicidology*, does mention that, among other responses, bereavement after suicide can sometimes include "flashbacks of painful memories, preoccupation with death, reversal to either extremes of behavior—excessive clinging and fearfulness or growing up overnight and becoming a parent to the remaining parent."

My friend's wife said something else that resonated for me: "He had no sense of danger—he couldn't even acknowledge that it existed." She felt that this was why she was the one who became "the worrier" in the family. Worrying was something he simply couldn't take seriously.

Perhaps it's also true that suicide survivors must make some sort of shell which they use to clothe their feelings of unworthiness; and that the world, seeing that shell and not understanding it (the second Alger), may assume that it's hiding something shameful or even criminal. What's much clearer to me is that, after meeting Holmes, at the wordless level where healing occurs, Alger and Donie no longer had to think of themselves as young men who'd never had a father. Alger and the Justice were by circumstance thrown closer together than previous secretaries—Holmes's beloved wife, Fanny, to whom he'd been married for almost sixty years, died five months before Alger took on the secretary's job, and it was Alger who persuaded Holmes to let him read aloud to him as Fanny used to do (Alger would read every afternoon for an hour if the Supreme Court was in session; for three hours if it wasn't).

"When he was in his usual high spirits," as Alger wrote in *Recollections*, "a regular greeting on coming back from the Court was, 'Shall we have some culture?' or, perhaps, 'Will it be murder, or shall we improve our minds?' The reference to 'murder' was in recognition of his frequent indulgence in mystery stories."

Alger's reading aloud was a hit with the eighty-eight-year-old widower, not surprisingly, since Alger was particularly good at it—listening to his Aunt Lila reading aloud to the Hiss family had been one of the great treats of his childhood. In order for the two men to continue their reading, Alger became the first secretary invited to accompany the Justice to his summer home in Beverly Farms after the Supreme Court had recessed for the summer (Alger boarded in a separate cottage, and it was his first separation from Prossy since their marriage the previous December). Whenever possible, Alger continued to read to Holmes thereafter, long after the secretaryship had passed on to others, even if in the hectic early days of the New Deal it meant breaking away from his desk at the Agriculture Department to fit in one more hour with the old man.

From Beverly Farms, on June 9, 1930, Alger wrote Prossy about Holmes, leading up slowly and casually to the thought that meant the most to him: "I must, must get on to bar exam work—last night Mary [Donnellan, the Justice's waitress and parlor maid] phoned just as I was starting in that she thought O.W.H. would like some reading. So over I hiked + read Birrell on Richardson v. Fielding + thought of thy love for Fielding. . . .

"The Justice in Boston told me he'd told F.F. [Felix Frankfurter] I couldn't have been more attentive + considerate this winter if he'd been my father whom I not only loved but whose society I enjoyed." (Holmes had rarely seen eye to eye with his own father, the famous—and somewhat self-important— "Autocrat of the Breakfast Table.")

The following October, Frankfurter forwarded to Prossy— with the added note, "Dear Pross: I'll let Alger's blushes be screened by you"—a letter he'd just received from Robert W. Wales, Alger's successor as secretary, and later a prominent New York lawyer, about his first day on the job in the Justice's house on Eye Street in Washington ("I thought you might be interested in my reactions while still fresh from the first few hours with the justice"). A few excerpts: "I approached his door with a sinking feeling as though the zero hour were at hand. . . . Alger's warm smile almost restored my confidence. The justice's words put me at ease, and I was left in Alger's care to learn the mysteries. I'm certainly glad that Alger was kind enough to spend this couple of days in initiating me [Alger was taking time off from his new job at a Boston law firm]. I've felt green and useless all day, but not one tenth as much as I would have with written instructions. The Justice is undoubtedly very fond of Alger—it is almost a shame to make him forego the attention and assistance Alger gave him, and that I can't replace even in part for a while yet."

"The afternoon," Bob Wales continued, which followed a "delightful" luncheon, "seemed too short for the first duties. When I left, the Justice was enjoying having Alger read to him." In a postscript, added the following day, Wales ended by writing about Alger yet again: "Alger left us this noon—I hope the Justice will not feel too lost without him. My admiration for Alger, always high, is now almost boundless."

The sixty-three years that separated them in age did not seem to strike either Holmes or Alger as any kind of barrier. A year later, during my parents' second separation—Prossy and Tim had moved to New York, but Alger felt obliged to stay in

Boston to finish a case he'd been working on—he wrote her about an unexpected evening with the Justice in Beverly Farms: "Last night I had a lovely time at Justice's. Bob called me in the morning to say he had to come into Boston for the evening and suggested that I come to dinner.

"I took a Personal Lending Library *John Henry* and it was a wow! The Judge enjoyed—and understood—all of it. . . .

"The Judge had got his color back and was ever so jolly and happy and affectionate. I felt big and strong and my feet didn't touch the ground when I left."

Several weeks later, Alger sent Prossy the much-crossed-out first draft of a letter he'd sent for the Justice to open on October 21, 1931. "It sounds awfully pompous now," Alger told Prossy, "but what I hoped to do was send our love unmistakably but briefly." He succeeded (displaying a depth of feeling that virtually disappeared from his letters until twenty years later in Lewisburg):

"Dear Mr. Justice,

"Tomorrow is Ball's Bluff Day and my wife and I, believing that it is proper on feast days to crystallize that which is most significant in the work-a-day life, send our love to you in this note.

"Massachusetts is given over to the fall fires. I assume that the tulip poplars of the Soldiers' Home have not yet been burned gold by the southward march of those fires.

"Yours devotedly, Alger Hiss"

ALGER WASN'T high-ranking enough to spend time alone with Franklin D. Roosevelt, but I've known since I was three exactly how much Roosevelt meant to both Alger and Prossy. My only memories of things that happened before age four are of days when the world changed in an instant—when I was a year and a half, my baby carriage got away from my baby-sitter, sped down a small hill, tipping over and spilling me out on my nose. No real damage at all, except to my sense of the world as a place you could always rely on. When I was two, the family moved a few blocks in Georgetown, from a house on Volta Place that seemed as big as a kingdom, to a tiny house on P Street I'd never seen before (the only house my parents ever actually owned in their thirty years together).

That was the morning I realized—to the extent any two-year-old can—that most things don't stay settled for long, that changes rain down on the world like a meteor swarm, that it takes an effort to stay true to what you know. I sat alone in the hot, empty, sunny front bedroom on the second floor of the new house, and watched out the window while downstairs my life was slowly catching up with me again as the movers brought in chairs and beds and books and toys and dishes. I was three—my own son loves this story about his Grandpa Alger the best—when I found out that my father was fallible. I asked Alger, at the National Zoo, "What noise do the elephants make, Daddy?" And he had just said, "Why, I don't think elephants make any kind of noise, Tony," when a big bull elephant lifted its trunk and began trumpeting ear-splittingly and (we thought) endlessly.

I was still three when President Roosevelt died. Both my parents were shattered. I can remember sitting very still; I had never seen grief so powerful or so jagged, hadn't known that such an immense force existed and that it could overwhelm strong, self-composed people from one moment to the next. They moved sluggishly; they talked slowly and very softly. Of course the whole country was mourning, or most of it—but I didn't know about that, wasn't interested. This was a private matter, a death in the family—of the head of the family, it felt like.

I never saw quite this kind of rawness in the house again; Prossy's beloved older brother, Dean Fansler, a teacher at a university in Manila who'd been interned by the Japanese during the war, died in 1945, shortly after the war ended. (He had stayed alive, but just barely, because former students smuggled him eggs every week.) Alger and Prossy were deeply saddened, but managed to hold themselves together because—I didn't have words for this yet, but I could already sense it—that was what you were supposed to do. But my parents had already shown me, a few months earlier, that there were some feelings you couldn't hide from and couldn't disguise.

Fourteen years earlier, as the Depression darkened, Alger's letters reflect, though spottily, his increasing awareness and concern about the hard times that had engulfed millions of Americans, and the beginnings of his own reaching out, by comparing notes with Frankfurter and other Boston-area liberals, toward some next steps the country might take:

"I have so much to tell," says one letter to Prossy, written February 3, 1932, "that I'll have to indicate most of it. 1. I gave some money to the Boston Unemployed Drive after much thought and consultation. I'll explain it all on Saturday. 2. I thought Edmund Wilson's article was grand. His integrity is a really moving thing. Has thee seen A. MacLeish's article on capitalism in last week's Saturday Review? Felix says it is soft thinking after Wilson. [My parents were always telling each other to read things in magazines, although by Lewisburg days it was generally Prossy alerting Alger to things she'd just read in *The New Yorker*, and Alger referencing pieces from either the *Friends Intelligencer*, a Quaker periodical he received through the chaplain's office, or the English *New Statesman & Nation*, for which he had an airmail subscription, while Prossy's copies came by freighter.] 3. We had a real Cambridge snowstorm all day yesterday."

(By the way, as I read their correspondence, I kept one eye out for any appearance of the word "communism." In all the letters they wrote each other, before, during, and after Lewis-

burg—751 from Alger to Prossy and 742 from her to him—I
did find it once, in a letter of Alger's from Beverly Farms, in
June 1930, during his summer with the Justice. It's a joking reference to the previous summer, when, while he and Donie
were living in Giverny, the tiny French village where Monet
had painted, Prossy was teaching at an experimental adult education summer program at Bryn Mawr for women factory
workers: "I loved thy calling Martha [Tim's baby-sitter] Eeyore
+ did thee call thyself a Wobbly with an I.W.W. tongue in thy
socialistic (I couldn't bring myself to write 'Communistic')
cheek?")

Perhaps, considering all the voids in the Hiss family history—
Alger's father's suicide was followed in 1926 by the early death
of his older brother, Bosley, and two and a half years later by
the suicide of his sister, Mary—Alger, or Donie, too, might,
even after the magic of meeting Holmes and enlisting in the
Great Span, have found themselves susceptible, as some may
have been, to the seeming solidarity offered by the Communist
Party. But they had both already been caught up by the
momentum of a different movement that also appealed to the
fearless, the young, and anyone who wanted to leave a mark on
history. And, as young lawyers, they had the skills to rewrite
the laws of a nation. As New Dealers, their days were long,
their minds busy and occupied and stretched by the country's
need; they were flooded with optimism, and their spirits were
at peace.

"I saw Roosevelt's victory," Alger wrote in the first draft of
Recollections of a Life (it was originally planned as a book just
about the New Deal), "as heralding a great national effort to
eliminate the root causes of the social ills I had found so dis-
tressing—and which to my chagrin I was doing so little about."
And: "My mood was one of elation and I was confident that all
over the country there were others like me who would join the

ranks of the New Deal with the same feelings. As I arrived in Washington, I felt I had come to join a band of brothers."

Nine months after Alger arrived in Washington, he got a glowing write-up in "Uncle Sam Grows Younger," an *American Magazine* tribute to the new administration: "In his twenties, he is one of the men chiefly responsible for the plan to buy $650,000,000 worth of commodities to feed the unemployed. He has too much spirit for his bodily strength and is in danger of working himself to death." As a salaried employee of the New Deal—a low salary, but his wants were modest—Alger gloried in having become something like an officially designated radical. (Donie, too young to have been a Happy Hot Dog—he was Holmes's secretary during Roosevelt's First Hundred Days—joined the New Deal shortly thereafter.) Labels weren't important, Alger liked to say; results were. This was a time (it became one of Alger's favorite stories, although when I was growing up he might as well have said "Once upon a time," it all sounded so long ago and far away) when Franklin Roosevelt, proud squire of a three-hundred-year-old Hudson River estate, took pleasure in opening cabinet meetings by poking fun at the names his enemies called him. He would flash his famous grin and declare, "Good morning, fellow socialists!"

"Youth is in the saddle," the *American Magazine* had declared, "riding hell-bent for victory or a fall." To me it's fascinating that one result of Alger's swashbuckling New Deal radicalism was that for a time he became as intolerant as any communist, and could be high-handed, smug, arrogant, and stinging in some of his dealings with those who were less fervent about Roosevelt than he was—such as the old-line civil servants he gave dressings down to at the Agriculture Department, or the business leaders he cross-examined caustically when he was counsel for the Nye Committee, the Senate committee set up to investigate war profiteering in the munitions industry during the First World War. He stepped on toes, he accumulated enemies, and, armed in righteousness, he never noticed. "The New Deal—it's amazing I ever got over it," Alger told me in the mid-1970s.

TIM ONCE remarked that, until Lewisburg, "Alger had no sense of evil"—meaning that he'd previously been unable to know when he was in danger or making trouble for himself. Lewisburg was also where Alger began to think again about the nature of evil. His younger, crusading conception of evil took on new dimensions; he now saw it not just as a presence to be combatted, but also as an absence, an aching hollowness inside, a thwarting of the completion people instinctively craved: " 'Destructiveness,' " he wrote home on November 1, 1951, quoting an "excellent statement" by Erich Fromm, " 'is the outcome of unlived (and, he might have added, unloved) life.' " Three weeks later, on November 22, Alger wrote: "Evil is not a separate force, but the negation of life fulfilled."

A month earlier, on October 16, he'd said: "The blight of our times is the betrayal of integrity by those who, when afraid, turn from the vision of man's potentialities (God in man) + 'sorrowfully' lament the alleged inevitable sinfulness of man (a rationalization for letting the cock crow thrice a thousand times . . .). This is the path of spiritual death, of suicide. It is neatly posed in Job. He, stalwart soul, rejected it. (In his agony he was advised by his wife: 'Dost thou still retain thy integrity? Curse God + die.' Job 2:9) There is a veritable orgy of cursing the God in all of us (+ many who don't curse, deny—which leaves the field clear to the cursers) + the spiritual death which falls on such blasphemers is visible to all but the wilfully blind."

"x-x-x Back to the theme of tests of essential personal *values*. These values are quite different from the optimum *circumstances* which allow them full expression. . . . For all who will so regard it prison can be an excellent test of one's basic values. . . . Meaningful realization of life is a complex blending of experience with understanding—inner growth without self-absorption. This is the concept which 'peace of mind,' 'inner light,' 'serenity,' etc. seek to convey. Bitterness comes from the inability of inner values to accommodate (+, more, to permit continued spiritual *growth* from) external events. Events that wound disarrange these values, but the healthier they are, the sooner the recovery. Circumstances may block the normal sharing + giving of the personality with consequent frustration. But complete blockage is rare + for the adult personality, the large of soul, there is always (though 'tis, indeed, 'sometimes hard to come at') the realization that those of good will are sharers in the ever-continuing high enterprise of man's endeavor. Satisfactions akin in scope + depth to those of the mystics are not denied to the rational in the middle of the 20th century" (November 24, 1951).

I find it extremely interesting that Alger's conscious memories of Lewisburg seem in later years to have been entrusted to the "public Alger" for safekeeping. A decade after leaving prison, when he was being interviewed by Meyer Zeligs for his book *Friendship and Fratricide*, Alger sent him a memo about the "self-analysis" he had undertaken at Lewisburg: "I wanted to know better what my capabilities were for the immediate future (in Lewisburg) and for later on. There was the occasion for a reconsideration of first principles, of values, of objectives and I welcomed the occasion. I had lived so actively that the reflective side of my nature had had only occasional chances to assess basic directions and motivations."

Earlier in the memo, he wrote, "The time available for these reflections resulted from the prison routine of 'lights out' at 10 p.m. (whereas I had long been conditioned to much later hours) and from the not infrequent periods when I was left alone in the storeroom."

Twenty years later, when writing *Recollections*, Alger could bring to mind only a solitary moment of joy from his years at Lewisburg—a morning when, on his way to the storeroom in the spring of 1952, he saw and heard a rose-breasted grosbeak singing from the top of a tree in the prison yard: "The bird's song was lengthy and repeated more than once. A small group gathered, watching and listening silently. When the grosbeak finished, no one spoke as we went on to our workplaces. I was refreshed; my senses were sharpened as if by a great aesthetic experience. I cannot think of another time when my spirits were so lifted that I was oblivious to my grim, oppressive sur-roundings." In some ways, curiously, the aftertaste of prison was more bitter than the experience itself.

My own feeling is that Alger, once he'd left Lewisburg, didn't need to recall the personal encounters and the sights from his cell window or the other glad tidings he'd set down in his let-ters, or to revisit the reflections that had poured forth into these pages, because his Lewisburg experiences had by then already entered his bones. He was now living what he'd learned, which meant that what he had been through was in some ways less important as a memory than it was as a skill he could make use of in the days that would thereafter unfold before him. He could connect to the special qualities in all kinds of people with the same ease and naturalness that twenty years earlier he'd brought to bird-watching.

As it happens, there's a powerful description in the Lewis-burg letters (on April 7, 1953) of the way Alger's world had expanded in the 1930s when for the first time he borrowed a friend's binoculars to look up at a bird in a forest clearing. "The first sight through glasses of a resplendent wild bird *is* breath-taking," Alger wrote. "The colors are so brilliant + alive, the bird itself so self-contained +, as Mommy puts it, 'competent.' You see the bird whole, as a fellow personality—

the way his (or her) 'friends + relations' do (at least that is the way it *seems!*)"

"My valiant dears," begins a post-Christmas, post-visit letter of December 28, 1952, "No wonder Venus sparkled so brightly last evening, as you two were homeward-bound, + today is crisp + flawlessly fair—even if it weren't that way outside we would be clear + bright enough inside to make up for it—after our wonderful loving visit. The brightness inside + out led me to wash my window this morning so there would be nothing between the joy within + the sparkle without."

Writing me at summer camp, on August 11, 1951, he asked: "Do the boys at Timberlake have lots of discussions? Here we have them all the time: about unions and strikes, about religion, about how the world began, about the best baseball team, etc. Right now three fellows beside me are discussing whether the earth is getting smaller or larger. One says volcanoes pile up more mountains, so the earth is getting bigger. Another says the rains and rivers and seas are always washing away mountains and fields and beaches, so it's getting smaller. Every now and then they interrupt my writing to see if I know anything about some point. (We are all nibbling from potato chips and peanuts we jointly chipped in.) All I know about their subject is that the earth (mankind) is getting better and wiser."

In early 1954, Alger wrote me that a new classification system for the items in the storeroom had required spending five months shifting around the entire stock of more than several thousand kinds of articles; to help out, a couple of new men joined the storeroom team: "Both have vigorous senses of the ridiculous + the storeroom has had more spontaneous roaring laughter in half a year than, I suspect, in all the 20-some years this place has existed. x Good, hearty, natural laughter is, as thee can imagine, not too common in jail. Yet it is, if anything, more enjoyable here than anywhere else. So, when it comes, it takes complete possession of the laugher—like a few cocktails for those who are light drinkers. We laugh until we are weak; the pleasure + the strength of the laughter are quite out of proportion to the humor of the incident. Just because so much of the tension + frustration of imprisonment are no laughing matters, the rocking laugh takes hold until it hurts. x The next time thee thinks thee hears thunder in the west it is just one of our gales of violent laughter" (March 11, 1954).

Sometimes Alger threw a suggestion my way. "Tony, my darling," he wrote me on February 25, 1953, "I have been thinking since thy visit to Boston + Cambridge that thee might like to try reading a fine recent novel about the 1850's in B. + C. That was a time when there were clashes of opinion as violent + as confusing for many people as there are in *our 50's*. It was also a time when Justice Holmes was exactly the age you are now—for he was born in 1841, just 100 years before you were. The book is Sin of the Prophet by Truman Nelson."

This led to another tale: "Thee might also be interested to know that when the Justice was a few years younger than thee is now, *his* father was bitterly + unfairly criticized for pointing out that the doctors of 100 years + more ago were themselves (unintentionally, of course) spreading the terrible sickness known as puerperal or child-birth fever. That was before Lister + Pasteur had discovered germs are the causes of most diseases; + many of the doctors went from one patient to another without even washing their hands! And they never sterilized their instruments or cleaned their long black coats. But when Dr. H. blamed the doctors—he was one himself—many doctors + their friends (+ lots of cranky, timid, unhappy people eager to condemn most anyone) called poor kind Dr. H. all kinds of mean + ugly + hateful things. But he didn't mind too much + his son, the Justice, after he grew up was very proud that the doctor had stuck by his views. He told me so himself."

The letter ends: "Mon. morning was bright here, so—having had my sonshine on Sun.—I got my sunshine on Mon. (This gave me an excuse to repeat what thee called my pun-shine, *my* brand of monkeyshine). All my love, Alger-Daddy."

Not pretending to be something other than what you were was a theme that Alger returned to in a number of his comments to me. "Mommy told me," he wrote me at camp, in the same letter about the earth getting better and wiser, "about the meeting when your camp discussed the story of Peter on the night when he was discouraged and uncertain about his ideals." (This was the Bible story of how Jesus had told Saint Peter, who thought of himself as the most faithful of the disci-ples, that, even on the very night of Jesus' arrest, Peter would find three occasions to denounce him.) "So that three times in one night he denied and turned his back on what he really believed in. And, of course, that made him very unhappy until he decided that from then on he would always stand up for his beliefs. As you told Mommy that story shows you mustn't be discouraged from following your goal or give up your objective."

I didn't need to be told that one day I would be proud of my father—I already was. But many of Alger's attempts to yoke me to the fixed lights of his life or to the shining discoveries he made at Lewisburg passed me by in the 1950s—it never seemed significant, for instance, that Holmes and I might be linked by birthdays, and there wasn't any special kinship I could feel with the giant thunderstorms that rolled across New York every summer. Just to assert myself, and not because I had any opinions pro or con about the matter, I actively rebelled against bird-watching. On the other hand, in the same way that I began clinging to sunsets, I was also, without ever quite letting on what I was up to, even to myself, slowly reorganizing my thinking around some of the bright spots that made repeated appearances in the letters—the moon, for instance, or the evening star, or the "full bowl of the sky," as Alger called it, whenever I caught a glimpse of a piece of it down at the end of a Manhattan street.

I thought about Simon Peter, over and over. As the 1950s moved forward, it seemed to me, with my grown-up-too-fast intellect, that the pressures on people—to recant, to pretend, to forget who they really were—were enormous. With my smaller-boy-than-ever feelings, I tried desperately to invent ways to protect myself from the onslaught. My basic thought, never discussed with anybody, was that I could stay safe by escaping into places where nobody would be looking. Some things I did were things that other children in trouble had already long since thought of—I tried, for instance, to drown myself in books. That doesn't mean drowning out the world by reading stories. It means throwing yourself so far into a story that that's where you actually live, curled up in one corner of a house belonging to one of the characters.

The best part—this I remember clearly—was that you could still stay in the story even when you weren't reading. There were rules, of course; you had to leave once you finished a book, but if you stopped in the middle because you had to do something else, such as setting the table, then that's where you actually remained, on that same page, for the whole time that you appeared to be setting the table. It's sort of the reverse of an out-of-body experience, because it felt as though you had sent your body out into the world while you stayed invisibly inside, next to the bookmark. It worked with *New Yorker* cartoons, too, although it took a long time and real concentration to stare at them until the lines in a drawing began to waver and get longer, and then you could jump into the drawing and walk right through it to the room *beyond* the one the artist had actually drawn.

My problem with this kind of retreat wasn't that it didn't work. It was that I had to be careful what kind of book I holed up in. (Books were best because they took longer to read than *The New Yorker*, which I then mostly flipped through, looking for the funny bits.) My favorite books when I was ten and eleven, for instance, were the Freddy the Pig series; Freddy, bright, overweight, and a newspaper editor (the affinities were obvious enough), lived on a farm of talking animals in upstate New York and had enough adventures to fill more than two dozen books published between 1927 and 1956. The books were lovable, as Michael Cart, the Beverly Hills city librarian who also grew up with them, has written, lovingly and accurately, because they were essentially teaching stories about friendship: "Freddy's friends were often in danger; yet, even if Freddy was so frightened that his tail was completely uncurled, he gritted his teeth and did whatever was necessary to help."

But even within this imagined domain of constancy and compassion, I had to look first at the copyright date in tiny print on the back of the title page; the only ones I wanted to read again were the early ones. It wasn't that Walter R. Brooks, Freddy's author, had run out of ideas toward the end, or that the postwar books, which had Martians as characters as well as animals and people, were any less believable. It was just that the new fears that were coursing through the world outside had leaked into Freddy's—the first books, mostly from the twelve New Deal years, were carefree and easygoing; animals and people got along, or, if things went wrong, everyone pulled together to bring them back into equilibrium. In the later books, the human villains were meaner and, for the first time, unredeemable and truly frightening. There was even the suggestion that by inciting the animals to subversion and riot, the crooks might ultimately enslave the entire United States.

The immediate world of my own neighborhood was darkening, too; the postwar building boom had just reached Greenwich Village. Once again, my reactions were split into parts I couldn't fit together. I could tell, accurately enough, every time I looked out the front window or headed off to school, that here was a physical expression of the same kind of heedlessness and recklessness that was already distorting other parts of people's lives. I also immediately overpersonalized what was going on, convinced that, as soon as Alger left New York for Lewisburg, Greenwich Village had been invaded by forces that totally ignored its needs—by which I meant, of course, the pleasures that children got from living there.

This was when the family apartment became a time funnel. The old red-brick mansion that stood at the next corner behind a curving brick wall disappeared, and what had been, looking west, the bowl of the sky was replaced by an awkward, brooding, gigantic white-brick apartment house. The Village's small community of elderly French people moved away: The Brevoort, a 110-year-old French hotel with a sidewalk café, the first in New York, and the town house next to it, which had once been Mark Twain's, were torn down for another enormous apartment building, this one in beige brick, that displaced another quadrant of the sky. The Lafayette, a French hotel that was only seventy years old and had newspapers hanging on racks in its café, was replaced by an apartment complex that covered an entire block.

In addition, the specialness of 8th Street, the Village's main street, dimmed or was dispersed. The Whitney Museum of American Art, where even a kid could walk in off the street to see the year's new paintings by Edward Hopper and Andrew Wyeth, moved uptown. Wanamaker's, a vast department store, "known throughout the world, a vital institution in Greenwich Village," as its local ads used to say, closed after giving the neighborhood less than two weeks' notice, and later burned in a spectacular blaze that sent a column of flames shooting more than a hundred feet into the sky. In the 1950s thousands of urban neighborhoods across the country were being picked apart in much the same way; the damage was so widespread and so wanton that historic preservation became a national movement in the 1960s.

Try telling that to a boy's burning heart. Just recently, when I rounded a corner coming home one night and saw that first white-brick apartment house out of the corner of my eye—a middle-aged man glancing up at a middle-aged building, its hulk sagging slightly and gone grimy gray—I felt again and with every bit of my old searing fierceness the grinding dismay and fury and helplessness that had overtaken me in the summer of 1951 when it was going up and I had watched as, floor by floor, it ate up the sky. I heard again in my head the echo of a voice that long ago had wanted to say, "You wouldn't dare try that if Alger were still here!" I wondered, had Alger ever heard a whispering voice in his head—or was he always too grown up for that?—a voice that kept insisting, "You wouldn't dare try that if F.D.R. were still here!"

When I was ten—this was, after all, the era of fall-out shelters, basement corridors, and boiler rooms, where people could supposedly escape the consequences of atomic bombs exploding above their heads—I put together in my mind a list of safety zones, places where the family would have immunity from attackers. It wasn't a long list at first—Peacham, of course, and Vi's, the Buttens', our apartment, and Robert Benjamin's apartment. Maybe also Anne and Gladys's apartment.

Anne Winslow, who ran the editorial department for the Carnegie Endowment, and shared a small flat with her old friend Gladys Peacock, wasn't famous the way Vi or the Buttens were, but she seemed like someone who could stand up to anything. Anne-and-Gladys, as my mother and I called them, treating them as a unit, had us over once a month for elaborate and warmly welcoming dinners where usually the dessert would finish cooking long before the main course, but never mind, just look at them. They were so ladder straight, so lady-like, and yet so stop-at-nothing that in their twenties they had helped establish the first visiting nurse service in rural Kentucky—on horseback. In their forties, they were the only cavalry that had come riding to our rescue.

Gradually the list of safety zones grew to include Washington Square, Central Park, theaters, museums, Carnegie Hall, the planetarium (a favorite). Places where people were so busy relaxing and enjoying themselves that maybe they wouldn't have the energy left for making other people miserable. There were moments when you could almost see them go out of one mind and into another—at a theater, for example, it was when the houselights were dimming and people suddenly sat up and stopped rustling their programs. At a New York Philharmonic concert, it happened just before the lights went down, when everyone was already onstage and Harold Gomberg, the principal oboist, blew an "A"—which always made his round face get beet red—so that the other instruments could adjust their tuning to his pitch. At the planetarium, everything changed as soon as you saw the first star on the dome overhead. At which point it wasn't a ceiling anymore, but a view straight up to the edge of the universe.

By looking at people, I came up with a new idea, and drew up a second list of safety zones—only these were time-governed, protected periods that depended on a watch or a calendar rather than on where you happened to be. This was much more helpful, because I not only didn't have to be anywhere in particular to get a breather, I could rely on these time-offs during which, while they lasted, the world wasn't going to get any worse. There were, for instance, weekends and holidays—days when everyone came to their senses, didn't they?—so right away two-sevenths of every week was accounted for, plus a little bit extra on the side. Then, too, there was nighttime, so that took care of about half of the five weekdays; and meals probably gobbled up a couple of hours of each of those days, as well.

Finally, even if you couldn't count on too many of them, there might be a blizzard or a hurricane to distract people who had built their days around cooking up more trouble. Maybe, maybe one of the snowstorms would be so hushed and clean and comforting it would make them feel so much better they would go into a business that left other people alone, or even one that tried to make people happier. From time to time I added on the thought or wish or prayer: They wouldn't even have to admit that Alger was innocent, just as long as they changed and wouldn't do it again to anybody else. Other times I took that one back and thought, No, they would have to apologize to him first, to show that they had changed.

Even at the time I knew this was a real long shot and probably just silly, because I could see how good people were at dividing their lives up into box after box after box, so that it was easy for them to see something beautiful on Sunday and do something ugly on Monday and not feel the contradiction. Still, the morning after Christmas was always the bleakest awakening of the year. The only thing I could think of was one of those ideas kids have that they know the adults will never do anything about—like the notion of putting a dome over the whole of New York City so it could be air-conditioned in the summer. Only this meant putting a dome around the year, so that the Twelve Days of Christmas became the 365 Days of Christmas (366 in leap years). Of course, you can't universalize a Christian holiday, and I was ignoring the question of how to reach out to people suffering from what Alger called "complete blockage" of the soul. But that's the way kids in trouble tend to see things.

When did I emerge from this way of thinking? As soon as I grew up, I would once have said. My new answer is: Just about now. I was walking down 8th Street a week after I'd finished working through all the letters and pictures. It was a minute or so after noon, a cool, partly sunny day. On my way to Krispy Kreme to buy my son an afterschool doughnut, I looked down the length of the street, saw tall clouds overhead, and without warning the entire perspective shifted, as if a giant hourglass had been turned upside down in front of me.

The sky, so huge a moment before, shrank to half its former size, while the bottom of the view—street, sidewalk, shops, cars, vendors, and neighbors—expanded, got brighter, moved faster. Edges were sharper, outlines had been filled in, faces showed more expression, and the end of the street seemed twice as far away as it had a few steps back. I had just returned to earth from a refuge in the sky that I must have climbed into a half century ago—and had long since forgotten about. So entirely that I don't remember inventing it and didn't know that I'd never left it. Which was why, five minutes earlier, I had not been able to sense that I was about to abandon it forever.

Since becoming a grown-up I haven't run across any other people who had discovered this particular mechanism—but then the only support group that exists for talking about exactly what happened back then—AlgerAnon, it could be called—has only me and Tim in it, and during the Lewisburg years Tim was in his twenties and handling things well, putting himself through college and then medical school rather than falling back on make-believe. One of Alger's letters home, however, from July 25, 1951, does seem to refer to my mother's finding a more constructive form of the concept I thought I had invented, which he contrasted with the lot of those who were truly unfortunate. So maybe the impulse behind what I was doing was more common than I had supposed:

"It's interesting that thee used the figure of speech 'island of time' in stating thy attempts to find the chance to write. Almost the same phrase (I noted in the Times) is used as the title of an account of years in a concentration camp. But where thee used it to describe a sought-for period of quiet, the novelist meant to convey a static, lost period—lost from the stream of life. Since the phrase caught my eye a few days ago I had been aware of how vividly the novelist's phrase synthesized the attitude of the overwhelming proportion of sentient inmates here (+ presumably in all our other prisons). I have never ceased myself to consider my stay here a part of (rather than apart from) the fullness of human experience. But the sense of frustration so predominant an element in the emotional atmosphere makes me capable of understanding the negative island *in* time (the novelist's variant) concept as clearly as I understand Tony's point of view when he sends love to everyone here."

IN THOSE days, even though I felt as though moving from one day to another was like scrambling from one iceberg to the next, I was also trying to be worthy of what Alger was showing me of himself in his letters. Which meant that I was extravagantly modeling myself, as I thought, on what he was doing. A couple of weeks before he wrote his "island of time" letter, I'd written him a letter from camp (signing it, as usual, "MUCH LOVE, Tony") which he described at some length to Prossy in Peacham on July 11: "The 'MUCH LOVE' was in 5 colors and, most typically Tonyesque, at the top he had added: 'P.S. Love to everybody there.' I shall try, after my fashion."

Since it was my goal to be more useful to Alger and more like Alger, I was elated whenever an occasional, casual comment in a letter seemed to make it possible to *be* Alger, or at least a presence of Alger in New York. As, for instance (on February 20, 1952): "x-x-x Will thee please try to see the Picasso show at the Mod. Mus. + be my eyes for me? I gathered from the notes accompanying the 'zoo' [of fanciful Picasso animals] that the showing is limited to prints. I hope not. But anyway I should especially like thee to compare it with the Matisse show for me." Or some months later (on June 29): "It is now 8.30 p.m. + the entire west is a copper bowl, burnished + gleaming. We have had a refreshing + relaxing evening stretched on the still parched grass. Thee + Tony must be making last minute preparations for the exciting + grown-up journey [on a train, without Prossy, to Camp Killooleet, also in Vermont, but a camp I'd chosen myself, unlike the one I'd been to the first summer Alger was away]. Please be my eyes + tell me of the scene in the station."

I volunteered for every one of these "be my eyes" or (as Alger sometimes put it) "be my eyes + ears" assignments, even when the letter indicated that they were directed to Prossy. As I did so, another piece of my adult life clicked into place. I already wanted to be a reporter—now Alger was showing me how to be a good one. As Alger's eyes and ears I had a roving commission that might take me anywhere, entrusted with a purpose that overrode my fears about what people might be up to. Alger needed information that couldn't find its way to him unless I went out and got it—I liked to think that, anyway.

While on the job for Alger, I had to use my whole mind for this kind of work. I needed to see and hear (and smell and taste) at least as many things as Alger would have if he'd been walking around the Picasso show or watching trainloads of kids dragging duffel bags bigger than they were through Grand Central Terminal; otherwise I wasn't being *his* eyes and ears, only mine. I had been handed the secret I sought—as Alger's extension, I could, like the other reporters, walk between the raindrops, talk to anyone, even say anything without being destroyed.

As a boy, I completely skipped over Alger's grave reservations about reporters, as he said, for instance, on September

25, 1952, "In a recent letter I mentioned the apartness from life of the reporter. It is not an accident that journalism has had such an influential part in modern life. As it has been developed in the past 3 or 4 generations it has epitomized the loneliness and separation from group solidarity that modern urban life has meant for the white collar class. Not only the reporter but his readers have been onlookers not participants."

On the other hand, I listened intently to his frequent comments on specific papers or magazines—such as his July 19, 1953, cheer: "x-x Bless the N.Y.er for its gay current cover of 'our' [Washington] Square alive in the crowded summer night, with the group chess games rightly taking pride of place. I shall save it."

I used to say that the one career decision I made in college was not to go to law school, as my father had. But down where the deeper choices get made there was certainly just one trade I had fitted myself for. About the only thing I studied closely in college was the extracurricular work I did for *The Harvard Crimson*, the student newspaper that came out six days a week. After graduation, I looked around only for journalism jobs, and that summer was lucky enough to find my way to *The New Yorker*—which, in addition to being a dream job for any young writer, brought together so many of the things I needed and craved: It was the place whose cartoons I had wandered through. As home base for Alger's good friend Joe Liebling, it was almost like joining a family business.

And now I could be the eyes and ears for William Shawn, *The New Yorker*'s famous reclusive editor, who hungered for information but rarely left his cell-like office. Yet I could also, by writing anonymously for decades in the magazine's "Talk of the Town" department, uphold my vow of silence. It was wonderful work—Alger's analysis of journalism's apartness had failed to notice how much group solidarity there was *among* reporters. Anyway, detachment was a useful way of handling the otherwise un-handle-able; at one point I even wrote a brash, youthful book about Alger, *Laughing Last*, because as a journalist I could ask him questions about his career and his case that as his son I thought I had to stay away from. Even later, after I had found a voice of my own, I was still feeling the tug from Lewisburg days. I was writing about neighborhoods and landscapes that badly needed help and could be helped, and how people changed dramatically inside as the places around them changed, even if they didn't always realize it.

It was from the asides in Alger's Lewisburg letters—sometimes introduced as "Nature Notes" or "Window Watching"—that I got the idea that places needed to be listened to every bit as carefully as people did: "Rewarding observation," as Alger said in defining this habit of the mind (on August 3, 1952), "is not the result of a rare 'something worth looking at,' but of one who is 'capable of seeing' the constant + ubiquitous marvels of life." Which meant that any landscape that was your constant companion could itself over time, if you befriended it, become another unheralded teacher. Alger's silent, daily conversations with the Lewisburg landscape had to be conducted in snatches—a moment at his window on waking, another at lunch, a glance out the storeroom window during an afternoon break, whatever outdoor time he was allowed in the prison yard, and perhaps a glimpse of moonlight after lights out. So his comments about this part of "learning + growing" are necessarily scattered throughout the letters home.

"It's strange to have country quiet of a summer night without the whirr of insect voices—a few Katydids reach the 'moat' between wall + building but so few that they sound artificial, like the rain effects in radio. But our seasons are sharply marked, as I have written before, by other signs" (October 13, 1951). "In this land of rolling fields + second-growth woods autumn seems to be a time of relaxation—spring everywhere has the energy of growth + here the summer is hot + brassy. The autumn is long + leisurely and full of ripe fruition, with none of the New England sense of summer's death + of urgency to batten down the hatches of life against the near approach of killing arctic winter" (October 30, 1951).

"Yesterday + today have been brisk + cold (in the low 20's)—yesterday's sunset was long + stunning, ending with numerous large purple clouds dominating the south + west, again drawing from my Italian yard-companion the awed comment: 'mysterious' (which means, of course, the 'mystery' of creation, not 'strange' or 'sinister')" (November 20, 1951). "Last week when we had day after day of heavy rain I began to worry about the middle-school rabbit (he is just about middle-school age, as rabbits grow, that is)." (I was now a middle schooler at Dalton.) "I wondered where in the leafless dripping world he could find shelter. And then Thurs. night at 10.00, in a steady drizzle, there he sat outside my window quite unconcerned by the wet. He didn't so much as sneeze—or even sniffle— + I had been fearful he would get pneumonia! I finished the apple I was eating + tossed him the core, leaving a good round core, too" (November 25, 1952).

Sometimes Alger's attention was drawn upward as well as outward: "Dear March came in quite spectacularly, with a baby (10 min.) blizzard, this morning. Soon after, the skies began to clear + we had a brilliant dazzling hour in cold sunlight (handball + walking) in the yard this afternoon. x Yesterday + today there was tremendous excitement among the members of the 'Astronomers Club.' The Harv. Observ. mag. had told us that Venus is now (1) so near, (2) so bright (nearly half moon in appearance—thru a telescope) + (3) so situated vis a vis the sun (setting about 3½ hours after the sun), that it can be seen in *BROAD DAYLIGHT*. That is something I had *never done before*, so I was one of the most excited members. Incidentally, our excitement was contagious + everybody else suddenly became members of the 'club.' The first sighting was yesterday just after 4 p.m.—when, of course, the sun was still shining brightly. At that time Venus just cleared the upper line of vision made by our windows' tops if we squatted below the sills, i.e., it was high in the sky—just w. + s. of the 'center' of the sky. A tiny, tiny white spot in the cloudless blue. We were all very proud of ourselves + watched as it 'swung' slowly west + got more + more distinct. Today we tried + tried to see it from the yard, but the glare of the sun was too great. Not until we were back in our cells + the 4.00 o'clock position was resumed could we repeat the experience" (March 1, 1953).

"Right now I want to share my afternoon Window Watching (+ Listening). This is a special Spring pleasure here. It can occur any time of the day or night but most regularly it is a 4.30 p.m. event. Then there is most doing. Take yesterday, for example. Even though the skies were close + a light Spring rain was falling the birds were as busily cheerful as could be. As this is also the time when I read my mail I have to do a good deal of looking up + down—down at the page, then up + out the window. The listening, of course, is continuously out through the open window. Robins, grackles, doves, red-wingers, song sparrows are busy singing as they eat supper + fly about in before-bedtime games. Yesterday I *thought* I heard a brief 'purity'—the bluebird's call" (March 19, 1953).

"There is still twist enough to share . . . today's positive ecstasy of the redwingers over the damp meadows—I have never heard such a chorus of Ker-ees as when I started to write this letter. The paper must have absorbed some of it. Perhaps if thee + T sit very still you can hear a faint repetition or continuation—it certainly still rings in my room" (April 16, 1953).

Occasionally, there was a reaching back into memories of Washington and New York: "The feel of a great city under a sea of heavy heat is unique. The air becomes as tangible as in a great wind; all are burdened, apathetic + ill as if the city were plague-bound or under siege. Motion + noise are lessened + the people really show in expression + carriage the 'quiet desperation' so many of them normally experience without realizing it. As in the stillness after a great fall of snow there is an air of unreality, of a cleverly compelling fantasy that gives the familiar strange, new appearances. Tony now knows what it is like + can imagine the discomfort of the great bulk of the overcrowded, amenity-less poor who endured the whole exhausting spell from beginning to end. . . . x-x Our heat wave ended yesterday. . . . By supper last night even the dining-hall had cooled off + this afternoon we have actually had 'jackety' weather (that is a word of Justice Holmes')" (September 6, 1953).

"The rising moon has been a fair sight but most memorable has been its setting at sunrise. Yesterday in the pale blue of the western sky as we got up just before sun-up the color was quick-silver, with the sheen of a fish's belly flashing under water + the craters like global maps" (September 24, 1953). "I hope that on Sat. thee + T . . . will have a real central Penn. autumn early evening sky. It is distinctive. . . . The Eastern Shore in summer is distinguished by an enormous orange-red setting sun that hangs for long minutes over the flat fields + tidal creeks. On any clear evening that swollen fiery disc is *the* distinctive feature that dominates all other concomitants of the day's end. Here in autumn the 'standard' clear-sky evening feature is a long-lasting radiance that arches widely till it merges with a powder-blue after-sunset sky. The luminosity is extraordinary + seems to have the pulsating quality, almost, of Northern lights. At the rim of the sky the intense light is seemingly colorless, higher in the arc it dims to amber which further aloft has a rosy tinge. I hope thy little group has a clear + 'typical' sky to light it homeward" (October 15, 1953).

. . .

JUST AS Pinocchio finally became a real boy, so did the Sugar Lump Boy. At least that was how I explained the extraordinary series of real-life stories Alger started sending home in October 1951, just when I had begun to wander away into fantasy worlds.

Almost a fifth of Alger's Lewisburg letters—87 out of 445— celebrate the determination, the joy of life, and the growing list of accomplishments of a man Alger saw every day: the "B.R.," as Alger's letters called him, both to save space and to disguise the identity of a fellow inmate. The nickname was later amended to the "B.R./M.R." and finally, as a graduation present, to the "M.R."; the initials stood for "Beginning Reader," "Beginning Reader/Middle Reader," and "Middle Reader," although we never knew the man's real name. We did find out, however, in the elongated, roundabout way of the Lewisburg years, just what the B.R. looked like.

Tim, on his way to Switzerland to begin medical school, sent Alger a color postcard of a portrait he'd liked during an unscheduled visit to the Louvre. ("Dear Alger, The ink for this card and the fact that I had shaving soap for this morning represent at least partial success with French. Yesterday was spent sightseeing Paris and this morning I had planned to see it all at once from le Tour Eiffel armed with a map but unfortunately it was gray and threatening rain so I spent the time at the Louvre instead.") Alger then wrote us (on June 14, 1953) that he'd just received a portrait of the B.R.: "x-x-x EXTRA! EXTRA! Moby's 1st card from Paris has just come! . . . Thurs. (?) he spent at the Louvre where he got the card (Antonello's Condottiere, a 15th century Sicilian who looks like a combination of the cabinet-maker [a Sicilian-born inmate who passed the time by making exquisite miniature furniture] + the B.R."

The card surfaced again in Alger's next letter (on June 16), because he had by then shown it to the "t.o.," the "tall one," Alger's nickname for his closest friend at Lewisburg, a man whom in *Recollections* he identified as the "leader of the Italian-American contingent and thus one of the two or three most important men in the prison population." The t.o. admired Alger tremendously. Like Justice Holmes, he was one of the people that Alger had in the letters told me I was linked to— "your twin," Alger called him, because we were both born on August 5.

I met the t.o. only once; Alger arranged it in the 1970s, when I was writing *Laughing Last*. Gravely polite, he made a point of telling me that Alger was not the kind of man who if he believed something would pretend he didn't. He knew this, he said, because he'd had to learn quite prematurely how to size people up in an instant; meaning, he explained, that when he was twenty-one he'd been given the job of running the numbers in three different Pennsylvania cities. That was in 1932, the worst year of the Depression, and he was making $1,000 a week.

The t.o. was a recurring figure in many of the B.R. stories, and Tim's postcard became his introduction to art appreciation: "x-x-x The t.o. has come to like the Antonello portrait that Moby sent me. He says that the more often he looks at it the more he sees in it +, very soundly, that 'It's so alive.' Because of his interest in it I showed him some of the 'Gallery.' I began with the Dutch—Vermeer, de Hooch— + Manet (ballet dancers + the little Zouave fifer). Then the charming 15th century French paintings of the duc de Berry's monthly activities—remember them? . . . thee sent me, last Feb. (i.e. 1952), the Fevrier scene of courtyard, fields + distant village covered with snow + thee circled the number 10 in the curved calendar because that was the day thee really learned to ride thy bike ('To START, STOP and RIDE without ANY HELP!!!!!'). Next, 2 Picassos, the poster-like child with a dove + the blue

Portrait of a fifteenth-century condottiere, a leader of mercenary soldiers, by Antonello da Messina; Alger thought it resembled his friend the Beginning Reader.

boy that Mommy + I like so much. . . . x He liked least the Picassos, because, as he put it, 'when pictures are distorted, how can you tell if they are good?' He meant that poor drawing is also distorted (but, of course, not on purpose + with no 'message')."

I didn't get to see Tim's card for another year and a half, until after Alger and all his Lewisburg mail had come home. Now, having finally looked at it with the kind of attention the t.o. gave it in 1953, I think I see what Alger saw in the B.R. A large part of Alger's "growing + learning" had to do with becoming quiet enough inside to look beneath the surface of anything. How right the t.o. was about the need for second thoughts when looking at this deceptively simple picture of a young soldier:

It shows a young man—brown-haired, slightly heavyset, with a squarish face, a strong jaw, and a bit of a five-o'clock shadow—who's seen against a darkened wall. At first, his face seems entirely still, as flat and somber as the background. It takes a moment to notice that he's looking straight at you. It's only when his eyes catch yours that you can see the unadvertised alertness that all along has been surging through this face. Then you get the disconcerting feeling that he began studying *your* face before you were even aware of his. As you look into his eyes, but not until then, you can see that his mouth, which had seemed so set and grim, is in fact pulled slightly upward at one corner into a hint or a ghost of a knowing grin.

I still don't know the B.R.'s name. I never asked Alger, which I think is exactly what he wanted; at any rate, in *Recollections*, which was published thirty-four years after Alger had left Lewisburg, he was still carefully protecting the B.R.'s identity, referring to him only as "Leo M."

The B.R. was a young prizefighter—quite a good one—who was himself a racket guy; he had grown up on the Lower East Side of Manhattan. One day when he was a boy and home cutting school, he saw a New York City truant officer slap his grandmother, who couldn't answer his questions because she spoke only Italian. The B.R. never went to school again. It was at Lewisburg, he told Alger, that he realized he had grown into a man who could only "talk with my fists." The reading materials in the prison's education department were incomprehensible to him. So he asked Alger, who was already writing down for him the letters he sent home, to teach him to read and write. They spent, off and on, the next two and a half years working together; at the beginning their sessions lasted two hours a day.

Early on, the Beginning Reader and the Sugar Lump Boy began to blur in my mind because I was being introduced to someone who although he was all grown up—exactly Tim's age, Alger wrote—couldn't do something I'd been good at for four years, and who sometimes felt so helpless and baffled and alone and stuck that, like the S.L.B., he needed a whole lot of encouragement just to get started. So here was a situation where Alger was actually being *me*! In one wonderful letter (of October 16, 1951), which ended with a new story called "The Sugar Lump Boy Teaches the Snow Man to Read," we all traded places:

"After the S.L.B. had been taught to read by Tony he was so excited that right away he decided the Snow Man ought to learn, too. The S.M. was very eager to learn but he didn't believe the S.L.B. had learned enough himself to teach others. But the S.L.B. was VERY insistent and asked Tony to write a little beginner's reader that would just suit the S.M. *So* Tony went to work + chose words like snow, boy, man, shovel, cold + drew pictures 🐧 🔨 that fitted the text. He had to write very small, of course." (Written in tiny letters.) "It was quite a hard job but when he had finished it the S.L.B. and the S.M. were 𝒟+ 💡+𝓁 (that's supposed to be a *light* bulb!). The S.L.B. then went over the words V...E...R...Y S...L...O...W...L...Y with the S.M.—first, of course, teaching him the alphabet with some alphabet blocks borrowed from Susie. 🎲 " (Roger and Susie Levin, my oldest friends, were kids who lived on the floor below; we spent so much time together that for years all three of us seemed to live in both apartments.) "And the S.M. got more + more interested + pleased. Soon he was able to read the whole book straight through—so fast that he was out of breath when he finished. And the S.L.B. was so PROUD he nearly burst. THE END of the story + of this letter."

A B.R. sampler:

"Tony, dear, one of the young New Yorkers in my dorm never learned to read or write. He is very sensibly using some of his spare time to do so now. A couple of weeks ago he asked me what was the best way of learning, in addition to the classes he goes to. I told him how good the new readers are + he got his wife to inquire at the school in their neighborhood. A few days ago he got 3 . . . and he is going through them so fast! Of course, he really had already learned a lot of words without knowing it—from signs, headlines, etc.—so that it's easier than he thought it would be. I hope he'll let me help whenever he gets stuck" (October 6, 1951).

"Today has been sunny + milder with another dashing sunrise + a glowing sunset. The new reader [not yet the B.R.] called the former to my attention as soon as he opened his eyes; and he + I + the amateur of misterioso clouds sat on the latter's bed before supper watching the blazing western sky, each of us *sure* that 'those in N.Y.' were watching the same band of rosy fire" (November 29, 1951).

"Now it's 4.00 o'clock Sun. afternoon—the [Mozart] Requiem [over the radio] was somewhat interrupted near the close, but not shattered, by a modest birthday 'gathering' in my cell for the non-reader. He got permission to come to our quarters [Alger had moved into semiprivate "honors" quarters in the "J Wing" in December; the B.R. followed five months later] + he + my Italian friend [not yet called the t.o.] constituted the 'gathering.' His studying has been zero for the past four months, but only yesterday he told me: 'I *must* learn to read. This way I am blind.' Since I moved to different quarters I have had no chance to help him + he went through a period of negativism toward the subject at the same time. Now that his interest has returned + we can soon be outdoors more, I may be able to nudge him along a bit" (March 15, 1952).

"x-x-x Tony, dear, each day I now help the Beginning Reader with his letters from home. He is improving fast + is very proud of his achievement. Today he received from his wife 3 readers + workbooks (just like the ones you used 1½ yrs. ago) to go with 2 of them. So I think that the slump that began about the time I moved out of the dormitory has come to an end + he should have another period of progress" (May 5, 1952).

"I still can't find nearly enough time for reading. The noon hour, regularly, + the pre-supper + pre-yard time, often, are now pretty largely monopolised by reading lessons. We do 2 new pages at noon + the B.R. (who works at night) reviews those pages during the afternoon while I am in the store-room. . . . x Really, the enthusiasm + perseverance is wonderful. The work, as Tony will remember very well, is hard + discouraging. The present zest can't last indefinitely at this level of intensity, so it's good to achieve as substantial an accomplishment as possible in this burst of earnestness. Then we will have that much higher a plateau to serve as the taking off point in our next assault on the peaks of reading skill" (May 10, 1952).

"Tonight those of us who are friends of the B.R. watched his [baseball] team play another inmate team + win easily. He is a Beginning Ballplayer as well as a B.R. + he was quite nervous at first. But he is improving + didn't get upset when he made several errors. The game was played with a lot of good humor + all of us laughed + laughed—a good thing to do almost any time, but especially in jail" (June 1, 1952).

"x-x-x A bat came into the building through some open window + is now sleeping peacefully, hanging head down as bats like to sleep, high up on a wall of the main corridor. I have just showed him to the B.R. + tried to convince the B.R. that the bat wouldn't get into his hair. x When I was your age, + younger, Donie + I + our Cousins Bill + Jack Wrightson used to carry old hats out on [Alger's Aunt] Tege's front lawn in the summer dusk + chant patiently: 'Bat, bat come under my hat,' as the little fellows swooped about in the warm Eastern shore air. But none ever did" (June 17, 1952).

"Yesterday + tonight the B.R. wrote the last 4 or 5 lines of his letters to his wife. This was a real accomplishment. It was his own idea + I was amazed at how firm + clear his handwriting is. His wife will be very pleased + proud—this will be the first time she has ever seen his handwriting" (June 26, 1952).

"The B.R. + I share a fondness for sunsets, incidentally. If one of us is preoccupied the other points out a particularly spectacular one. After supper in the yard this evening while I was in the midst of a close handball game, the B.R. who was on a nearby bench, interrupted me + pointed to the west. . . . One of the men playing with me looked in the direction in which the B.R. was pointing + said: 'That's just the sun. Didn't you know it always sets over there, that's the west.' But the B.R. was right—the colors were intense + glorious. It *was* worth seeing. The colors were so strong that 20 minutes later when we had come in + had found the evening star from my window, the sky about the planet was still salmon-tinted" (September 29, 1952).

"This morning the B.R. came in as I was dressing about 7.00 to get me to cross to his side (the east) of the corridor to see a fiery sunrise. I heard him tell someone at breakfast that he didn't use to pay attention to sunrise + sunset but that it is a good thing to do, 'it helps you understand the way of nature, going on all the time' " (November 25, 1952).

"My tall friend + I are using the current clear nights for much star-study. As luck would have it he started Sun. to read the Rey book. (He always has Mon. off so yesterday he went on with Rey.)"

One of the books that meant most to Alger at Lewisburg was H. A. Rey's *The Stars*. Rey was the author of the famous *Curious George* children's books, and the dust jacket of *The Stars*—I still have Alger's Lewisburg copy—lists several curious facts about his life (he sold bathtubs up the Amazon River, and had escaped from the Nazis on a bicycle). Just as wondrous was the fact that his work had made a nightly Alger-led constellation out of Alger, the t.o., the B.R., Prossy, and me (we had our own copy of *The Stars* so we could make observations from our back windows).

Rey had redrawn the constellations. He didn't move the stars around, but the lines he used in his drawings to show how they were connected made the sky figures look real, something astronomers had never bothered to do. Gemini, for instance, as drawn by Rey, looked like twins, instead of like a broken umbrella. Alger's copy (it's now in my son's room) still has its Lewisburg stickers on the front endpapers—"THIS AUTHORIZATION IS ISSUED ON THE GROUNDS THAT THE SUBJECT IS ENGAGED IN THE STUDY OF Nature Studies." "IF THIS LABEL IS ALTERED OR REMOVED THIS ITEM WILL BE CONSIDERED CONTRABAND."

"And last night about 9.00 the B.R., who had seen us going over the charts, burst in to tell us to 'come see the *wonderful* stars' from his window. You guessed it. There was Orion, faithfully followed by his big dog, spread out brilliantly in the east on the first clear night we've had in weeks" (December 16, 1952).

"x-x-x Tony, darling, the B.R.'s progress in his studies—he can now spell + write over 350 words—has led to a new interest in words + in spelling by some of my other friends. They will 'casually' slip into a conversation some $5.00 word like 'fastidious' + wait expectantly for a rise from someone. The Barber [who indeed was a barber; in later years Alger and I used to visit the barbershop he worked for in the basement of Rockefeller Center], very sensibly, has started a vocabulary list— words he comes across in reading that are unfamiliar. We have impromptu spelling bees—at the table, in the middle of a general conversation, in the yard. (Unfortunately the bees are usually occasioned by some one person having looked up a stumper which he hopes will lay everyone low. The Barber's favorite stumpers are 'phlegm' + 'vacuum.') x-x Do you remember that for a couple of weeks you had some kind of block about writing themes for school? Some of my friends here are *always* blocked by writing. It makes them very self-conscious + their good, quick brains just freeze. Whenever the Barber has to write a letter of any importance he is miserable, for days. He called for help the last time, saying he was worn out: 'My back is killing me,' he said, as he sat all tightly hunched over his paper on which he had written only a few lines in over an hour. x The t.o. and I asked quietly what he wanted to say. He gulped, sighed + quite naturally + sensibly told. We then said 'That's fine, go ahead + write it just that way.' He looked at us in great surprise, saw we meant it, relaxed + finished in 10 minutes" (December 30, 1952).

(When I was in my thirties, a novelist friend of mine and I started a writers' workshop that based itself on the principle Alger and the t.o. had discovered. Our motto was: "If you can talk, you can write." People gulped, sighed—and wrote.)

"The B.R. is now getting interested in long words. 'Possibilities' is the latest + he gets me to have the tall one challenge him to spell it—then very proudly spells it correctly" (January 20, 1953).

"Tony, luv, the B.R. was pleased to hear that thee was impressed with his mastery of 'possibilities,' but a little disappointed that I hadn't also mentioned 'audacity,' which he quite rightly regards as still trickier even though p. is 'so full of i's.' Last night he was justifiably proud of having written for the first time a letter to his wife entirely without help until it was finished—then he got me to read it over for mistakes. He said he had a kind of feeling he had never had before + that the words came to him as if he had always known them" (January 25, 1953).

"The B.R. has an active + eager mind. He bubbles with questions. Many of them are new to him—suggested by his steady progress in reading + writing + diction, e.g., Was there a time when people couldn't talk? How did people first learn to write? Did some very bright man figure it all out + teach it to others? x Some come from the t.o.'s having become engrossed in Nehru's Glimpses of World History—Where did the Pilgrims come from? Was Napoleon a greater general than Alexander the Great? Others, I think, he has carried around with him for a long time but was shy about asking lest he appear ignorant—What is a cocktail made of? What is a high-ball? (He has been in many bars but likes only cokes + ginger ale + orange juice.) Is the White House inside the Capitol? Does a new President have to buy all new furniture for the W.H.? What's the name of that star—and that? Why do they twinkle? Why isn't the moon always round + bright? How did the world begin?" (January 27, 1953).

A day of two entries: "I am taking time-out from our eclipse [of the moon] watching. . . . The view from the B.R.'s room is perfect. All day there were clouds + it seemed that the weather would be unkind. But at sundown the clouds began to break up + now it is black + clear. The t.o., the B.R. + I have been quite excited ('maniacs,' the B.R. calls us) + a string of our friends has come in + out of the B.R.'s cell to view the show. I do hope it is just as clear in N.Y. + that thee + Mommy are also watching—if you are on the roof *I hope it is warmer* than here. x I hadn't realized that during the period of totality the moon would be quite fully visible, dully orange like the sun [in Peacham] on the day of the great Canadian forest fires."

And: "Today the B.R. got a grand Am. history book from the Education Department. It is called 'Heroes, Heroines + Holidays.' The B.R. is delighted with it. He read over several pages with me right after supper, before we turned into astronomers. Since then he hasn't been able to leave it alone—he finds it so amazing that he has gone forward so fast that he can now read something he is himself interested in for what it tells him, not just to practise reading. A few minutes ago he looked in on me with his face shining + said, 'That book's like a toy' " (January 29, 1953).

"The B.R. is certainly going ahead in his studies with a rush. . . . He has learned so much about writing that he won't let me speak any more of 'a line' to show that a word is continued from one line to the next. 'You mean a hyphen?,' he says severely" (February 3, 1953).

"The lengthening evenings have staged a stunning sky: at 6.15 the crescent + Venus were silver-white in a light blue sky still luminous at the horizon from the sun's afterglow. Moon + star stood out so sharply, with no other stars as yet for distraction, that I could see clearly why the B.R. calls a semicolon (which he has met but recently) 'the little moon + star' " (February 18, 1953).

"The B.R. has just surpassed himself in writing, unaided, a letter to his brother. He is— + rightly—especially pleased with the absolute straightness of the margin. Recently I showed him the sample pages of Harold Laski's + the Justice's letters that are reproduced in Mark Howe's new book. He was shocked at Laski's slanting left-hand margin. Tonight as he showed me his letter he said 'It's even straighter than the Judge's!' Later he said he was so proud of the letter he almost hated to mail it + he *hoped* his brother would show it to his (the B.R.'s) wife" (March 12, 1953).

"The *BIG* Easter news here is that one of my friends (the young ex-consul [whom Alger had enlisted as a *second* teacher for the B.R.]) discovered an Easter Rabbit's nest. Really. In a remote corner of the yard. No bigger than a large robin nest + in it *not* Easter eggs but 3 tiny, soft, gentle baby rabbits. The round nest (scooped out of the ground, flat bottomed + about 2 in. deep) seemed as full of silky brown fur as a bread pan is of rising dough. They were neatly 'packed,' alternately head to tail. Mama, of course, fearful of Man, was nowhere in sight. How good they were!, never moving—but staring hard—as we lifted off the dry grass cover to see them. Practically no one could resist touching the soft fur with one finger, but still good little Peter + (goodness, I've forgot the names of Peter's brothers + sisters: please supply 2 names) _____ + _____ didn't move; though Mama was away all afternoon they did just as they had been told. They were only about a week old; eyes open but ears still quite small (good thing, too, or they would have stuck out of the nest!). Not as big as hamsters" (March 29, 1953).

"Last evening the ex-F.S.O. [or ex–Foreign Service Officer, the B.R.'s second teacher] was translating the four lines of Li Po that tell of the absent one who finds moonlight gleaming on his bed, compares it to frost on the ground + is moved to think of home. We were comparing a literal translation with Witter Bynner's version that appears in Lin Yutang's collection of Indian + Chinese texts when the B.R. burst in + earnestly called us from a moon of 12 centuries ago to see from his window last night's rising full moon. It was dimmed by light clouds + crossed by thin streamers of dark ones and fully lived up to the B.R.'s enthusiasm. The misty glow + the distortion caused by the clouds had made him uncertain of what he was seeing but he wanted to share the beauty anyway" (April 30, 1953).

"A pleasant Thurs. evening, this: now 7.15, I have just had a shower after 2 fast games of handball (in which the B.R. was my partner) + I'm starting in on a 'chat' with thee + Mommy (while keeping my ears cocked for unusual bird calls outside my open window). The B.R. has devised our standard warm weather evening drink. Recipe: melted orange life savers (about ¼ of a pkge. per cup of water) plus—at my request—the juice of ⅓ of a fresh orange. . . . We all agree that the B.R.'s product is superior to Nedic's!" (May 14, 1953).

"The B.R., like Uncle Donie, has a keen (+ merry) eye for noting resemblances between people + animals. Like Donie, he confides his observations only to a few close friends so that no feelings can be hurt. It is amazing how close his names (Moose, Hen, Crow, Pig) fit. Today he said with a grin: 'I wonder what we look like to them?' " (May 17, 1953).

"I am trying to help him get the feel of syllables. So far he learns words—even long ones—as units, without relating them or their parts to other words he already knows. So I have given him lists of all the words I can think of that begin with 'pre,' that end with 'sion' or 'tion,' + so on. He is really much further along than he realizes + I think the new emphasis . . . on the way words are built by syllables, as a house is built with bricks, will show pretty quick results. . . . When he said to me a few days ago, 'What does this spell: e-x-a-c-t-l-y?', I shuddered at the labor of learning arbitrary collections of letters by rote. Poor boy. It's as if you + I memorized the order of qxslrtoof + a dozen more typesetter's accidents! Think how hard it would be" (May 28, 1953).

"I was, *not without good reason*, apparently beaming all afternoon as a result of our jolly + close visit of this morning, for several people commented on my notably happy appearance. (Do not assume from this that I am usually morose. *Au contraire.* Several weeks ago the B.R. asked me one day if I had had bad news + when I assured him I had not, he said: 'I noticed you didn't smile at breakfast and when *you* don't smile something *must* be wrong')" (June 24, 1953).

"Dearest Tonesy, I delayed my weekly letter [to Camp Killooleet] from last night so that I could have a 'chat' with thee on thy BIRTHDAY. This let me celebrate the day twice: (1) last week when I wrote thee a letter that was to arrive by today + (2) again on the day itself. Also the delay will let me tell thee about the birthday 'party' for thy 'twin,' the t.o., which the B.R. + I are planning as a surprise for later this evening. . . . x-x-x *LATER:* The 'party' was a complete surprise + a very considerable success. While I kept the t.o. occupied in the yard, the B.R. + 3 or 4 others decorated the t.o.'s cell. His bed was moved out + 2 card tables placed in the center of the room were covered with paper. Streamers of colored paper from the diagonally opposite corners crossed above our heads. The long center table was piled with cookies + oranges + candy. Each 'guest' was standing at his place in the darkened room when the t.o. returned + casually snapped on his light. It was really a very well organized affair. There were 10 guests, 11 all told present in the small room. The t.o. said he hadn't had 'such a party since I was 6.' x And the cleaning up, before lights out, was just as cooperative + speedy. Most of the men were surprised that they had enjoyed so much the collective preparation. x-x-x Cool here all week; must be *BRISK* at camp. Stars + constellations + worlds of love. Daddy" (August 5, 1953).

"x-x Tony, the B.R. has at last come up with an animal likeness for me—a giraffe" (September 1, 1953).

"x The B.R. now thinks that a kangaroo is better for me than a giraffe. I think so, too, doesn't thee?" (September 3, 1953).

"The B.R. is back to his books, like any good scholar after a vacation. He is reading Robinson Crusoe in what I judge to be about a 5th grade vocabulary. It goes all the faster for the holiday during which his quick brain—on the basis of his regular letters to + from home plus occasional scanning of newspapers + magazines—has without his knowing it added to the foundation of reading skill that he so faithfully built last winter + spring" (September 15, 1953).

"The early part of the evening has been spent rewardingly in reading with the B.R. a fine new book of his—The Mountain Book by John Y. Beaty (Beckley-Cardy Co. of Chicago), much sound geologic information interestingly presented + illustrated. Under this stimulus, progress is so marked that he must hereafter be known as the Middle Reader!" (November 15, 1953).

"What a jolly Thanksgiving evening thee + Mommy are

having. I think Vi would be just about my first choice for a Thanksgiving guest! My day has been very pleasant, too (+ like thee, but unlike Mommy, I have tomorrow as an additional holiday). We had cheerful early services: the choir much improved over recent levels in morale + volume (we have a new director. Believe it or not, the chaplain asked *me* to direct: we were as hard up as that! But I reminded him of one of our former members, a good baritone. . . .)"

"x Our mid-day dinner was really good—fresh (!) fruit cocktail, *plenty* of turkey, smoothly whipped potatoes with giblet gravy, fresh celery, peas + quite tolerable pumpkin pie. I don't recall such an ample + well prepared meal since I came here. Oh! I forgot—we also had a slab of cranberry jelly + rolls + oleo. For once I could have eaten no more of any delicacy that I could have imagined. Next Mon's weighing in ceremony should show a record gain! x But the real holiday event (apart from this 'chat' with thee + Mommy) was the terrific achievement of the M.R. (after today there is no further doubt about his having left the Beginning class). He read *25 pp.* of The Mountain Book which is listed as 5–6 Grade but in maturity of subject + in much of its vocabulary (crevasse, terminal + lateral moraines, strata) is up to 7th Grade standards. He is planning at least an equal advance each of the remaining 3 days of our holiday weekend. His enthusiasm, progress (actually from day to day), + his pleasure in accomplishment + in scientific information are pretty to see" (November 26, 1953).

"We got outdoors again this afternoon—a bright cool yard it was. The *M*.R. made good on his ambitious schedule for constantly higher reading achievements: Fri. 26 pp., Sat. 32 + today 44. Indeed we have only about 30 pp. more to the mountain book. Fortunately it is continuously interesting—yesterday we learned, among other things, that when the rate of flow (speed) of a river is doubled it can move rocks 64 times bigger (in bulk) than before! Today we read of mountain flowers, birds + animals. Our mountain is an 8,000 ft. peak in the Rockies so that the species are all western—e.g. marmots instead of woodchucks, black-throated humming birds (whose amazing powers of flight astounded the M.R.), ground squirrels instead of chippies. The M.R. is as exhausted as after one of his 10 round bouts in his boxing days! It has been some grind for him" (November 29, 1953).

"　And now it is bright, cold + fair on Christmas morning.　The M.R. must have squandered his commissary funds for weeks to amass the presents he had hoarded (+ hidden in this place of no privacy) for the t.o. and me—a pipe, razor blades, pipe cleaners, tobacco, cigarettes for me + equally useful items for the t.o. x Lights were on till 11.30 + we talked late + toasted the season in hot choc" (December 25, 1953).

"Last night a very important event occurred: the M.R. wrote a letter for a friend who is unable to write. It is really remarkable, the progress he has made— + last night's performance was an important symbol to the M.R. himself of how much he has accomplished. I read the letter, a fine well-organized, well-expressed two-page one it was. It came at a good psychological moment, too. The M.R. will soon go to the farm, perhaps tomorrow (at least we are having a farewell cocoa party tonight on that assumption) [the prison had its own large, inmate-staffed working farm; it stood well within the enormous Lewisburg reservation, but because it was beyond the main prison walls only inmates who were going home soon got sent there], + it is good for him to realize that he no longer needs help, *but on the contrary can give it*" (January 21, 1954).

"The M.R. did go to the Farm + the t.o. + I miss him already, though we see him when he comes in to church services + other less regular trips" (January 24, 1954).

"Very good news: the Middle Reader has made parole on a reconsideration of his case. He called the news up to me yesterday just after he had heard it + then skipped + danced happily down the road to the farm, turning from time to time to wave at the storeroom window where I stood applauding the celebration" (March 4, 1954).

"x-x-x The M.R. went home Tues. morning—a very happy + self-possessed young man. I shall miss his cheerful, turbulent vitality" (March 25, 1954).

ALGER'S LETTERS from prison seldom spoke about the people who had worked to put him there—and when they did it was usually a comment in passing, or perhaps a blithe one-liner that had occurred to him after running across a familiar name in the newspapers. In a single mention, for instance, of Thomas F. Murphy, the successful Hiss case prosecutor, Alger said that a photograph he'd just seen of Murphy made him look like "a sea-sick sea lion"; Murphy, who became a prominent public figure after Alger's conviction—serving first as New York City's Police Commissioner and later as a federal judge—was a hugely tall man who took pride in a large, drooping walrus mustache. During the 1952 presidential elections, when Richard Nixon's standard campaign speech as Republican nominee for Vice President veered between family values and the role he'd played in the Hiss case, Alger wrote home (on October 14), "This era's Poor Richard (what a far cry from the original) seems to have but two topics of conversation: me + his wife. I hope he speaks more accurately when he refers to 'Pat' than when he refers to me."

Alger was similarly offhand about Nixon only a month before leaving Lewisburg, as he savored (on October 24, 1954) that weekend's final family visit before his homecoming: "To combine our delicious visit with observance of UN Day + successful birding gave the occasion authentic touches of family interests! The most tactful of hosts could hardly have been expected to provide a tame hermit thrush, with a jay's cry + a visible and audible chickadee thrown in. They are, incidentally, 3 new additions to my Lewisburg list. . . . x-x-x We talked about almost all the important + interesting events + developments but we forgot to mention Adlai Stevenson's witticism that Nixon represents 'white collar McCarthyism.' "

Although Alger also had only a few things to write about Whittaker Chambers, his comments about his principal accuser seem to have undergone a gradual transformation, as his Lewisburg "learning + growing" progressed. Alger's early remarks on Chambers were brisk and satirical: "Gleaned from the Feb 3, 1951 New Yorker: 'Although intimately connected with the State Department for many years, Mr. Sayre's integrity has never been questioned.—Lawson Y.M.C.A. News, Chicago.'! (One might add, except by Whittaker Chambers)" (April 18, 1951).

Chambers, in 1940, had accused Francis B. Sayre, former Assistant Secretary of State, former U.S. High Commissioner to the Philippines, Woodrow Wilson's son-in-law, and Alger's first boss in the State Department, of having been associated with a communist underground movement in Washington; he later abandoned the story. On September 19, 1951, Alger wrote, "I assume Bob [Benjamin] + Chester [Lane] saw . . . the Her. Trib. for Sept 14 with its interesting quotation of poor witless Whittaker Chambers." Six months later, on March 16, 1952, after Alger's lawyers had filed a motion for a new trial, I wrote him—I was ten, and enjoyed loathing and making fun of Chambers—saying, "Tomorrow Helen [Buttenwieser] is coming to school to explain the trial to me," and under this sentence included drawings of a scroll, a gavel, an English judge's curly wig, and a fat man, labeled "CHAMBERS." A balloon coming out of the man's mouth said, "Yakity Yakity."

Alger wrote back, on March 18, "*Now* I know why you wanted to know what Chambers looks like; you must have had your letter in mind at the time of your last visit. Well, you made him look much nicer than he is, but the 'Yakity' part is just like him." In the first half of 1952, Chambers took on a new role before the world, as a spectacularly successful author. His book, *Witness*, an instant best-seller, earned him more than a quarter of a million dollars. Even before reaching bookstores it spent almost three months on newsstands, when (as "I Was the Witness") it was serialized in ten consecutive issues of the *Saturday Evening Post*.

It was during this period, I think, that a new question arose in Alger: Which of the two men was more severely punished—Alger, confined to Lewisburg, or Chambers, wrapped in new acclaim on his farm in Westminster, Maryland (which was about one hundred miles due south of Lewisburg), but deeply isolated within his own mind?

"Yes," Alger wrote home on February 7, 1952, "thee must read what the Sat. Eve. Post has added to the Great Books. . . . Any enlightened layman will realize at once that it is the product of a seriously disturbed psyche. I read it this evening after a visit to the library where I beamed through chap. 1 of Bleak House. The contrast between wholesome Charles + doomed W.C. is that between liberating affirmation + self-imprisoned despair." At the end of the month, on February 26, he returned to the same theme, this time more obliquely: "On clothing-change-Tues. one letter is about all that there is 'time' for, strange though that sounds when in so many ways + for so many people time in prison is a tantalizingly slowly melting obstacle to all spontaneously natural manifestations of life, an obstacle so large in dimension that it seems like a bitter jest to complain that there is not enough of it. But, as thee well knows, bitterness is a product of ignorance + self-imprisonment."

. . .

Two and a half months later, on May 15, Alger wrote me the one Lewisburg letter I secretly resented for years—for its leap into sermonizing, for its holding back of feeling, for what I saw as its typical Algerish trick of redirecting sympathy onto people who hadn't earned it and had no use for it. On May 12, I had been robbed after school—of only ninety cents, but it was my haircut money and all I had. Two bigger boys, probably them-selves only twelve and thirteen, had stopped me—on the corner of Park Avenue and 77th Street, which was as scary as the theft itself, because this had happened close to Dalton (a safety zone in my mind) and also well within the heart of angel territory, since it was only a few blocks from both Vi's and the Buttens'.

I can now, belatedly, apply the letter's advice (learn how not to take things personally), and read it not for what it seemed to be saying then, but as a unique summing up of the many over-lapping, and conflicting, and not quite fully resolved, thoughts that Alger had looked at and considered as he worked, day after day, on how to come to terms with what had been done to him:

"Tony, my boy, that business on Park Ave. last Mon. must have been quite a shock. Actually, like most cases of aggression or hostility it will cease to bother you as soon as you under-stand what made those two boys pick on you. Once you under-stand why someone does something strange or unfriendly it ceases to be strange; + it even ceases to be unfriendly when you see it isn't really directed at you because you're you at all. It is caused by something sick in the other fellow or by his being mixed up about something. Actually, I have met in here a great many fellows who have done things just like what was done to you + almost all of them have, nevertheless, some very, very good qualities. If those 2 boys had known you, I'm sure they would have liked you so much that they would have wanted to be your friends + then they wouldn't have dreamed of doing anything against you.

"x One thing I'm sure of—they certainly needed the money even more than you did, poor as we are! Another thing I'm equally sure of—there must be people, grown ups, who have been much, much meaner to them than they were to you. That's how they got that way, there's no doubt of it. So, seriously, I'm much sorrier for them than I am for you, though of course what I really mean is that I'm sorry people are so treated that they act that way. On the next visit you + I can compare our ideas of what they are really like and who or what taught them to be bullies, which is a very unhappy thing to be."

"Your father," people have sometimes said to me, "must have been very bitter." But it's resentment, as Alger was trying to tell me, that saps your strength—"resentment," as Malachy McCourt, Jr., the Irish-American writer, has said, "is like taking poison and then waiting for the other fellow to die." Forgiveness, as Alger did say, does not banish sadness, and so it is only (as he did not quite say) the first of many steps toward understanding.

To untangle the Chambers case people needed information as well as energy. Here was a seldom encountered, most contagious psycho-political disorder, you'd have to call it, that occasionally sweeps across whole countries for a year or more, ensnaring minds and disrupting lives. This still nameless "X" syndrome is such a rarity because it represents a confluence or a yoking together of two forms of unhealthy behavior that are themselves unusual. Since the two components of this asymmetry—let's call them "A" and "B"—are seen so infrequently, most people in the modern world have trouble recognizing or neutralizing either one by itself. This vulnerability then leaves people even less prepared for coming to grips with the enormously toxic potential both forces exhibit if they find and feed on each other.

. . .

In the last thirty years, Americans have, unfortunately, become aware of the fact that a very few individuals among us are crazed and tormented enough to commit multiple murders; now we even have a name for such people—*serial killers*. We have not yet focused on the existence in our midst of a parallel group of people—*serial liars*. Meaning people who are compelled to use untruths either selectively or indiscriminately to try to ruin a series of relatives, friends, acquaintances, or well-known figures they have never met.

Similarly, we haven't seen the commonalty among a certain class of "hot button" public issues that arise from time to time and that are extremely hard to find solutions for and so deeply troubling that they simultaneously arouse anger and fear within people. The issues are seemingly disparate, since some are moral concerns and some are law-enforcement matters, while others are thought of as political or constitutional questions. When enough anger and enough fear are mixed together in people, they create the most potent biochemical weapon known—because then the mind can poison itself, without any outside intervention, and in certain cases can override reason, memory, and empathy all at once. In such a state people are in great danger of seeing things back-to-front or upside down, so that a friendly smile is perceived as a hostile scowl.

Then their actions may be both unjust and without humanity, while at the same time they may feel they have been dealing honorably, even nobly, with their neighbors. In our own time, for example, the increasing attention paid to the very serious problem of child molestation has, because it also brings up anger and fear, sometimes led to a distortion of people's abilities to judge a particular situation clearly. Panic and frustration about this subject are necessarily brought together because we can't simply look at other people and instantly know whether or not they are potential molesters.

Shortly after Alger's death, I got a long letter from a man I've never met, an ex-schoolteacher who said he was moved to write because of what had happened to him—he'd been accused, unjustly and maliciously, of molesting children, and a court trial had convincingly established his innocence. Afterwards he was, nevertheless, no longer able to work as a teacher—the accusation itself, in too many people's minds, had proved his unfitness, tainting him indelibly. So he had moved to another state and, having changed professions, was now a minister and a counselor.

When I was growing up, after World War II, the thing you couldn't tell about other people just by looking at them was whether they were now, or had ever been, a communist, or a spy, or a traitor. There have been at least some communists in every country since the *Communist Manifesto* was published in the middle of the nineteenth century, and there have been spies and traitors throughout the world since long before countries even existed, dating back most probably to at least the founding of the Mesopotamian city-states such as Ur of the Chaldees almost 5,500 years ago.

But in postwar, mid-twentieth-century America, this commonplace situation of living in a country that has in it a mix of people, the contented and the discontented, suddenly became something to be scared and angry about: One reason, in the late 1940s, was news that communist Russia, the only other superpower left in the world, had developed an atomic bomb of its own. There was also the suggestion that the American government, or people within the American government, were plotting to give communist Russians information about how to make atomic weapons and possibly even to gain control of the United States.

Here was a generalized atmosphere of suddenly swirling

mistrust—a kind of "B" force in the making—which might have melted away, as sometimes happens, or could perhaps have persisted at its initial level of intensity, becoming, like our own need to learn more about how to protect children from victimization, one of the troubling, unresolved issues of the day. Instead it met up with an "A" force, a small group of compelling storytellers. And because "A" + "B" = "X," there was a rare, full-scale "X" outbreak. Anger and fear, for many people, became the mind-set with which they evaluated the accusations put forward by several people who claimed to have access to inside information, among them Whittaker Chambers and Senator Joseph R. McCarthy.

McCarthy became famous by inventively and inaccurately telling an audience in Wheeling, West Virginia—this happened less than three weeks after Alger's conviction—that he had proof that the State Department was "thoroughly infested" by 205 card-carrying communists (pressed by reporters, McCarthy later reduced the number to four). Alger Hiss, McCarthy said at the time, "is important not as an individual any more, but rather because he is so representative of a group in the State Department." The "X" outbreak that followed this speech has a well-remembered name—McCarthyism. Some liberals, because McCarthy was a Republican and claimed to be fighting communism, like to imagine that they could never become McCarthyites. Of course that's not true: Anger, fear, and lies can flow together within anyone. What no society remembers is that McCarthyism is only a single, modern-day instance of a recurring pattern of explosive, corrosive human behavior that, until we outgrow it, will haunt everyone's future.

In college, I became fascinated by an "X" episode in England—the Titus Oates case—that did so much damage in a few months it's still remembered and studied about more than three hundred years later. In Protestant England in the late seventeenth century, the invisible sickness that could not be detected just by looking at someone was not communism, but Catholicism. It was a politically unbalanced time—the English monarchy had recently been restored, after Oliver Cromwell's Puritan revolution, and was considered "soft" on Catholicism. The French king, Louis XIV, a Catholic, was financing intriguers who hoped to replace Charles II, the English king (and a kind of underground Catholic), with his avowedly Catholic brother, James. A serial liar named Titus Oates became, for a while, the most important man in the country, because he seemed to be an expert on anti-Catholicism, telling a series of judges, in effect: *You can believe me, because I used to be a Catholic myself, and I participated in their secret plots to overthrow the King.* (In fact Oates had pretended to be Catholic for four months, long enough to gain some firsthand knowledge of Jesuit practices.) Hundreds of people that he implicated—falsely—were executed, and he was stopped only when he overreached himself and accused the Queen of being a Catholic plotter.

McCarthyism in this country was itself a damaging episode. According to one estimate, ten thousand people in and out of government lost their jobs over the course of a decade which began even before McCarthy added himself to the picture in February 1950. Philip Roth, who was an undergraduate at Bucknell University in Lewisburg during the years of Alger's imprisonment there, has said that this was the time betrayal of friends and colleagues became respectable. Waters changed, but then, with the exception of several large pools, changed back once more. Some of the wrongs done during this recent "X" episode have not yet been righted.

At its height, McCarthyism had so much power that Clarence E. Pickett, then honorary secretary of the American Friends Service Committee, the national Quaker relief organization, wrote Prossy (on December 15, 1953) that patriots should prepare for the likelihood of prison terms: "With the growing sense of fear that there is in the country, one wonders whether others of us may not be called upon to pay a similar price to purchase again the spirit of courage and freedom in this country."

The preceding year Uncle Tommy had written Alger a letter (on November 16, 1952) telling him that prison was now actually his only reliable refuge and safe haven:

"I know that you want to be home again to Prossie + Tony and all of your friends, and I too long to see you. But I honestly think this would be a most awkward time to get your release. Such is the temper of the country—if I read the signs right—that I think you would be hounded mercilessly from the moment of your release. You have a degree of protection at present which you would not have outside Lewisburg's gates. Perhaps you do not realize that you are a symbol and no longer a person—to many people, that is. And a symbol with 2 sides, a dark side and a bright side. And to those who look at the symbol and see that rather than the person—to *all* such the passionate feelings against and for are great. Unfortunately the overwhelmingly large number of those against are aided and abetted by all the mighty power of mass communication media. As of this month of November 1952 you will have no place to go, and not a moment of peace. . . .

"There is a war on and the fight is to the death. The war is not a war between *haves* and *have nots* but between the grabbers and the givers, between the aggressives and the passives, between the haters and those who love. Unfortunately, the commies have made political capital out of lining themselves up with many of the 'causes' for which those who love strive. Hence *all* that side is now coming to be labeled with the tag of communism. Everyone who isn't 100% *for* aggressive, dog-eat-dog, cynical grabbing is now in grave danger of being

Prossy's drawing of the Lewisburg Inn and of the wallpaper in our room

tagged. The former amused toleration with which the grab-bers used to regard the 'causes' is now turning to almost rabid hatred. In fact, the 'hate boys' are really on the march, and I fully expect as bitter a period of rabid witch-hunting and per-secution as this country has ever seen.

"Chambers was able to slap a label on you and the label stuck, and the reason why the label stuck is that you are not oily enough or greasy enough for it to slide off harmlessly. You were much too clean, too forgiving, too gentle, too honest, too loving. Such persons refuse to be slippery and so the labels *stick*. More on this another time. Meanwhile all our love and courageous thoughts. Yours, Tommy."

I BEGAN grappling with the subject of anger, fear, and lies sometime during the early spring of 1952, in an upstairs back bedroom of the Lewisburg Inn—a room I considered "our Lewisburg home." I'm sure it has taken me all of the forty-four months Alger spent in Lewisburg plus all of the forty-four years since then to grapple with it further. But it was in the Inn—a sweet little building that's still a fixture of downtown Lewisburg—that I got a sense that it's possible to recognize the "X" phenomenon, should it occur again in our lifetimes.

Lying on my bed in the Inn on a Saturday night and looking at the flowered wallpaper inside and two flowering dogwoods on the street outside, I felt a sting of sadness I had never felt before. Was it really true, I wondered, that some people in the world, like Whittaker Chambers, felt so lost that they could only make themselves feel better by bearing false witness against others? Next to this sting was its twin—Why did so many people want to believe him? Could they really be pulled so far away from their senses that they cherish falsehood and punish truth? How could they hear the ring of truth inside hollow, empty words?

The Inn—it's the only building in the whole town of Lewisburg that I can visualize—was such a friendly, cozy place, a place that made a fuss over you whoever you were, that I had added it to my list of safety zones the first night I stayed there. It was like a lodge within sight of the summit of a high, faraway mountain. My mother and I had figured out that we could make a two-hour visit with Alger seem to last for almost a day by seeing him for one hour on a Saturday afternoon; then we'd head for the Inn, pretending it was a kind of extra-long intermission in the middle of a two-act play, and take our second hour with Alger the following morning.

The Inn had a subscription to the *Saturday Evening Post*, the magazine serializing "Witness." The *Post* was a magazine I never saw at home because my parents thought of it as mediocre. But under the double protection of a Saturday night in Lewisburg—tucked away in the Inn's back bedroom and all the while still so much in the middle of a visit to Alger that it felt as though *he* was the one who had left the room momentarily—I could in complete safety (as long as I kept it to just every now and then, and for only a few minutes at a time) finally look and see exactly what it was that Whittaker Chambers had been saying about my father.

The easiest way to do this was to curl up on the little bunk bed tucked into one corner, and then leaf slowly backwards through a stack of recent *Posts*. The final pages were fun to look at anyway—there was always a cartoon about Hazel the maid, who was twice as smart as the people she worked for, and a silly story in a box that was supposed to teach you about manners and had drawings of a creature called the Watch Bird who was looking at you to see if you'd been listening to the story. Then, after lingering on these back pages as long as I could, I would take a deep breath and flip forward to Chambers's words.

Some of what he was saying made sense: "The outstanding fact about Alger Hiss"—the *Post*s I looked at belonged to the Inn, so I've taken these quotes from the book version of "Witness"—"was an unvarying mildness, a deep considerateness and gracious patience that seemed proof against any of the ordinary exasperations of work and fatigue or the annoyances of family or personal relations." But then, in the next sentence, Alger would disappear—or everything about Alger except his name would disappear—and somebody I'd never met (someone else Chambers knew? someone made up entirely? some part of Chambers's own mind?) would step out, looking like Alger, wearing Alger's clothes and walking around through Alger's house. And you weren't supposed to notice that a substitution had just taken place.

In this paragraph the next sentence said: "Only very rarely did a streak of wholly incongruous cruelty crop out." How did this cruelty manifest itself? Alger's "strange savagery cropped out in a conversation about Franklin Roosevelt. Hiss's contempt for Franklin Roosevelt as a dabbler in revolution who understood neither revolution nor history was profound. It was the common view of Roosevelt among Communists, which I shared with the rest. But Alger expressed it not only in political terms. He startled me, and deeply shocked my wife, by the obvious pleasure he took in the most simple and brutal references to the President's physical condition as a symbol of the middle-class breakdown."

The two Algers do-si-do-ed in and out of sight, although it seemed that the real Alger was described rather hurriedly, as if by someone who hadn't known him well or long enough to pick up more than a few hard-to-miss facts: "A gentleness of character . . . in the Hisses . . . found one expression in an absorption in nature, especially in the life of birds. When I first knew them, the Hisses used to rise at dawn on Sunday and take long rambles out along the Potomac River, around Glen Echo and Great Falls."

The imaginary Alger was shown in vivid detail with much talk about "the simple pleasure that all of us took simply in being together," and about how "toward the Hisses, we felt a tenderness, spontaneous and unquestioning." At the same time, Alger was characterized (and why was this?) as someone whom clearly no one would want to spend much time with:

"Despite his acknowledged ability in the legal field, which I was not competent to explore with him, Alger Hiss is not a highly mental man. Compared to the minds I had grown up with at Columbia, free-ranging, witty and deeply informed (one has only to think of Clifton Fadiman or Meyer Schapiro), Alger was a little on the stuffy side. Ideas for their own sake did not interest him at all. His mind had come to rest in the doctrines of Marx and Lenin, and even then applied itself wholly to current politics and seldom, that I can remember, to history or to theory."

And: "I particularly remember Alger's opinion of Shakespeare. In 1936 or 1937, Maurice Evans played *Richard II* in Baltimore. It was the first time that my wife or I had ever seen Shakespeare acted. We were deeply impressed, not only by the new life the play took on for us on the stage, and the new texture given the verse by Evans' elocutionary style, but by the aliveness of the politics of the play. During the opening scenes, my wife whispered to me with awe: 'It's just like the Comintern!'

"A day or so later, I was trying to convey some of that to Alger. 'I'm sorry,' he said at last, somewhat less graciously than usual, 'I just don't like Shakespeare—platitudes in blank verse.' He quoted some Polonius, and I realized, for the first time and with great interest, that he disliked Shakespeare because the platitudes were all that impinged on his mind."

This was strange reading—a nonfiction novel we would call it now, although the term hadn't been invented yet. Equally, it was part of a strangely unbalanced situation. Hundreds of thousands, maybe millions, of people were, like me, happening on these words as they picked up copies of the *Post*. The reality of Alger as a living contradiction of what the *Post* wanted people to think was something that only my mother and I, and two lawyers (Chester Lane and Bob Benjamin), and twelve hundred prison inmates and several hundred prison guards and officers could at that point encounter in person. Only my mother and I were receiving, in our three letters a week, first-hand written reports setting down the thoughts and feelings that were welling up every day within the real Alger.

Of course, Alger's letters weren't being written to refute Whittaker Chambers. But it's interesting to look now at some things Alger was thinking and doing during the first months of 1952, the precise moment the world was first offered a chance to purchase Whittaker Chambers's fully drawn portrait of the "third Alger," the kit of parts presented as a living being, the considerate-gentle-tenderly-remembered-cruel-fanatical-platitudinous traitor and spy.

Alger was writing home about F.D.R., Holmes, and Shakespeare—and also about the B.R., the t.o., the Sugar Lump Boy, and sunsets. He seemed to be spending whatever spare time he had trying to construct a modern theory of esthetics and conscious evolution—"Thy thoughtful comments about the psychic role of British Royalty apply, I think, to the place

F.D.R. held in the emotions of the great mass of Americans. Those who say that our present confusion + unmanageable problems would not have arisen had he lived speak more profoundly than they themselves realize. So much of o.p.c. + u.p. arise from loss of the belonging + togetherness that he symbolized" (February 22, 1952). "I was struck to find in the Edwin Arnold version of the legends of Buddha's life the same aspiring figure of speech that Fry rises to in Sleep [meaning Christopher Fry's play *A Sleep of Prisoners*]. . . . As the Buddha leaves his princely pleasure dome to share mankind's ills in an effort 'to save / . . . all flesh, if utmost love avail,' he exhorts his steed: '. . . Be still, / White Kantaka! be still, and bear me now / The farthest journey ever rider rode.' . . . / Fry's phrasing is more meaningful to our times—vide O.W.H.'s aperçu that the wisdom of the past had to be constantly reformulated in the idiom of the present in order to be valid (and valuable) currently—but strikingly similar in its imagery + spirit of affirmation: 'Thank God our time is now when wrong / Comes up to face us everywhere, / Never to leave us till we take / The longest stride of soul man ever took.' And, of course, the truly significant parallel is the confusion of moral values then + now; and the comparable need for an arching spiritual affirmation that man can be what the seers + prophets have glimpsed" (March 15, 1952).

"Art for Art's Sake . . . is but Eastern withdrawal from the contest for the improvement of man's lot + classical philosophical detachment from ditto, thinned with Trilling treacle [this refers to Lionel Trilling, the literary critic] for an age in which our physical equipment for eliminating the squalor of ancient times is so tremendous that the old + noble lament for man's misery is patently outworn. More bluntly, that creed is dead + an esthetic wrapped about it naturally smells of decay. Lord give us ever an eye for life + love" (March 24, 1952).

"Next Tues. a Bucknell prof. is to speak on how to read

poetry. As source material he has had mimeographed + distributed in advance Keats somewhat turgid + callow Ode on Melancholy (but it does have the lovely simple words: 'She dwells with Beauty'), Marvell's dexterous sophisticatedly robust allurements to his coy mistress, parts of Prufrock + Sonnets XXIX + LXXIII. I tried out the Sonnets . . . on my friend [the t.o.]. As I expected, they spoke to him without barriers of any kind (the few inversions, ellipses + word meanings quite easily explained) because of the ecstatic simplicity + sincerity of the emotions that fuse + irradiate the structural complexity—which becomes the supple skeleton of a living creation not confining boundaries to ideas or artificial forms for word games. He (the Italian) approaches all new experiences with natural dignity + psychic candor; as a result he suffers little from confusion of values induced by self abasement, over-assertiveness, self consciousness or preconceived cultural fads based on the psychic wobblings of others" (April 13, 1952).

"In art as in mental health respect for man's potentialities + the attempt always + everywhere to further their growth are basic. Form in art is largely determined by cultural conditioning (with some outside biological limiting factors such as physically painful sounds in music) + in turn vastly affects communicability. Form, therefore, necessarily proceeds in styles + reflects the preoccupations + concepts of current civilization. But the emotional impact (Holmes' 'trigger') of art (as opposed to expertise in writing or painting or music) derives, I feel certain, from the sincerity, intensity + maximation of the artists-+-their-respondents' visions of man's perfectibility" (April 22, 1952). "Tomorrow's picture [on display in the "gallery"] will certainly be the almond branch [of Van Gogh] with its bold integrating stripe of carmine + its contrastingly delicate sprig of nascent life. But often, very often, I shall return to Picasso's even more compelling evocation of the angelic endowment of life (the child + dove) which only lack of nurture can prevent from glorious fulfillment. How pathetically neglected the divine substance of those for whom Prufrock's lament remains still pertinent, that they have measured out their lives with coffee spoons" (April 26, 1952).

"Does thee remember a search we made in 1945 for poems of stature on peace? And how we found that our inability to recall any was due to their virtual non-existence? Man had never been sufficiently at peace within himself to have any vigorous + concrete concepts of peace with his fellows. Similarly there is a dearth of words to express the affirmative outreach + aspiration of spirit which is the natural accompaniment + source of wholesome human growth + maturation. The obstacles to realization of man's potentialities have been so overwhelming that the most articulate + whole men of history have never, until very recent times, grasped those visions of the potentialities except in mystical raptures which were largely uncommunicable. In stating the problem I have almost exhausted the common vocabulary of fully realized human growth. There are to be sure words borrowed from physical analogies: vaulting, climbing, soaring, expansive, constructive. And there are a few others of much more generalized origin that can serve, limpingly, (purposeful, meaningful, avowal) to express aspects of the subject. Some essential elements (cooperation, love, understanding) have been partially understood + their names have come into the language, but only as imprecise + ambiguous terms.

"x The [psycho]analysts have, quite simply, had to coin new terms or earmark existing ones for specialized use: think of the newness of the concepts of sublimation, affective attitudes, integration, conditioning, psychic trauma, security—to mention only a tiny fraction of the discoveries that have made the obstacles to growth identifiable + manageable. But even they have not gone far in their thinking beyond the now surmountable barriers to the 'peaceable kingdom' which is man's long sought + intuitively sensed potential state. Will thee see if thee can find words of affirmation, outreach + aspiration which I have overlooked? Remember thy remarking on the paucity of psychiatric thought about the nature of the emotionally healthy man?—he appears only as one free of various mental ills, a most negative fellow indeed!" (May 20, 1952).

Uncle Donie, unlike Alger, was cheerfully, almost exuberantly, unforgiving of Whittaker Chambers's writings, telling Alger (on February 25, 1952):

"I came down [to Washington] on the train with Bob Benjamin and his wife (whom I had never met before). It was a pleasant trip indeed. Bob got from me a splendid article appearing in the newsletter of the Baptist University Church in Austin, Texas. The letter consists of four pages and I presume is sent to the minister's parishioners. One article is entitled, 'Whittaker Chambers, God and the Saturday Evening Post.' It starts off by referring to a letter from the Post to the minister announcing that the first of a series of 'I Was the Witness' would appear that week and suggesting (a) that the minister read it and (b) use it in his sermon the next Sunday. Then the article continues with the minister saying that he did read the article but will not use it in his sermon. Then there follows a discussion in which the minister concludes that Chambers is still a Communist—'prove it,' he asks; 'no but I am convinced that he is,' he answers. One final paragraph refers to Chambers' attitude toward God and he says he will write more the next week on that but makes a few remarks about Chambers' idea that he is serving God. The last line is: 'Poor God! What would he do without Whittaker Chambers and the Saturday Evening Post?'"

My mother's response to the *Post* pieces was more oblique. When events in America seemed overwhelming, she often looked abroad—to England—burying herself in *Punch*, or the *Countryman*, or the *New Statesman*, or buying a new batch of English paperbacks (Penguins, Pelicans, and Puffins) at the British Book Centre on East 55th Street. "It is quite understandable I should think," she wrote Alger (on February 18, 1952) about funeral services for King George VI, "that we have all been so interested in the full reports of the English tradition + ceremony because the scene in our rootless urban centers is always changing so disturbingly. And the stability + mutuality of much English tradition provides a sense of belonging too many people don't have."

Two of the English paperbacks she read over and over were detective novels by Josephine Tey. In one, *The Daughter of Time*, a bored Scotland Yard detective stuck in a hospital bed, recovering from a humiliating fall through a trapdoor, singlehandedly reexamines the evidence against King Richard III, the most hated king in English history. The detective concludes that Richard was a decent man and a good, magnanimous king who after his death became the victim of a vicious propaganda campaign by the Tudor kings who had supplanted him, a strategy so successful it was still assumed to be an accurate account of Richard's life almost five hundred years later. In the other Tey book, *The Franchise Affair*, a middle-aged English woman and her mother who live by themselves in the countryside are falsely accused of kidnapping and beating a fifteen-year-old schoolgirl; for many months the girl's story is widely accepted as truthful, because she seems to have such detailed knowledge about the women and the inside of their house, The Franchise. And why would she make up such a story? (To conceal an illicit affair with a businessman, it turns out; and she could invent plausible stories about the women and The Franchise because she had seen just enough from a bus that passed by the house.)

I remembered *The Franchise Affair* recently when an American Cold War historian, Bruce Craig, sent me a copy of Donald Hiss's F.B.I. file, which he had just obtained after filing a Freedom of Information Act request. As I was reading through the papers, a moment in the book came back to me so suddenly and strongly that I went and looked up the passage (my mother had eventually passed the book on to me). In her darkest hour, as she despairs of ever establishing her innocence, the unshakable reserve of Marion Sharpe, the book's immensely resourceful heroine, cracks: " 'I wish,' she said passionately, 'oh, how I wish that we had one small, just one small piece of evidence on our side! She gets away—the girl gets away with everything, everything. We keep on saying "It is not true," but we have no way of *showing* that it is not true. It is all negative. All inconclusive. All feeble denial. Things combine to back up her lies, but nothing happens to help prove that we are telling the truth. Nothing!' "

These were words that *exactly* summed up a feeling I had harbored for years when I was growing up. How I had longed then to find even one small, no-way-to-get-out-of-it lie in a Whittaker Chambers story. Now I actually had one in my hand: Six weeks after Alger went to prison, Donie became "desperately ill," as Prossy wrote Alger (on May 7, 1951), with double pneumonia so severe he lapsed into a coma for three days. "They all thought he was going out yesterday," she reported, "but he has responded to the pneumonia drugs." The following day she was able to send "the most terrific good news"—Donie "completely came back today from Nowhere, ate two meals, sat up + shaved himself. Even started worrying about the exams he was supposed to set for his class."

The F.B.I. document I held, a typed memorandum to J. Edgar Hoover from the special-agent-in-charge of the agency's Baltimore office, is dated May 24, 1951: "WHITAKER [sic] CHAMBERS, while being interviewed on other matters on May 22, 1951, advised that he had recently heard a report to the effect that DONALD HISS had recently attempted suicide and was in 'Emergency Hospital' in Washington, D.C. CHAMBERS did not know as to what Hiss' condition was except that he had heard that he was still alive."

How extraordinary, how appalling, how sad. Alger Hiss was already in jail, and Donald Hiss had nearly died—and with nothing left to gain or prove, Whittaker Chambers still couldn't stop lying about the Hiss family, casually, promiscuously, almost at random. There is a Central Asian proverb which takes off from the old Western fairy tale of the emperor's new clothes and goes it one better. Sometimes, the proverb suggests, the question that needs to be asked is not, "Is our emperor actually wearing no clothes at all?" The question, instead, is: "Can that man riding around naked in public really be an emperor?"

Yet, in a curious residue of our postwar "X" period, there are those who find Chambers more believable today than when he first told his stories. Although the emphasis of the story seems to have shifted, so that, at least for some, it has become of somewhat less importance to keep discrediting Alger and far more important to elevate Chambers into a heroic role, seeing him as a founding father and the Paul Revere of the Cold War. *Witness*, the autobiography of a facade, a vendetta presenting itself as a life, has been echoed by more recent books, several by scholars and journalists trained in analysis and investigation, that begin the Chambers story with the second chapter, so to speak. They take Chambers's assertions about himself and others at face value and, having accepted them in advance as factual and rational, restate them rather than subjecting them to the kind of rigorous examination that in other cases is second nature for these writers.

The life of the "second Whittaker Chambers"—meaning a setting forth of what he really did and what went on inside the tortured individual who invented the third Alger, among many other destructive fictions—has yet to be written. Over the years I have of course wondered why Chambers included Alger among the more than 150 people he accused of communist activities. I've heard many theories—some ludicrous, some plausible. It's been suggested, for instance, that perhaps Chambers was never a spy but only a gifted storyteller. One man I know of spent decades trying to show that if Chambers was a spy, he worked for the Nazis, not the communists. In 1949 Chambers acknowledged to the F.B.I. that from 1933 or 1934 to 1938 he had anonymously engaged in "numerous homosexual activities," and some have suggested that Chambers and Alger were lovers. Another theory is that because the dates of Chambers's underground sexual experiences bracket the entire time he claimed to have been a spy, perhaps his stories about underground communist activities were basically a metaphor.

I've come to think that it was the *idea* of Alger that appealed to Chambers—that he felt drawn to Alger not so much because he wanted to be with him but because he wished he could somehow *be* him and possess his serenity. Chambers bought his Westminster, Maryland, farm after Alger had once considered buying it himself. In his basement Chambers carefully preserved a small, ragged piece of cloth, dry-cleaned and folded, that had once covered an old chair in the apartment he had sublet from my father.

In the early 1980s, President Ronald Reagan, who liked to say that the writer who had most influenced his life was Whittaker Chambers, presented Chambers to the nation as someone to cherish, posthumously awarding him the Medal of Freedom, America's highest civilian decoration, in a White House ceremony. Also in the 1980s, Chambers's Maryland farm was designated a National Historic Landmark. Perhaps there was a greater need then for larger-than-life Cold War figures than there had been in the 1950s—some historians call the 1980s the "Second Cold War," because it was a reintensification of tensions between the United States and the Soviet Union following a period of détente and relative restraint during the Nixon and Carter administrations.

The final years of the Cold War were also expensive. "Between the beginning of the Cold War in 1946, and its end in 1989," according to *Billions and Billions*, a posthumous book of essays by Carl Sagan, "the United States spent (in equivalent 1989 dollars) well over $10 trillion in its global confrontation with the Soviet Union. Of this sum, more than a third was spent by the Reagan administration, which added more to the national debt than all previous administrations, back to George Washington, combined."

Or perhaps, as with me, when attitudes I adopted in 1948 froze in place and thereafter felt natural and spontaneous, other people have been stuck in one spot, too—only of course their attitudes are the mirror image of mine. Astonishingly enough, the Hiss case, more than fifty years after Alger's indictment, is still a current event; in 1997, for example, two Republican Senators told the Senate Intelligence Committee that, whatever his other qualifications, Anthony Lake, President Clinton's nominee to be director of the C.I.A., was probably unfit to take over such an office simply because he had once said on television that he wasn't entirely convinced of Alger Hiss's guilt.

AFTER SEVEN months in prison, Alger wrote home (on October 27, 1951), "I have known since I first came to jail how much harder imprisonment is on the families than on the prisoners themselves—and this disparity is far greater than the average in my case for I have learned so much that I could not otherwise have learned, whereas thee has no such compensation for thy greater strain + hardship."

Prossy during the Lewisburg years

A year later, on October 19, 1952, he returned to the subject, this time in another three-way dialogue with Uncle Tommy: "Tom's letter repeats an attitude he has, to my embarrassment, stated before. He writes that *my* 'courage + steadfast faith' gives *them* 'a great deal of strength.' . . . All I am called to do in the courage line is to sit here like a bump on a log, learning + growing as much as I can. And as for faith, what's it for if not to be steadfast? That's the minimum standard for faith (which should also have a few other characteristics). The obvious point, which I have mentioned before, is that thee + Tony are the exemplars of courage + purposiveness. My embarrassment arises from Tom's misplacing, misdirecting his well-meant + affectionate tribute."

"x There is always so much to learn," he added several months later (on February 8, 1953), "that it keeps one a little breathless reaching out for the next experience!"

My mother, in the winter of 1951, struggled to find a measure of Alger's balance and bounce. When Alger had written her, on December 4, that "as thee so well learned this fall, a serious illness can indeed be a suspension of living," that was Algerish shorthand. Returning to New York in September from Peacham, Prossy came down with pneumonia as Donie had in the spring. While she was never hospitalized, her spirit was more deeply wounded than her body. She was, I think, so deeply ashamed to find herself suddenly laid up, frail, not regaining strength for week after week that she sank into a depression that didn't lift for several months. After the cheerful, nothing's-changed hubbub of Peacham, with its old summer routine of swims and hikes and picnics, this may have been when the full weight of Alger's absence descended on her.

The summer of 1951, I can now see, had its own glow and momentum. Even though Alger was already in Lewisburg, this time was a high-water mark for Prossy—for her, the worst had happened and she'd met it head-on. An unexplored land lay ahead—and now so many people were trying to be helpful, acting almost like guides through foreign territory. There's an extraordinary letter to Alger—from an unauthorized correspondent, so why did the censors pass it along?—that embraces the sweetness that lifted the summer of 1951. It's from Lucie Stephens, an old friend of Dardar's who'd come to Peacham for a week; as far as I know it's the only letter she ever wrote him:

"The house is very quiet this Sabbath afternoon because your Prossy and your Doris [Dardar] have hied themselves over the hills to see your Tony [I was at summer camp for the first time]. And so because you have been ever present, tightly woven into the sunny fabric of our lives here, I shall talk to you for a bit. . . .

"The other afternoon I fared forth alone . . . opening all my pores to the beauty about me. . . . On the way back . . . I heard a Maryland yellow-throat singing in maddening concealment

Prossy's drawing of Andrew Wyeth's sketch

from within a bush. I stood for once patiently until at last I saw him. I had never been so close before or watched one sing. He darts quick little looks about, then throws his head back and you see him pour his ecstasy literally from his golden throat. It was the crowning moment of the afternoon and took the 'trudge' out of the last steep hill. At the top, I came upon three men . . . [and] out of my intoxication I dared say to one of them:

" 'Aren't the views glorious today?' He replied with a quiet smile, 'It's Vermont.'

"I . . . returned home filled with the beauty of 'small, unconsidered things.'

"And here it all is waiting for you and until your return all who love you are seeing it with your eyes.

"I just must add that you will never know the uplift I have derived from touching, for all too short a time, your and Prossy's life lived with no bitterness, with dignity and self-lessness, enhanced here in Peacham by Doris's ever present love and solicitude. It is a rare example of the triumph of the spirit and I am privileged to witness it.

"This brings my very best wishes tho you don't need them for you are already creating what I would wish for you."

That summer also gave Prossy a special treat, a vacation within her Peacham vacation. While I was still in camp, Dardar took her off for a dash through Maine, where they ran into Andrew Wyeth in a coffee shop, and Wyeth later, in Alger's honor, took out his fountain pen and added a small, impromptu black-ink sketch of a lighthouse to the plain white cover of the catalogue for his latest show. This simple Wyeth drawing—a tower, window, turret, light, and two clouds—still sits on the mantelpiece of my apartment, exactly where my mother put it the day she came back to the city. On the windowsill is a jauntily carved wooden duck that also came home from Maine—it opens up and becomes a box that long ago was just big enough to hold the first stack of Alger's letters. In tribute to Andrew Wyeth, Prossy named the duck "Andy."

All this information is recorded in carefully observed detail in Prossy's letters to Alger; her narratives of that summer are fresh and unfaded: "I don't know whether I ought to try to share with thee the smells or the sounds of the part of the Maine Coast we were in. I think I will remember a mixture of gulls + foghorns + sweet peas + strong lobster smells—and then visually the peculiar carpentry. Not simple clean lines like Vermont houses but a lot of fancy fret work around the eaves or porches, paper doily style, + a lot of the churches suffer from this. Wyeth has painted a lot of this, like Hopper, but always with a tremendous Flemish interest in detail plus a strong sense of human drama of man's life here below" (August 16, 1951).

Prossy found her feet in the fall of 1952, when she finally found a job after more than a year of searching, working in the un-air-conditioned basement office beneath a Doubleday Book Shop on Fifth Avenue. (She had to work downstairs rather than on the sales floor because the head office didn't want people coming into the store to be shocked by a sudden glimpse of Mrs. Alger Hiss.) Teaching jobs were of course not available; she almost got one office job where a friendly boss told her, "Don't worry, the fact that you're the Mrs. Hiss leaves me completely non-pulsed."

The Doubleday pay was meager—she took home thirty-seven dollars a week—but it was just enough to supplement a couple of small inheritances and a continuing stream of generous gifts from family and friends and angels. Her co-workers were young and enthusiastic and welcoming. They were writers and editors trying to break into publishing, or aspiring actors working in a bookshop instead of waiting tables. They were nonpolitical and nonjudgmental, so the Hiss name didn't scare them; Prossy was simply the new member of the overworked, understaffed basement team—people who though scrambling for the time being, knew they would be doing something else next, maybe something they were looking forward to.

It was the kind of friendly, makeshift world my mother could fall into easily; she knew exactly what she was looking forward to. She made close friends with the jolliest of them, taking them on bird walks in Central Park and treating them to balcony seats at Carnegie Hall for New York Philharmonic concerts, and her letters to Alger echoed the lyrical quality of the trip to Maine: "The flight of the wild swan was very startling. I heard a lot of calling and soprano sounds and expected to see four or five seagulls instead of which an enormous V of very large swan, thirty-five counted, which broke into a Y as they neared lower Manhattan—the skyscrapers?—and then made a V again and veered off southwestward across to New Jersey. This happened about a quarter past eight on Wednesday or Thursday morning. I could follow them for a long time from the bedroom window and it was very wonderful indeed" (October 18, 1952).

I'd hoped my mother's letters would help me reclaim some missing memories in the same way that Peter Pan could get his shadow sewed back onto the soles of his feet. Sometimes it did—I had, for example, forgotten all about Andy being the name of the duck, and I could now attach a date (March 21, 1953) to a memory that's never left me: of the night that, returning home half-asleep after a visit to Lewisburg, my small gray suitcase, until then my talisman on the weekend trips to see Alger, got all sliced up in the exit turnstile at the local Sixth

Avenue subway station. I also learned that when I received a treasured, only-to-Tony letter from Alger, as sometimes seemed miraculously to happen just when I craved one most, it was my mother's doing. Earlier in the week she would have written Alger that "Tony is very needy + I think a letter all to himself will help."

But there are places in my memory that cannot be repaired. Interestingly, these gaps are not about anything my parents did; all the blanks have to do with things that were of special importance to me. I discovered, for instance, that one spring we got a cute black kitten to be a companion for Putter, my cranky old tabby, and the two cats, who detested each other on sight, fought battles for months. And that just after turning thirteen, I was allowed to make my first solo trip away from home: On the morning that Hurricane Carol roared through New York, I took a train to Baltimore all by myself to visit my grandmother and Aunt Anna and dozens of cousins, and stayed two nights with Dr. Esther Richards, a famous psychiatrist I greatly admired. Alger's friendliest cousin, Elizabeth Hiss Hartman, drove me all the way to Gettysburg so I could see the battlefield. And the previous spring, when I was twelve and in seventh grade, my Dalton classmate Bobby Fisk threw a party at his parents' country home in Tuxedo Park, and he and I and another close Dalton friend, Bill Harris, were able to save the life of a three-week-old fawn, cowering in some bushes, that Bobby's retriever, Robin, was trying to kill.

I'm not quite sure where to put these episodes that belong to me, because they happened but I can't see myself reflected off any of them. It's as if other people could see me, but I was invisible to myself. So parts of who I was now exist only in letters and postcards.

One of the letters says that Vi thought that once my family had been split apart I had sought safety by diving into communities that couldn't so easily be torn asunder—particularly Dalton and Peacham. I think that's an accurate, shrewd insight, and typical of Vi—goodness, how much that woman did for me without my ever registering it: making time to talk and listen to my problems; telling Prossy that my fears were "not whimsical or to be ignored"; paying for the Dalton-run camp I longed for instead of the Quaker-run camp Prossy had her eye on. I know—the angels have drummed it into me—that the only way to thank someone is to help out someone else. But what a lot of helping out I've got to do!

A great deal about the Lewisburg years in fact wasn't particularly memorable. My mother and I followed routines whose simplicity almost paralleled Alger's inside—Doubleday and Peacham for her; Dalton and camp and Peacham for me. And once a month we took the eight-hour trip to Lewisburg. The world offered few signs that life had changed. Nobody harassed us and there were no threatening phone calls, although sometimes we'd get late-night hang-ups, and the F.B.I. clicking on the phone continued. Many people were extraordinarily kind—Lester, the young owner of Maison Louis, the dry cleaners around the corner, always asked to be remembered to Alger; and Jimmy, the elderly guard at City Bank–Farmers Trust, close to retirement, once a week said to be sure to tell Alger that he'd said, "How's my boy?"

After our apartment got painted one spring, I reported to Alger that "gradually things are getting better and 'back to normal' (whatever that is!)." When in seventh grade it was time for Dalton's Father-and-Son night dinner, an annual spring event, I could tell Alger, composedly, "As usual, I am going with the Engels"—meaning George Engel, my best friend, and his father, George Senior. From time to time, there were stories about Alger in the newspapers—his motion for a new trial had been denied; he'd been turned down for parole; a Congressman had been told (erroneously, of course) that Alger had tried to pack the United Nations Secretariat staff with communists.

The tabloids sometimes passed on a hostile, spicy rumor about Alger. Alger seemed not to mind: "Last night," he wrote home early on (October 2, 1951, before he'd been transferred to honors quarters), "there was much humor in the dorm when someone discovered [Walter] Winchell's column in the Mirror (+ presumably other papers) stated I am 'ailing' in the hospital; and today as I labored alone (my colleague absent for Rosh Ha-Shannah holidays + services) polishing the storeroom floor there were numerous quips about my 'convalescent routine,' etc. I haven't been within 25 yards of the hospital since I got the sulpha tablets last June. It is pleasant to contribute to the de-bunking of Winchell in any milieu."

Prossy, on the other hand, got thrown off stride the following winter by a "regrettable and repulsive" Sunday phone call "from a mid-afternoon Daily Mirror reporter inquiring about the 'story' that I was leaving or had left for Reno for a divorce." She wrote Alger that I'd found the call funny—"though I noticed he was needing me right by him for the balance of the day." But such calls were infrequent, and the single act of direct discrimination we encountered (if you don't count my mother's long job search and the fact that she had to work in a basement) was when several members of a Quaker Meeting in Manhattan strongly opposed our application for membership. We were urged to try again at some later date.

THE VISITING room at Lewisburg, a result of one of the New Penology reforms that James V. Bennett felt proudest about, was actually almost a cheerful place: "The grim screens and barriers," as Bennett wrote in *I Chose Prison*, "through which prisoners and their families had peered at one another during visiting hours, were torn down. We re-equipped the visiting rooms with sofas, tables, armchairs, and other furniture so that men and relatives could enjoy one another's company." That's in fact understating it—the sofas and chairs, which had bamboo frames covered with big, green, jungly prints of leaves and vines, had a sort of sprightly, cozy, veranda feel to them. The racket guys and their families had exuberant reunions, while wide-eyed toddlers wandered happily from group to group.

Because handshaking, embracing, and kissing were permitted only at greeting and parting, the three of us sat as far forward in our chairs as possible, and looked closely at each other's faces. For two hours a month, no other room in the world existed. A visit, as Alger wrote (on February 20, 1952), "is such an exhilarating intense experience," adding two months later (on April 17) that he wanted to make sure that the trips to Lewisburg went easily so that nothing would interrupt "the rightness of those singing moments." Two months after that (on June 19) he reminded us—and himself—that "There is always so much more to say on a visit than comes to the surface during the brief joy of being together. . . . But the relaxed beamishness of being together is more important than any particular exchange of ideas," so he could leave the room "sure my love + pleasure were as evident in my face as yours showed in your faces."

At the beginning I kept hoping that Alger could still somehow make everything okay:

"I miss you very much! [I wrote Alger on June 18, 1951.] Last night I had a dream. I don't remember what it was, but I do remember that you made it come out right." In one of the longest letters I sent to Lewisburg, dated May 18, 1952, I told him: "The horse-chestnut tree in Washington square is in blossom with its elegant white candles. I learned how to spin a top today and my record is 58 seconds! Tops are the fad in school this year as yo-yo's were last year. . . . Your letters are taken by us very warmly + thankfully. We both love them very much. We know + think that you are the most wonderful father that ever was or will be and love that magical wave that surges through us can never part us no matter where on earth our bodies are."

Alger replied (on May 22): "What you wrote is very true about how we in our family love each other so much that it is a very real living force within us + is present when we are separated as well as when we are together. This feeling of certainty in counting on others, of knowing that they will always be the same (except for constantly growing in sweetness + understanding) is one of the most wonderful things that people can give each other, isn't it." He faithfully updated his clairvoyance every few months—"What time," he wrote me at camp (on July 3), "do you (1) get up in the morning, (2) have your meals + (3) go to bed? I want to be able to think of what you're doing at different times during the day." At the end of the summer (on August 28), he wrote me in Peacham: "When does Dalton begin? I like to know your schedule so I can figure out what you + Mommy are planning + thinking + in that way share your thoughts."

But by that time I had become bitterly ashamed of my thoughts, and none of the dreams were coming out right. The thing that was tearing me apart was something that everyone agreed was tremendously important and quite wonderful—my mother's new job. I wasn't bothered by the fact that I would probably be Dalton's first latchkey kid. But an empty apartment was my breakdown point:

Every afternoon that I came home after school to a dark and vacant apartment was for me an unavoidable, unanswerable, unbearable reminder that, no matter how resplendent the sunset beyond my bedroom window, even if it exploded into colors the world had never seen before, and no matter how many times I wished upon the evening star, Alger would not be home that night or that year or the one after.

What could I do? Once again it felt as though talking about this feeling would be the wrong thing. Stopping Prossy from working—I couldn't even imagine another solution—would be letting the family down and pulling my parents off course. So the best thing, the grown-up thing, the only thing, would be to stop thinking about it. I told myself that that was what I had done. I didn't know that a heartache that follows prolonged stress will find a language and make itself known.

I didn't start failing courses, or get dangerously sick, as both Donie and Prossy had in the aftermath of Alger's arrival at Lewisburg. Instead I had a fluky series of accidents.

The first one came in Peacham, right before Prossy started work; I was already anticipating trouble. It happened on August 29, 1952, the day after Alger was writing to ask what I was "planning + thinking." As Prossy wrote him the next day, "Tones had a sad spill on Howard Smith's new cinder driveway causing a serious gash in the palm of his left hand, much gore." The thin, white "Y" of the old scar sits at the base of my palm, almost exactly in the middle of my lifeline.

A couple of months later, playing basketball after school, I tripped and sprained my toe badly. When it was being splinted my pediatrician noticed that I now had large plantar warts on both feet. I told everyone I was all right and not to worry. They didn't. "I'm delighted to hear that your eye + your aim are on the basket this year," Alger wrote me cheerfully (on November 9). "Tough luck about the toe! But I'm not a bit surprised to find out from Mommy that you are a toe-tal hero about it! Toe-ny has a toe-ken of basketball. This is going to affect my spelling strangely: you will eat toe-ma-toes; your favorite stoe-ne will now be toe-paz; you'll cross only toe-ll bridges to islands become atoe-lls; there are toe-boats + a city, Toe-kyo

+ toe-tem poles; bells will toe-ll; cloth will be toe-rn; Fabre wrote about entoe-mology; there are forest fires at High Toe-r; autoe-s have motoe-rs. I seem to be having a case of toe-mania!"

Later in the same letter he told Prossy: "How typically serene was thy + T's reception of the mishap of the broken toe, mentioned in a practical + sympathetic way after the more engrossing topics of a good-all-through issue of Punch." Prossy wrote back, "Tones loves all thy fooling about his toe."

The most serious accident followed a month later. Prossy's letter of December 9 filled Alger in: "Just after he had left for school at 8, he reappeared dripping blood from his mouth with teeth hanging loose (top front) having tripped + fallen smack on the cement pavement." The family dentist was smart enough to cram all three teeth back into my head, so they survived, but they had cracked diagonally, like fangs, and quickly turned black as soon as the nerves died.

Over the next few years, after being fitted with horrible temporary caps, I learned to smile without moving my upper lip. On the day of the smash-up I tried to be as brave as I thought my parents would have been if this had happened to one of them; I told the dentist that he was now an accidentist, and told my mother we could still make it to school if we hurried. The next day I wrote Alger a card that began, "I AM REALLY NOT AS BAD AS I SOUND," and ended, "PLEASE DON'T WORRY."

Alger was shaken—"Tony's lacerations," he wrote on December 14, "make very meaningful the biblical phrase 'child of my flesh'—I *felt* the pain + shock." He told me he was proud of my bravery: "Thee + Mommy were simply superb (talk about 'persons of the 1st magnitude'! That's you two to a T— + a P) last Tues.— + since (+ *before*, too, of course, because people react to emergencies with what they already are; they can't suddenly become different, 'add a cubit' to their stature)." He also, Algerishly, reminded me that someone else he knew was in even worse shape: "Isn't it lucky the bones were tough + strong? One of the nicest boys here broke his jaw just cracking it on another fellow's shoulder during a touch football game (some 'touch,' eh?). It was a nuisance. To have it knit properly, his jaws had to be wired together for 6 weeks + he could 'eat' only through a straw."

In another letter (on December 11) he tried hard to reach out: "You've had to take on a lot of responsibilities for many years now + that must sometimes be a bit of a strain, in spite of how well + how easily you measure up to your responsibilities. But, my darling Tony, remember that you can relax, that Mommy + I simply love you to pieces + that being our wonderful Tony should be a singing, happy-making affair—there's nothing to feel strained or anxious about, really!"

Vi was the only one who could see the mangling inside. I don't remember any of the part that happened next—I've reconstructed it from Vi's notes of a talk with Prossy on February 20, 1953 (Dr. Kathleen Kelly, one of Vi's executors, has been kind enough to make these notes available).

Someone must have told me that if you touched railroad tracks, you could feel them vibrate if a train was approaching. So in Peacham I had tried this once, a couple of minutes before a train was due. Nothing happened; there was no vibration. On a trip to Lewisburg just after Christmas, I again put my hand on the tracks, this time not stepping back until fourteen seconds before the train reached the station.

The previous weekend, when Prossy and I were going to Providence to visit Bobby Alford, I pulled my hand away only a split second before the train thundered in. The next day, on the way home, I asked Prossy to hold my hand so I wouldn't do it again. When she loosened her grip for a second, I tightened mine.

Vi convinced Prossy—who had said that my priorities should be piano lessons and orthodonture—that I might benefit from some therapy. Vi and I were already having occasional talks—I had told her about the recurring Peacham dreams, where the monster fish swam across the ocean in our basement. And I'd told her a dream of George Engel's—he'd come to our house for dinner, and Prossy had served him a glass of sweet white wine. He hadn't wanted to drink it, because it was full of black specks, but Prossy insisted. Vi and I agreed that the dream was saying that I got upset when Prossy tried to force a sweet attitude on people. A year later, when I was in seventh grade and studying the Civil War, I told Vi about a dream in which my teachers had falsely accused me of giving away secrets to the South while the class was escaping to the North. In jail, I was visited by a lawyer who believed me but wouldn't help me. I began to wonder, was he a lawyer or a prisoner like me?

Vi arranged for me to start seeing a young psychiatrist, Louis J. Gilbert, twice a week after school. I wrote Alger a postcard that ended, "P.S. Dr. Gilbert is fine!" Prossy wrote Vi that I'd said, "He doesn't look like a psychiatrist, he looks like a father." Things got somewhat better—from Lou Gilbert's office, in his presence, I was able to phone my mother and tell her how greatly I dreaded coming home to a deserted apartment. She began leaving work earlier—and I got home later, at least on the days I saw Dr. Gilbert. (Instead of being the only kid in my class who came home to an empty house, I was now the only one who saw a psychiatrist twice a week.)

Both my parents could see that I was in pain; it was not whimsical, they were not ignoring it, and to my great relief they did not see me as someone who'd been undermining the family or Alger's quest for vindication. Alger even wrote home (on October 11, 1953), "Of course the empty rooms are depressing to return to regularly—a grimly cold symbol of my long absence, in addition to the boredom of loneliness for any outgoing, active pre-adolescent. I wish the plan had been thought of last year; surely it would have minimized much of the strain—the avoidable strain, that is, for much is unfortunately inevitable."

Lou Gilbert was helpful to me for years. The terrifying train phobia, which I can't even remember, disappeared. Equally scary thoughts and feelings emerged—these I remember, probably because I could talk them over with someone. There were nights at Carnegie Hall when I had to hang on tightly to the balcony railing to keep from jumping over the edge. It wasn't that I wanted to die—I didn't, that's why I was hanging on. But I had the feeling that I was supposed to jump. Lou Gilbert helped me understand that I didn't have to make every trip to Lewisburg—that it was okay to want to go to a friend's house for the weekend even if that meant not seeing my father for a whole month. Living a life, he impressed on me, was as noble as being noble. He talked me through recurring dreams based on *The Borrowers*, the children's book about little people who live behind the walls of a house and are helped by a girl who lives there. I was always one of the little people—only in my dreams the girl was just one more threat to their existence.

Another dream still comes back. I'm walking through an unfamiliar part of New York City, turn a corner, and find myself in a meadow that leads to a tiny village exactly like Peacham. I just *knew* this was here! I tell myself. The city grew up around it and never displaced it. All I have to do is remember what street I came down, what corner I turned—and then I can find my way back.

Vi found me another psychiatrist when I went to Harvard, but when I was in my twenties I returned to the steadying, thoughtful Lou Gilbert. In this and other ways, my family has

Tim in uniform with Alger and Tony

always been exceptionally fortunate. One of Alger's Lewisburg letters rejoices in what he calls "the luck of the Hisses"—specifically meaning that we had all been lucky to meet up with Helen and Vi just at the time he would be away. I think he also meant that there are worse things in life than going to jail for a crime you didn't commit.

As Alger wrote from Lewisburg (on May 20, 1952) to the Rev. Duane Wevill, the Episcopal minister who long ago had prepared him for confirmation, "The essence of tragedy is the unfulfillment of life's basic aspirations." And again: "This blockage of the healthy, normal dynamism of life is, to my mind, the essence of tragedy."

WHEN MY brother and I talk these days, it's usually to get caught up; Alger's name may not come up at all. Tim has a thirty-two-foot sailboat and a half-interest in a half-chow named Smoky, and he's taken up writing. He is seventy-two and has seven grandchildren. He separated amicably from his wife several years ago after thirty-five years together and has now found happiness in a stable gay relationship. But in one conversation since Alger's death he began turning over in his mind some of the imponderables of Alger's life. "I have always felt guilty and resentful," Tim said, "about the fact that I wasn't allowed to testify at Alger's trials. In a way, my troubles were of my own making—I was too honest, but maybe that was part of my upbringing." In 1945, when Tim was eighteen and part of the Navy V-12 cadet program, he felt himself under intense moral stress to come to terms with his homosexual inclinations. He went to a Navy doctor and asked his advice: "He looked it up in the book—and then he threw the book at me."

Tim spent about three months in St. Albans Naval Hospital, where, it turned out, he was treated by a gay doctor, and then remained in protective custody for nineteen days—first for several days on an old hulk moored next to the *Queen Mary*, and then in what amounted to solitary confinement, in the brig at the Brooklyn Navy Yard, before being given an "undesirable" discharge after medical evaluation. "It's the only time I ever spent in prison," Tim said. Alger and Prossy were totally at sea, Tim remembers, when it came to the subject of homosexuality. "They were supportive, but concluded it was a neurotic disorder I would grow out of with counseling."

After Chambers's charges surfaced in 1948, the F.B.I. spent "I don't know how many man-hours interviewing everyone I had ever lived with or slept with—I know this because my friends told me that they'd been questioned." Twice, two F.B.I. agents came to Tim's apartment to talk about Alger. "So, in effect, I feel as though I was blackmailed into not testifying in the Hiss case. I wanted to testify, but Alger wouldn't have it. He told his lawyers, 'I'd rather go to jail than see Tim cross-examined about his private life.' That's the way Alger invariably behaved—throwing himself in front of the dragons.

"Maybe it wouldn't have made much difference if I had testified, but then it would have been three-against-two at any rate—my word added to Alger's and Prossy's against the testimony of the two Chamberses. That might have been enough to produce at least a deadlocked jury in the second trial as well as in the first—and maybe it would have led to acquittal.

"I could have told them, under oath, everything I've always told you, that Chambers's story is mostly poppycock. Of course, I still know what I saw and heard, but at my age the historians had better get to me fast. There wasn't anything in Alger that wasn't a good, decent, honest man. If anything, he had an unfortunately strong respect for the law—he couldn't even jaywalk without being horribly upset. Roosevelt was a god in our house. If F.D.R. had failures and weaknesses, they were not recognized; everything was forgiven. Holmes's presence hung over us like a direct representative of the Lord. Alger focused in on every important decision by asking—what would Holmes have done?"

Tim felt that if he had testified, and Alger had been found innocent and continued at the Carnegie Endowment, speaking out on behalf of the United Nations and other New Deal ideas, maybe that could have exerted a moderating influence on the Cold War, and helped keep McCarthy from gaining a foothold. "Maybe we might even have been spared the Korean War or the Vietnam War!" Tim said.

"But on the other hand, Tony, think about it—if Alger hadn't gone to jail, it's likely that he would have been stuck being just a stuffy and limited Alger all his life, and would never have been more than the starched-shirt, upstanding Boy Scout that Alger let everyone see. I think the playful side of Alger got buried alive some time during his childhood; it never withered, but also never developed. Alger died a happier man with Lewisburg behind him—he got closer to other people, he got closer to his soul. Jail is a funny place to come up for air in your life, but jail is where Alger became a human being. How could you want to take that away from anyone?"

THE DAY I was allowed back inside Lewisburg—the institution Alger called a "citadel of lonely men" in an early letter home and a "fortress of frustration" several weeks before he was released—I got the sense that the prison has become an even sadder, grimmer place than it was when Alger was there. Outwardly, it's much the same—still the largest single pile of bricks I've ever seen, assembled from the full output of a gargantuan brickworks over several years. Every surface and every corner is still scoured and scrubbed with the same kind of single-mindedness that was in place when Alger was polishing the storeroom floor. The inmates, as in Alger's day, don't wear stripes (that went out almost a century ago, and survives only in the imagination of cartoonists); they wear gray work shirts and blue jeans.

But Lewisburg is no longer a place that many people come home from. Most of the inmates Alger knew were serving short or intermediate, five-to-ten-year ("nickel-and-dime") sentences, and everyone, as Alger could still vividly remember when writing *Recollections*, could point out "Tiny, the placid, uncommunicative, lumbering ox of a man, the only lifer in the prison, in for killing a guard." Most of the inmates nowadays are serving long-term or life sentences, in many cases for crimes of violence; many men are considered "incorrigibles" who have already placed themselves beyond the reach of any rehabilitative services. And rehabilitation is no longer the byword among federal prison officials; money is the currently preferred incentive. Working in a prison industry, an inmate can make as much as $400 a month—for his family, for paying off a fine, as seed money for a business outside.

Drugs and drug money, prison officers told me, have

changed the nature of both crime and punishment—"No one would sign up for choir practice these days," one officer said. The prison farm was eliminated twenty years ago as a cost-cutting measure. Visiting hours have been vastly expanded—the current maximum is five visits a month, and each visit can last as long as seven hours. The old visiting room, because it was up a flight of stairs, didn't have handicapped accessibility, so it's been turned into a law library for inmates; the comfortable, old, oddly festive, Bennett-era patio furniture has been thrown away. The still new ground-floor visiting room, which has fluorescent lights and long, straight lines of unmovable, molded plastic seats, feels more like a waiting room, a last resort, the end of the line.

There are no more honors quarters at Lewisburg—the only reward offered for good behavior is to be transferred to another institution. The old "J Wing" where Alger lived was emptied out in 1995, no longer considered secure; during an almost system-wide insurrection in October 1995 in federal prisons after the Million Man March—an event that went unreported in the press—J Wing, where inmates could move freely from cell to cell, proved hardest to retake. The protest was about a Supreme Court decision on sentencing, which mandated that shorter-term sentences are handed out for powdered cocaine use (most of these offenders are white and middle-class) and much harsher sentences are given to crack-cocaine users (most of whom are poor and African-American).

J Wing was about to be remodeled so that each cell could be individually locked down from a central location in the prison. Because I happened to get to Lewisburg shortly before the contractors did, I was able to enter Alger's cell, nine feet by fourteen feet, the room he had lived in for 1,090 nights, and look out his window. The window opened out. It was covered with steel bars deliberately thinned down so that, from both the inside and the outside, they look like the strips of lead that hold the glass in castle windows or cathedral windows (a Bennett-era reform). The self-contained westward view from the window was the same—green grass in the yard, then the gray wall beyond and the blue sky above. But I was told that a sight Alger had counted on—a glimpse of a pheasant rocketing over the wall—was now a rarity. Pheasants are not faring well in the Buffalo Valley—they have no place to hide now that farmers no longer let cornstalks stand in their fields through the winter.

So here was a place that, when I was a boy, he couldn't leave and I couldn't enter. Now I could stand in the spot where all the letters had come from. My father, looking for parallels, had written that his room was almost as big as mine. It was. It did have—Bennett at work again—many of the proper attributes of a real room, including plaster walls and a wooden door.

Here, in this particular almost-room, of all places on earth, the cell that was, in his words, "near and far"—a place that was both ordinary and cursed, humanely designed and yet enveloped by a 2,500-year-old spell of disdain—my father made so much progress at becoming a human being, as Tim put it. Alger found within these walls a way of living honorably and of reconciling mind and heart in the face of a world that had turned on him like something out of Dickens, or a Hitchcock nightmare.

I also peeked into the cell directly across the hall—it had been the B.R.'s, and from its east-facing window my father had waved at my mother and me as we crossed through the yard after a visit, sometimes signaling us by flapping a sock the B.R. had been drying on his windowsill.

One of the prison officials taking me around asked what I was feeling. So many things. On my first visit to Lewisburg I'd been so unsure of what to expect or how I should behave that on the way through Pennsylvania I picked a bunch of roadside dandelions and violets and presented it to an enormous, blank-faced guard at the desk just inside the main gate, who accepted it without comment.

This time I could take home my own mementos—I had already been shown a caseful of Lewisburg souvenirs that are sold to raise money for the families of prison employees. I bought a Bureau of Prisons golf umbrella, a United States Penitentiary Lewisburg mouse pad and coffee mug, and a small portrait of the prison that was hand-painted on carved wood. On the back is printed "The United States Penitentiary in Lewisburg, Pennsylvania was activated November 15, 1932. The 'Centerpiece of the Federal Bureau of Prisons' reflects Italian Renaissance architecture. The free-standing wall encompasses twenty-six acres and has served to protect society from such infamous criminals as—Al Capone, Jimmy Hoffa, John Gotti, the World Trade Center bombers, international terrorists, murderers and National Spies."

The language is not quite clear, but I suppose "National Spies" is meant to include Alger. Still, it's a cheerful little plaque, despite its mistake, and the red-tiled roof of J Wing can be seen peeping over the prison wall. The plaque now sits on a shelf only a few feet away from Andrew Wyeth's lighthouse sketch.

Though not a liar or a National Spy, Alger had led something of a double and sometimes a precariously balanced life before Lewisburg—there was the maddeningly obtuse, hopelessly naive side that got him into terrible trouble and kept him there. There was also the wise, gentle, kind (and frighteningly vulnerable) person Alger always had been, even when in terrible trouble.

Lewisburg did not perfect Alger, but it was where his best self grew; he entered prison an expert in foreign policy and international organization, and left possessing deep intuitive

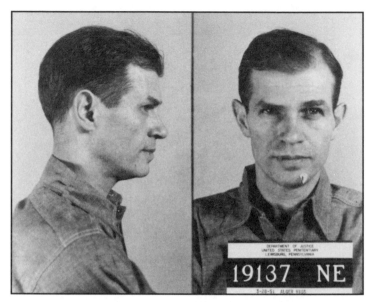

Alger's prison mug shots, taken on his first and last days at Lewisburg

understanding in many oddly assorted areas—the intersection of esthetics and ethics; the needs of prisoners; the awkwardness of young people. Afterwards, even as he nurtured others, he was often still out of his depth, so that his good qualities could never help him take effective action on his own behalf. Twenty years after leaving Lewisburg, when, with Nixon's downfall, the world seemed ready to listen to Alger's story, he opened his heart and all of his files and papers to a historian who then wrote a book re-blackening his name—even though a blind colleague of Alger's in the printing business (which quietly became his full-time work for eighteen years, two years longer than he had spent helping Roosevelt and Truman) warned him against trusting this man. The blind printing salesman had never met the historian but had once heard his voice on television.

Even after Lewisburg, Alger, despite an "alpha-double-plus intellect," as a writer once characterized his mind, continued

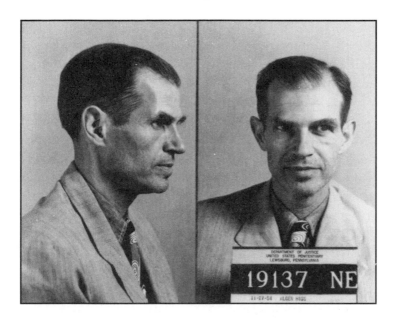

to navigate through life with one sense missing. He still couldn't, or couldn't let himself, sense when someone, either inadvertently or deliberately, might hurt him.

As his son, what a complicated legacy, what a pointing-in-so-many-directions-at-once role model! We're all more of a mix than we want to think about, but my father was so brilliant and so dumb, so brave and so foolhardy, so caring and so oblivious. But as I stood in Alger's cell that was about to be obliterated, I felt fully content with this mixed-blessing inheritance.

I was allowed to walk up the stone staircase that inmates in Alger's day had used to enter the old visiting room. Always before I had to get to this room from a visitors' staircase at the other end. As I reached the middle of the large room, it felt like something of a reunion.

It wasn't until some months later that I learned that Alger's Lewisburg file—inmate number 19137, to them—still existed.

Most prisoners' files are destroyed thirty years after the expiration of their sentences, but in recent years archivists at the Bureau of Prisons have set aside the paperwork on a few "notorious offenders," as they're called, that the archivists suspect future generations may want to know about. Fortunately, Alger made the cut.

No one outside the B.O.P. has looked through the 661 pages (out of 664 in Alger's file) that were sent to me, and probably not a lot of people would want to, since much of the information is routine and bureaucratic (for instance, Alger had to write out a special "INMATE REQUEST TO STAFF MEMBER"—a "cop-out form," in prison slang—every time he wanted anything even slightly out of the ordinary, such as to write to his lawyers or to have his name added to the list of men eligible for the official prison portrait sent home to families).

There is a complete list of the sixty books he'd had in his cell, books he brought home—a mix of titles, including *The Meaning of Shakespeare, Anne Frank: The Diary of a Young Girl, The Best Loved Trees of America, Our Amazing Birds, Walls Are Crumbling, Time in New England, Our World from the Air, Migration of the Birds, The Trouble Makers, The Judges and the Judged, Witch Hunt, I Go Pogo, A Book of Ducks, The Size of the Universe,* and *On Being Human.*

There are many letters that complete strangers had written to him, or toward him, that he was never told about—some of them hostile, some cranky, some odd, one from a Swedish publisher hoping to commission a book, several that were touching. A Cleveland woman (her name is not part of the record) wrote the warden on July 11, 1952, to see if she could write to Alger because "I have had my personal doubts many times as to the guilt of Mr. Hiss. I am not a Communist just a plain every day citizen a Mother."

In Alger's "MONTHLY WORK REPORTS," filled out by the head of the storeroom, Alger always gets thirty-five out of a possible thirty-five rating points—for "care of equipment, comprehension of job, dependability, interest, progress, attitude, and cooperation." "Very outstanding," wrote his supervisor during his last month at Lewisburg.

Alger's "ADMISSION SUMMARY," the extensive, typed evaluation form that had to be completed in early 1951 when he entered Lewisburg, sounds as though the institution didn't quite know what to make of him. Here are a few excerpts: On an "Occupational Interest Inventory" he placed in the ninetieth percentile for "Personal-Social" and for "Level of Interests"; in the eightieth for "Verbal" and "Art"; and in only the first for "Business." He "shows no pathological personality traits." "Intelligence is superior." "The record indicates some ambivalence about assuming an aggressive or passive role in life." "Subject's present approach to his situation is one of calmness and self-assurance. He undoubtedly should be able to function at a high level institutional assignment although the range of possible assignments may be limited by external pressures." "He seems to be taking his incarceration in the form of an enforced vacation rather than a penitentiary sentence." "An objective evaluation is not possible at the present time." There's also one penned-in interpolation: "The modern 'Benedict Arnold.' "

Reading one cop-out form, dated January 25, 1953, was like getting a final letter home from Alger:

"Will you please authorize the Visiting Room to let me bring to visits which I receive from my 11 year old son 2 or 3 books. The books would, of course, be either institution Library (or Education Dept.) volumes or my personal property. They would be chosen with reference to the interests of an 11 year old + in each instance would be submitted for examination, as to suitability, to the visiting room officer. The purpose is to lighten the tedium of a full two hours of unrelieved inactivity for a child, a tedium increased by the amount of adult talk beyond his level of interest which is a necessary part of my visits with my wife who always accompanies my son."

(The request was turned down: "Sorry; this practise would be feasible only if possible on an institution-wide scale; which it is not.")

"This letter," Alger wrote me on March 10, 1953, "is going to be mostly about a very big subject that we will often discuss, thee + I. The subject is: What makes people really happy inside themselves?—the kind of happiness that keeps on shining day after day, not just now + then; and the kind of happiness that lasts in spite of discouraging disappointments + sad events. I don't mean that sorrow isn't real; I do mean that it doesn't continuously darken the skies of a truly happy person. x The answer isn't simple + various ways exist for stating it. I'm forever changing, at least slightly, my way of saying it. Thee will in time decide on thy preferred formulation of it. The important part, which is itself quite simple + has been understood for a long, long time by wise people, is that happiness is a natural result of a full + healthy growing. In that respect men + women + children are like flowers; when they are healthy they grow continually— + they blossom. The blossom is our happiness. Or it can be compared to a bird's song— the natural result of living fully. So, if there is continuing sorrow or anxiousness or crossness or even boredom, this is a sign that something is wrong. The Romans knew this long ago. The wise Emperor Marcus Aurelius said: 'A man's happiness,—to do the things proper to man.' The ancient Chinese knew it. One of the followers of Lao Tze said to keep the mind easy (not worried) + the body healthy 'since both mind + body have no inherent defect or trouble.'

"x-x But the really important words in all these statements are 'proper,' 'full,' 'healthy.' This is where so many people, even kind + intelligent ones, get confused + this is where the question gets more complicated, where the more the world learns the surer the answer. This is the part of happiness that for a long, long time only the most wonderful + remarkable men understood, men like Buddha + then, later, Jesus. They learned that no one person can live fully or healthily or properly (or happily) by himself or for himself. Now more + more people have come to understand this. We are lucky that we live at a time when this is no longer hard to grasp. x Perhaps you remember a kind + quiet older woman, Dr. Richards, who visited us at Peacham with Aunt Anna for just an hour or so in the summer of 1950. Dr. Richards is a psychiatrist + she says her pleasure in life comes from 'pumping air into other people's tires.' No one can live well with out both giving to + getting from other people that kind of help.

"x-x These are not normal times in our country. Many

Alger after Lewisburg

people are confused or frightened so that they are not naturally— + *happily*—helping each other. And—a strange thing—
it is so natural + necessary for all to love + help that one who
stops gets twisted. The energy for helping is still there, but
when it doesn't get a chance to be used naturally, it sours +
turns to hate or miserableness. When President Roosevelt was
alive he encouraged most people to bring out their natural
kindness; he 'pumped' lots of 'air'—good fresh air—into people's spirits. And Adlai Stevenson had some of this quality as
thee + many others realized. Thee knew then how happy-
making it is to wish others well. Just because there came, after
Roosevelt's death, so much confusion + twisting of love into
hate, there is much to be done by all of us who know what people need to be happy. As long as some are hungry + cold + sick
+ rejected no one can feel as good about life as he should,
because we are all like members of one big family. But those of
us who are fortunate in having enough to eat + to wear (+
MUCH MORE than merely enough), who are well + strong +
loved, we can find great happiness in pumping friendliness +
cheerfulness into the lives of others—*including each other,* of
course!

"x-x-x That is why I thought thee would now enjoy the
book about Boston during the years when Justice Holmes was
just the age thee is now. His friends, young + old, were the people who did most to end slavery in our country. And they didn't
lose heart though there was even more confusion + fear + hate
than there is today."

MY PARENTS separated in January 1959, about four years
after Alger's return from Lewisburg. She kept the family apartment, and he stayed first in a friend's guest room and then
moved into a furnished room in the West Village only a little

bigger than his old J Wing cell. About a year later, he found work as a salesman in the printing business. (His first job after Lewisburg had been as office manager at Feathercombs, Inc., a company which made women's hairpins out of piano wire.) Alger liked to say that he wasn't a particularly good salesman, but he could always get in the door, because when the boss heard that Alger Hiss was in the lobby, he had to come out and take a look.

At first my parents corresponded regularly after their final separation, from one side of the Village to another, just as they always had when they were apart. And Prossy kept these painful last letters, too, as she kept all the others. One of them, dated October 22, 1959, says: "Despite our past beautiful hopes, our lovely past closeness and our wonderful loyalties to each other, our children, our friends and our common aims, it is psychically, emotionally wrong and destructive for us to live together. This is the clear lesson of the past unhappy five years." Other letters sound like one half of an argument— Alger saying that he'd been worried about Prossy's anxieties and dependency on him even before prison, evidently in reply to Prossy's having insisted that there hadn't been any serious problems before Lewisburg.

Although I was in boarding school in Vermont for most of the time my parents' marriage was failing, I've always felt that they split up not for the reasons they fought over but because, as sometimes happens, they had simply been through too much together. I think there came a time when, looking at one another, what each came to see was only the suffering that the other had been forced to endure.

Prossy, after the separation, worked in an art gallery and later as a children's book editor, and the high point of each year became a short vacation in England. She would never agree to a divorce—and I used to think that, if they actually had, as

Prossy in Greenwich Village with Assemblyman Bill Passanante

communist co-conspirators, shared a guilty secret, she could have made my father come back by holding that threat of betrayal over his head. In fact she continued to express faith in Alger and his ideals. She suffered a stroke in 1981 and was physically incapacitated during her last years. She spoke out publicly about the Hiss case only once—after a newly published anti-Alger book implied that she had always harbored doubts about him. So on March 10, 1978, she wrote a letter to the editor of the *New York Times:*

"For more than a quarter of a century, I have kept silence amid the clamor concerning the conviction of Alger Hiss. Recently, statements have appeared in print to the effect that I have made remarks indicating that Alger Hiss was guilty. I fear that if I do not now speak out, my silence will be interpreted as confirming these statements.

"At all times, and with my every fiber, I have believed in the innocence of Alger Hiss. I have never spoken a word to the contrary. To me the conviction of Alger Hiss represents a cruel miscarriage of justice.

Alger and Tony in front of the Puck Building, early 1970s

"I do not intend to make any further statements concerning this painful subject."

It wasn't until my father's memorial service that I realized that Mrs. Tillie Novick, whose husband, Abe Novick, had been his boss in the printing business for almost fifteen years—at S. Novick & Son, Inc., in the old Puck Building, on Lafayette Street—lives down the block from me, in one of the high-rise buildings that went up while Alger was in Lewisburg. Mrs. Novick asked me over for a cup of tea some afternoon, because, she said, it would give her pleasure to talk about my father. I took her up on her invitation—it turned out to be only a couple of weeks before her ninetieth birthday—and her daughter, Lynn, dropped by as well. "I had to be here," Lynn said. "I had a prolonged adolescence, and it was my many talks with your father that helped me climb out of it. He made me feel valuable and special and convinced me I could be seen and loved by other people."

Mrs. Novick pointed to a prized possession—a framed 1975

Associated Press photograph of a hugely grinning Alger. He's standing in front of the Puck Building and being hugged by two smiling women, one of them Mrs. Novick, the other an Argentinean accountant who worked at the company. It was the day after he was readmitted to the bar in Massachusetts; Mrs. Novick had traveled to Boston to appear as a witness on his behalf. It was oddly touching to think that, by standing at my own front window, I could see the front window of someone who looked at Alger's picture every day.

"It was such an honor to have your father working for us," Mrs. Novick said. "As a person, that is—I'm not interested in politics. Although I will say this, that I never heard anything from your father except the truth. Which could mean very little to you, but means a great deal to me, because honesty has always been a very important component in my life, at home as well as in business. My father had always told me that I must tell the truth, because that way I'd only have one thing to remember. Your father was the epitome of honesty and truthfulness. There was never any question about anything with him. Whatever he said—that was it."

Was Alger really a decent salesman? "I think he enjoyed the work," she said. "He had a wonderful coterie of customers. When he started going to colleges to give lectures, his customers wouldn't re-order until he came back. It amazed me and troubled me all the time. I would see these miserable magazine and newspaper articles about what a villain he was, and I would say, 'They don't know this man.' "

Alger lectured at colleges during the 1970s; in all, he appeared on seventy-five American campuses, including Boston University, Michigan State, Brandeis, and Cornell, and seven English universities. His subjects were the New Deal, the Yalta Conference, the United Nations, and the Cold War—he refused to lecture about the Hiss case, although he would answer questions about it after a lecture. He liked to spend several days at a college, rather than dash in and out the way so many celebrity lecturers do, so he could get to know a variety of students and teachers.

After Alger's death, I received a condolence letter from a man I'd never met, a venture capitalist outside Boston (I keep letters, too, just as my parents did, only not so many):

"I met your father only once. When I was an undergraduate at Cornell University, he came to Ithaca to speak to a graduate seminar on the cold war. . . . Your father spoke for one or two hours. In particular, I remember his description of the Yalta Conference, and FDR's behavior there. In 1975, he was the sole surviving senior American participant in those talks. His recollections and thoughts were so interesting, and his articulation of them so useful to us, a group of 21 year old college students. After the session I was transfixed: to me, Alger Hiss was just a brilliant, thoughtful, and reflective man who was willing to share his recollections of history-in-the-making.

"My only knowledge of your father is what I gained in that session. Other than reading an occasional article about him, I have never studied the facts of the case in his long battle with the courts. But I walked away from that 1975 session truly inspired, very impressed, and frustrated that our system of laws and politics could have squandered such a resource as your father. The raw intellectual power he possessed could have been so much more usefully deployed, on behalf of our great nation, than it was."

While in his seventies, Alger also helped set up and then served on the board of a small grant-making foundation based in Tucson, Arizona, that specialized, among other things, in environmental and social justice issues. The idea for the foundation, and for getting Alger involved, came from Agnese N. Haury, who'd worked with him at the Carnegie Endowment

Alger on Long Island, 1980

almost forty years before. "He was a natural," she told me. "After all, Alger had been a foundation president. At our meetings he was the one who would hold back and not say anything until the end. And then he would keep us on course, by asking, 'Is this a project that will have helped the world twenty years from now?' "

During this time, I was floundering upwards, writing "Talk of the Town" stories and then longer pieces for *The New Yorker*, and then books as well. Alger and I would generally meet every week or two for a long lunch or dinner, when he wasn't off lec-

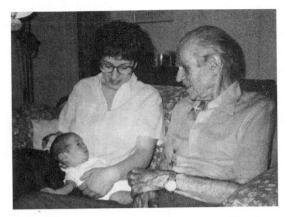

My wife, Lois Metzger, with Alger and Jacob,
one month old

turing or down at his tiny house in East Hampton. It felt almost like a continuation of the old Lewisburg pattern. After my son was born, his grandfather greeted his birthdays by sending him sketches of birthday cakes with tiny candles on top; these drawings were almost identical to the ones he had once sent me from Lewisburg.

Joe Liebling had introduced Alger to East Hampton long before it became fashionable, and my father began spending more and more time there every summer. I think he found the still sleepy oceanfront village, which had a summer colony of writers and artists and a year-round population of fishermen and farmers, a cross between Peacham and the Eastern Shore. In his eighties, Alger's eyesight deteriorated badly—he had macular degeneration, as Donie also did in his last years. Relays of friends, both in New York City and in the Hamptons, volunteered to read books and magazines and the *New York Times* to him, as he had once read aloud to Justice Holmes. Another letter that came after Alger's death, this one from a middle-aged New York lawyer I'd never met, described the experience of being one of Alger's readers on an almost weekly basis over the course of five years:

"These were among the most enjoyable and rewarding hours I have ever spent. His responsiveness was often more enriching than whatever text was at hand. I learned as much, if not more, from him about history, government, and literature than from most of the professors who taught me. But I have learned more from him as a human being. Pain and disappointment never seemed to dominate his life. Rather, what I saw was excitement about a new book, passion about the events of the day, and pleasure—easily and warmly expressed—in friendship. The fineness of his daily contacts is what conveyed his breadth, depth, and reach."

In his final year, when my father, his body almost completely worn out, became a prisoner of his own physical frailties, he asked me to start reading from Boswell's *Life of Johnson*. Since I estimated that, in weekly sessions, this would easily take us several years, I thought this was a sign that Alger was planning to stick around awhile longer.

Reading Boswell was actually a long-postponed project—I can now pinpoint the day it came to him. On May 20, 1951, two months after he went to prison, Alger wrote, "Some time I shall add Boswell's Johnson to Don Q. as among my Lewisburg accomplishments of deferred 'improvements of the mind' [a Holmesian allusion]. I noted it in browsing the [library] shelves today—also Herndon's Lincoln + Van Paasen's Days of Our Years + a to-me-new Nehru (the title of which slips my mind—it is essentially a history of India written after the first 20 months of his 9th prison term)."

My father and I made a good start on Boswell, but he often interrupted to ask for news of the world. During his final summer, we stopped to talk about the comeback no-hitter Dwight Gooden had just pitched for the Yankees and about a Law Day ceremony I had attended on his behalf in coastal New Jersey. The sixth-grade class at the East Dover Elementary School had spent a year studying the Hiss case, and re-enacted Alger's second trial in an ornate, restored, 1850s courtroom in front of their parents and almost all the judges from Ocean County. Their rendition was completely as-it-happened—except that the jury, after its deliberations, found the defendant not guilty. Alger was very pleased by both stories, but the one he wanted to hear again was the one about Doc Gooden, a man who, heading into the twilight of his career, had learned to pitch better than he had at the height of his powers.

Since Alger's death he has been the subject of a new series of magazine and newspaper articles attacking his character and patriotism, written by a new generation of people who "don't know this man." Alger seemed to offer his own comment on the subject. In his final year in prison, he wrote home, on May 25, 1954: "Letters are, for me, the most effective biographies + almost equally valuable as history—not only the writers but their social settings come alive more truly than through any other form of literature."

ACKNOWLEDGMENTS

Many people very generously contributed their time and thought during the writing of this book, and I am deeply touched by their helpfulness. My gifted editor, Ann Close, has been a guiding star. Charles Patrick Crow, now a senior editor at *Audubon* magazine, is the best friend a generation of New York writers ever had. Amanda Urban, my agent, saw the book clearly long before I did. Hugh Eakin, now an editor at *Art News*, was a superb fact checker who also tightened the thinking in the book.

Everyone I've worked with at Alfred A. Knopf and at Random House has eased my path: Sonny Mehta, Pat Johnson, William Loverd, Paul Bogaards, Paul Kozlowski, Katherine Hourigan, Virginia Tan, Carol Devine Carson, Elise Solomon, Karen Mugler, Dorothy Schmiderer Baker, Jill Morrison, Nicholas Latimer, Kathy Zuckerman, Bette Graber, Asya Muchnick, and Jason Zuzga.

For permission to quote from family and other papers, I am most grateful to David Warrington, Librarian for Special Collections at the Harvard Law School Library; to Ellyn Polshek, Esq.; to my cousins, Cynthia Hiss Grace, Joanna Hiss Hoople, Cynthia Fansler Behrman, and Gillian Fansler Brown; and to Alan Levine, Esq., and Michael Zak.

Many people at the Department of Justice and the Federal Bureau of Prisons have gone to extraordinary lengths to make it possible for me to visit the United States Penitentiary at Lewisburg and to get copies of Alger's Bureau of Prisons file. I am indebted to Jeremy Travis, Director of the National Institute of Justice; to Page True, Warden of Lewisburg Penitentiary, Edwin Claunch, Executive Assistant to the Warden, Laurie Cunningham, Esq., Attorney Advisor at Lewisburg, and Richard Wagner, who has recently retired as Case Management Coordinator at Lewisburg. Anne Diestel, the Archivist of the Bureau of Prisons, Elizabeth M. Edson, Chief of the Bureau's Freedom of Information/Privacy Office, and Kathy White, one of Ms. Edson's most dedicated staffers, found, reviewed, and photocopied the 664 pages in Alger's inmate file.

Two old family friends in New York shared their lifetimes of thinking about Alger: Mrs. Tillie Novick and the late Viola W. Bernard, M.D. The intervening decades disappeared whenever I talked to old family friends in Peacham, including Thelma White, Eloise Miller, Jean Kemble, and, most especially, Nancy Bundgus and her daughter, Juliette Azots.

I can never forget the kindness and insights of so many other people as well, including Dr. Willa Bernhard, Dean Jo Ivey Boufford, Paul Buttenwieser, Peter Canby, Robert Cormier, Dr. Bruce Craig, Nancy Crampton, Frank Curtis, Esq., Liz DiGiorgio, Michael Garabedian, Suzanne Goel, Agnese N. Haury, Ann Hobson, Judith Kelly, Dr. Kathleen Kelly, Rita Kelly, Jeff Kisseloff, Rhoda M. Kornreich, Tammy Jo Kreiter, Jonathan Lampert, M.D., Jeffrey Lewis, Judith Livingston, Esq., Susan Logan, John Lowenthal, Esq., Harry Mazer, Norma Fox Mazer, Rob Michaels, Thomas Moore, Esq., Anne Mortimer-Maddox, Prof. Mitchell Moss, Victor Navasky, Sharyn November, Judith Papachristou, Linda Wheeler Reiss, William A. Reuben, Kim Stanley Robinson, Virginia Robinson, Philip Roth, Peter Shepherd, Letty H. Simon, John Stonehill, Judith Stonehill, Edith Tiger, Amy Tonsits, Mike Truppa, Richard Tyler, Dr. Roger S. Ulrich, Harriet Walden, Irene Williams, Winnie Zeligs, and Judith Zimmer.

My wife, Lois Metzger, made the most important contributions of all, as she always does.

PERMISSIONS ACKNOWLEDGMENTS

Grateful acknowledgment is made to the following for permission to reprint previously published and unpublished material:

Harvard Law School Library: Excerpts from the Alger Hiss Family Papers. Used by the kind permission of the Harvard Law School Library and of the President and Fellows of Harvard College.

Alfred A. Knopf, Inc.: Excerpts from *I Chose Prison* by James V. Bennett, copyright © 1970 by James V. Bennett. Reprinted by permission of Alfred A. Knopf, Inc.

Octagon Press Ltd.: Excerpt from "When the Waters Were Changed," from *Tales of the Dervishes* by Idries Shah (London: Octagon Press Ltd.). Reprinted by permission of Octagon Press Ltd.

Random House, Inc.: Excerpts from *Witness* by Whittaker Chambers, copyright © 1952 by Whittaker Chambers, copyright renewed 1980 by Esther Chambers. Reprinted by permission of Random House, Inc.

PHOTOGRAPHIC CREDITS

CORBIS: pages 17 and 78

Federal Bureau of Prisons: pages 9, 226, and 227

All other photographs are from the collection of the author.

A NOTE ABOUT THE AUTHOR

Tony Hiss is the author of nine previous books, including the award-winning *The Experience of Place*. He began writing for *The New Yorker* in 1963, and his work has appeared in many other publications, including the *New York Times*, the *Atlantic Monthly*, and *Gourmet*. He is a Visiting Scholar at the Taub Urban Research Center at New York University, and he lectures frequently about how people are affected by their physical environment.

He and his wife and son live in New York City.

A NOTE ON THE TYPE

This book was set in Janson, a redrawing of type cast from matrices long thought to have been made by the Dutchman Anton Janson, who was a practicing type-founder in Leipzig during the years 1668 to 1687. However, it has been conclusively demonstrated that these types are actually the work of Nicholas Kis (1650–1702), a Hungarian, who most probably learned his trade from the master Dutch typefounder Dirk Voskens. The type is an excellent example of the influential and sturdy Dutch types that prevailed in England up to the time William Caslon developed his own incomparable designs from them.

Composed by North Market Street Graphics,
Lancaster, Pennsylvania
Printed and bound by Quebecor Printing,
Martinsburg, West Virginia
Typography and binding design by
Dorothy Schmiderer Baker